A WORLD BANK COUNTRY STUDY

Slovenia

Economic Transformation and EU Accession

Volume II: Main Report

The World Bank
Washington, D.C.

...nt © 1999
...ernational Bank for Reconstruction
...evelopment/THE WORLD BANK
...H Street, N.W.
...shington, D.C. 20433, U.S.A.

World Bank Country Studies are among the many reports originally prepared for internal use as part of the continuing analysis by the Bank of the economic and related conditions of its developing member countries and of its dialogues with the governments. Some of the reports are published in this series with the least possible delay for the use of governments and the academic, business and financial, and development communities. The typescript of this paper therefore has not been prepared in accordance with the procedures appropriate to formal printed texts, and the World Bank accepts no responsibility for errors. Some sources cited in this paper may be informal documents that are not readily available.

The findings, interpretations, and conclusions expressed in this paper are entirely those of the author(s) and should not be attributed in any manner to the World Bank, to its affiliated organizations, or to members of its Board of Executive Directors or the countries they represent. The World Bank does not guarantee the accuracy of the data included in this publication and accepts no responsibility for any consequence of their use. The boundaries, colors, denominations, and other information shown on any map in this volume do not imply on the part of the World Bank Group any judgment on the legal status of any territory or the endorsement or acceptance of such boundaries.

The material in this publication is copyrighted. The World Bank encourages dissemination of its work and will normally grant permission promptly.

Permission to photocopy items for internal or personal use, for the internal or personal use of specific clients, or for educational classroom use is granted by the World Bank provided that the appropriate fee is paid directly to Copyright Clearance Center, Inc., 222 Rosewood Drive, Danvers, MA 01923, U.S.A., telephone 978 750 8400, fax 978 750 4470. Please contact Copyright Clearance Center prior to photocopying items.

For permission to reprint individual articles or chapters, please fax your request with complete information to the Republication Department, Copyright Clearance Center, fax 978 750 4470.

All other queries on rights and licenses should be addressed to the World Bank at the address above, or fax no. 202 522 2422.

TABLE OF CONTENTS

Abstract ix

Currency and Equivalent Units xi

CHAPTER I.   **Economic Performance in the Transition**.................................1
Introduction...1
Stabilization and Recovery 1
The Initial Response 2
Fast Turnaround but the Recovery Slows Down 3
The 1997-98 Revival and EU Accession..6
Fiscal Sustainability and the Transition 7
The Size of the Public Sector...10
The Need for Pension Reform 11
External Balance and Capital Inflows..12
Coping with a Volatile External Environment 13
The Challenges of the Pre-accession Period 16

CHAPTER II.   **Sustainable Growth and Income Convergence** 17
Introduction...17
European Integration: The Experience of Ireland, Greece, Spain and Portugal........18
Bridging the Income Gap with the EU 19
Loosing Ground in the Transition 20
Stimulating Alternative Growth-Accounting Scenarios 21
Sustainable Growth: Alternative Policy Reform Scenarios 22
The Challenge Ahead: Accelerating the Structural Reform Agenda........25

CHAPTER III.   **Complying with the European Union Environmental Directives**........29
Introduction...29
Slovene Environmental Policy and the EU Accession 29
Institutional Changes and Investment Costs..32
Main Environmental Areas 34
Water Supply and Treatment...35
Waste Management 37
Air Quality..39
Industrial Pollution, Control, and Risk Management 42
Implications for Households 42
Recommendations..43

CHAPTER IV.   **Foreign Trade Sector**..45
Introduction...45
External Equilibrium...46
An Impressive Record of Maintaining Macroeconomic Stability...46
Quick Re-adjustment of Foreign Trade Patterns 46
But Low FDI Inflows 47
Export Performance in EU Markets...49
Diversification in Export Offer: Moderate Change After 1995 50
Commodity Chains: The Move towards Final Stage Products 50

Factor Content: The Move towards Skilled Labor and
Capital Intensive Products..51
Comparative Advantage of Pollution-Intensive Sectors.............................52
Competition in the Single Market...53
Contestability of Domestic Markets..53
Tariff Structure: Diversification in Protection......................................54
Access to Markets for Agricultural Products..55
MFN and Preferential Rates: Growth in Reverse Discrimination................56
Competition Policies..57
State Aids..57
External Access to Government Procurement..58
Implications for a Pre-Accession Strategy...59

CHAPTER V. **Financial Sector**...61
Introduction..61
The Banking System...61
Evolution Since Independence...62
Structure of the Banking Sector...64
Market Concentration..65
New Bank Groups and Strategic Alliances..65
Banking Sector Assets and Balance Sheet...67
Efficiency and Profitability..68
Capitalization and Asset Quality...68
Money and Credit Developments..69
Capital Markets..72
Securities Market and Ownership Transformation...................................73
Role of Foreign Investment..74
The Bond Market..75
Capital Market Development..75
Other Institutional Investors: Security Brokers and Mutual Funds..............76
Insurance Sector...77
The Legal Framework..78
EU Accession and the Insurance Sector..79
Legal Harmonization with the EU..79
Banking Sector..80
Capital Markets...81
Insurance Sector..81
The Pre-accession Agenda...81

CHAPTER VI. **Enterprise Sector in Transition**...85
Introduction..85
Ownership Transformation...85
Privatization Slovenian Style...86
Outcome of Privatization..88
The Unfinished Privatization Agenda...90
Enterprise Sector Performance in the Transition...92
The Enterprise Sector Still Generates Losses...93
Enterprise Restructuring is Slowly Taking Place.....................................96
Investment Climate Remains Weak..97
The Role of Foreign Investment..99
Concluding Remarks..101

CHAPTER VII. **Labor Market and Social Policies** 103
Introduction..103
Labor Market Characteristics...104
Labor Market Adjustment..106
Constraints to Effective Labor Market Performance.....................................107
Social Protection and Active Labor Market Policies......................................108
EU Accession and the Labor Market..113

CHAPTER VIII. **Agricultural Sector in Transition**...119
Introduction..119
Overview of the Agriculture Sector..120
Agro-industrial Sector Policies..124
Rural Finance and the Cooperative Sector...126
Private Sector Development in the Service Industries to Agriculture.............128
Adjustment of the Central Administration..128
Strengthen Private Sector Links 129
Agriculture and the EU Accession Process 129

CHAPTER IX. **Public Services and Municipal Infrastructure**........................131
Introduction..131
Infrastructure Development at the Municipal Level..131
Current Status of Economic Infrastructure Development.........................131
Energy Sector 133
Transport and Telecommunications...133
Municipal Services 135
Investment Needs and Funding Gap 135
Key Issues in Municipal Infrastructure Development.....................................136
Legal and Institutional Framework...136
Financing of Local Communities 137
Price Setting for Public Services and Tariff Structures 139
Financial Performance of Municipal Public Utilities................................140
Recent Trends in Municipal Infrastructure Investment..............................141
Compliance with the EU Legislation...143
Strategy for Municipal Infrastructure Development..144
Introduction of Cost-Reflecting Prices of Municipal Infrastructure Services...144
Competition and Private Sector Involvement...145
Legal Framework and Institutional Support..146
Regulatory Framework 146
Concluding Remark...147

Statistical Appendix 149

Map IBRD 26882

Tables

Table 1.1   Annual Inflation and GDP Growth in Selected CEE Countries, 1992-97.....................4
Table 1.2   Selected Economic Indicators, 1992-98 5
Table 1.3   Index of Real Net Wages and Productivity, 1992-97..7
Table 1.4   Summary of General Government Operations, 1993-98..8
Table 1.5   Sustainable Fiscal Deficit – 1997 Conditions...9
Table 1.6   Selective External Balance Accounts, 1993-98...13
Table 2.1   Income Convergence of Ireland, Greece, Spain and Portugal 18
Table 2.2   Per Capita Income Level in Europe, 1997..20
Table 2.3   Years Required to close Per Capita Income Gap with the European Union..............21
Table 2.4   Growth Rate Required to Achieve EU Parity..22
Table 2.5   Growth Determinants for EU Candidate Countries...24
Table 2.6   Years to Close Income Gap Under Alternative Policy Scenarios..............................25
Table 2.7   Major Components of the Slovene Pre-accession Reform Agenda............................26
Table 3.1   Total Estimated Investment Costs, 1998-2005..33
Table 3.2   Investment Costs – Water Quality Sector EU Compliance, 1998-2005.....................36
Table 3.3   Investment Costs – Waste Management Sector EU Compliance, 1998-2005............39
Table 3.4   Investment Costs – Air Quality Sector EU Compliance, 1998-2005 41
Table 3.5   Investment Costs – Industrial Pollution Sector EU Compliance, 1998-2005............42
Table 4.1   Slovenia's External Performance, 1992-97 46
Table 4.2   Geographic Composition of Slovenia's Exports and Imports, 1992-97.....................47
Table 4.3   Cumulative Foreign Direct Investment, 1990-97 48
Table 4.4   Changes in Slovenia's Exports to the EU in Individual Commodity Chains............51
Table 4.5   Factor Content of Slovene Exports to EU over 1992-97 51
Table 4.6   Selected Features of Slovenia's 'Dirty' Exports to the EU, 1992-97........................53
Table 4.7   Share of EU Imports in Total Imports and Estimates of Customs Duties.................55
Table 4.8   Types of State Aids and Their Evolution Over 1993-98 58
Table 4.9   EU Imports from First-Wave EU Applicants, 1989-97..59
Table 5.1   Number of Banks and Saving Banks in Slovenia..64
Table 5.2   Market Share of the Seven Biggest Banks, 1995-97 65
Table 5.3   Banking Groups, 1997 66
Table 5.4   Structure of Banking Sector Assets, Selected Items, 1991-97...................................67
Table 5.5   Structure of Banking Sector Liabilities, Selected Items, 1991-97.............................68
Table 5.6   Indicators of Bank Efficiency...68
Table 5.7   Classification of Balance and Off Balance Sheet Assets of the Banking Sector........69
Table 5.8   Monetary Aggregates, 1992-97..70
Table 5.9   Domestic Credit, 1991-97..71
Table 5.10   Market Capitalization, 1992-97..73
Table 5.11   Initial Public Offerings, 1994-97...73
Table 5.12   Net Capital Flows from Foreign Direct and Portfolio Investments...........................74
Table 5.13   Market Capitalization by Company, October 1998..75
Table 5.14   Structure of Security Brokers Assets..76
Table 5.15   Development of the Insurance Market, 1991-96 77
Table 5.16   Insurance Business in the European Union and Slovenia, 1996.................................78
Table 5.17   Financial Sector Directives..80
Table 6.1   Corporate Ownership Structure after Privatization, 1997..89
Table 6.2   The Impact of Different Privatization Techniques 93
Table 6.3   Ownership Structure of Enterprises and Selected Indicators, 1995...........................95
Table 6.4   Comparison of Performance Indicators by Ownership Categories, 1995....................96
Table 6.5   Profitability of the Enterprise Sector, 1994-96..97

Table 6.6	Profitability of the Private Enterprise Sector, 1994-96	97
Table 6.7	Investment by Ownership Structure, 1995-96	99
Table 6.8	Comparative Performance of Foreign and Domestic Enterprises, 1994-96	101
Table 7.1	Annual Percentage Change in GDP and Employment, 1993-97	103
Table 7.2	Employment Rates by Occupation and Sector, 1996	107
Table 7.3	Accession and Separation Rates: International Comparison	107
Table 7.4	Social Security Contribution Rates in 1997	108
Table 7.5	Unemployment Benefits, 1988-96	111
Table 7.6	Social Assistance, 1988-96	112
Table 7.7	Statutory Social Contributions Rates in Slovenia, Europe, and the OECD	116
Table 8.1	Structure of Food Industry (Private and Public Sector)	125
Table 9.1	Infrastructure Investment Needs and Funding Gap, 1997-2000	136
Table 9.2	Financing of Local Communities, 1992-98	138
Table 9.3	Average Prices of Municipal Services, 1991-96	139
Table 9.4	Municipal Sector Enterprise Performance, 1997	140
Table 9.5	Selected Performance Indicators for Enterprises, 1997	141

Boxes

Box 1.1	Status of Main Economic Reform Legislation	16
Box 2.1	Equation and Parameters used for Convergence Simulation	23
Box 3.1	Environmental Development Fund	30
Box 3.2	Environmental Accession Strategy	31
Box 5.1	Structure of the Financial Sector in Slovenia, 1997	62
Box 5.2	Public Sector Ownership in the Banking Sector	64
Box 5.3	The New Ljubljanska Banka Group	66
Box 6.1	A Privatization Bill Dilemma	87
Box 6.2	The Privatization Gap and the Privatization Investment Funds	92
Box 6.3	The Increasing Role of the Slovenian Development Corporation	98
Box 7.1	Social Protection Programs	110
Box 7.2	Slovenia's Labor Market and the Acquis Communautaire	115

Figures

Figure 1.1	Annual Inflation Rate	2
Figure 1.2	Private Sector Share in GDP	3
Figure 1.3	GDP Recovery in Selected CEE Countries	3
Figure 1.4	Trade and Current Account Balance	4
Figure 1.5	Savings and Investment Rates	6
Figure 1.6	Fiscal Balance in Selected CEE Countries	8
Figure 1.7	General Government Revenues and Expenditures	10
Figure 1.8	General Government Expenditures in Selected CEECs	11
Figure 1.9	Stock Exchange Index (SBI)	14
Figure 1.10	Current Account Balance, 1997	14
Figure 1.11	Index of Speculative Pressure	15
Figure 2.1	Convergence in Per Capita Income	21
Figure 3.1	Overall Expenditure on Environmental Protection	32
Figure 3.2	Impacts on Households Income	43
Figure 5.1	Real Interest Rates	71

Figure 5.2   Interbank Market Real Rates 72

Figure 6.1   Ownership Structure by Value of Capital...88

Figure 6.2   Insiders Control after Privatization..89

Figure 6.3   Cumulative FDI in Selected CEE Countries, 1992-97 100

Figure 6.4   Private Sector Share in GDP...102

Figure 7.1   Labor Force Participation Rates...104

Figure 7.2   Employment and Output Growth..104

Figure 7.3   Differences in Survey and Registry Unemployment, 1996 105

Figure 7.4   Unemployment of Household Heads...106

Figure 8.1   Distribution of Agriculture Lands...120

Figure 8.2   Labor Productivity in Agriculture and Industry...................................120

Figure 8.3   Agriculture Trade Balance..121

Figure 8.4   Structure of the Cooperative Sector..127

Abstract

This country study is based on the findings of several missions that visited Slovenia during the second half of 1997 and 1998. The report analyzes economic developments of the past few years and policy options linked to the challenges faced by Slovenia in its pursuit of European Union membership.

The report is composed of two volumes. Volume I is a summary report that condenses main findings and conclusions. The report focuses mainly on the elimination of the remaining structural weaknesses as means to maintain the macroeconomic stability while increasing the competitiveness of the Slovene economy abroad, and redefining the size and roles of the public and private sectors.

Volume II is the main report. It provides the assessment and technical analysis of selected key sectors of the Slovene economy. While each chapter is sector-specific in nature, the EU accession process dominates them. Volume II is structured as follows: Chapter I reviews the economic performance during the transition, focusing on the stabilization and recovery of the early years and the revival of output growth impetus in 1997-98. Chapter II analyzes growth and income convergence issues in relation with the EU accession process. Chapter III studies the environment sector and the costs of implementing the EU directives. Chapter IV provides an assessment of the foreign trade sector, focusing on trade policy, export performance in the EU, and the contestability of domestic markets. Chapter V covers the challenges of the financial sector, reviewing mostly banking, but also capital and insurance markets. Chapter VI reviews enterprise sector issues: it concentrates on the privatization process, the remaining privatization agenda and the performance of the enterprise sector post-independence. Chapter VII studies the labor market and social policies. The chapter analyzes the trends in the labor market and assesses the degree of adjustment and constraints to effective performance. Chapter VIII analyzes the agricultural sector in light of the fragile Slovene ecosystems. Finally, chapter IX studies the capacity of the municipal governments to deliver efficient and cost effective public services. The chapter focuses on the state of public utilities and the infrastructure investment needs at the communal level.

The report was prepared by a World Bank team composed of Carlos Silva-Jauregui (ECSPE, team leader), Marcelo Bisogno (ECSPE, labor market), Julia Bucknall (ECSSD, environment), Rita Cestti (ECSSD, environment), Michel Debatisse (ECSSD, agriculture), Bozo Jasovic (consultant, capital markets and insurance), Bart Kaminski (DECRG, foreign trade and FDI), Philipe Lefevre (consultant, legal framework for banking), Tina Mlakar (ECSPE, enterprise sector), Nathalie Moreno (ECSPE, competition policies), Mojmir Mrak (consultant, banking and municipal infrastructure), Robert Palacios (HDNSP, pensions), Rossana Polastri (ECSPE, macroeconomics, FDI and growth), Claudio Sapelli (consultant, labor market and social assistance), Helmut Schreiber (ECSSD, environment), Marko Simoneti (consultant, capital markets and insurance), Carlos Rivas (consultant, finance sector) and Milan Vodopivec (consultant, labor market and social assistance).

The report benefited from valuable comments and suggestions received at different stages from Hafez Ghanem, Michelle Riboud, Bernard Naudts, Frank Lysy, Carlos Cavalcanti, Ana Revenga, Robert Palacios, Michael Nightingale, Deborah Wetzel, Nathalie Darnaut, Borut Repansek, Kevin Ross, Roberto Rocha, Roger Grawe, Hennie van Greuning, Maureen Lewis, Frank Sader, Anthony Wheeler, Slovene government officials, and participants at the ECSPE seminars on Slovenia's Labor Market and Foreign Trade and Investment.

The authors also benefited from the effective collaboration with government officials and had the opportunity to discuss the main findings of the different missions at the Bank of Slovenia, Ministry of Agriculture, Forestry and Food; Ministry of Economic Relations and Development; Ministry of Economic Affairs, Ministry of Labor and Social Affairs, Ministry of Environment and Physical Planning, Ministry of Finance, Ministry of Foreign Affairs, Ministry of Science and Technology, Agency for Privatization, Institute for Pension and Disability Insurance, National Employment Office, Statistical Office of the Republic of Slovenia, Institute of Macroeconomic Analysis and Development (IMAD), Slovene Export Corporation, Slovene Development Corporation, Securities Market Agency, Environmental Development Fund and the Agricultural Institute of Slovenia.

The missions had the opportunity to discuss key issues with academicians at IMAD, University of Ljubljana, Institute for Economic Research, Central and Eastern European Privatization Network, Center for International Competitiveness and GEA College. The report also benefited from discussions with representatives from four trade unions, Chamber of Economy, Deloitte & Touche, SKB Banka, Nova Ljubljanska Banka, Banking Association, Ljubljana Stock Exchange, Bank Societe Generale, National Financial Company, Banka Celje, Triglav Insurance Company, European Commission, International Monetary Fund (IMF), Organization for Economic Cooperation and Development, and European Bank for Reconstruction and Development. Special thanks to the IMF for its cooperation with the statistical data.

The different mission members would like to express their gratitude to all our Slovene counterparts in the government, academia and business community, for the time they spent with us in open and friendly discussions. Their cooperation made this report possible. In particular, special thanks are due to Irena Sodin and Bojan Pogacar, International Department, Ministry of Finance for their effective support and organization of the multiple agendas. Rossana Polastri and Tina Mlakar provided research support. John Karaagac provided editorial assistance. Dolly Teju processed the report.

CURRENCY AND EQUIVALENT UNITS

Currency Unit = Slovene Tolar (SIT)

	1991	1992	1993	1994	1995	1996	1997	1998
SIT/US$	55.60	81.28	113.24	128.81	118.52	135.36	159.69	166.14
SIT/DM	34.81	52.03	68.43	79.37	82.66	89.98	92.12	94.41

WEIGHTS AND MEASURES

Metric System

ACRONYMS AND ABBREVIATIONS

APR	Agency for Privatization and Restructuring	KBNG	Komercialna Banka Nova Garica
ATM	Automatic Teller Machine	Kg.	Kilogram
BAT	Best Available Technology	LB	Ljubljanska Banka
BOS	Bank of Slovenia	LDC	Less Developed Country
BRA	Bank Rehabilitation Agency	LFP	Labor Force Participation
CAP	Common Agricultural Policy	LFS	Labor Force Survey
CAR	Capital Adequacy Ratio	LSE	Ljubljana Stock Exchange
CEE	Central and Eastern European	MEPP	Ministry of Environment and Physical Planning
CEECs	Central and Eastern European Countries	MFN	Most Favorable Nation
CEEPN	Central & Eastern European Privatization Network	Mg.	Milligram
CEFTA	Central European Free Trade Agreement	MOAFF	Ministry of Agriculture, Forestry and Food
CEM	Country Economic Memorandum	MOERD	Ministry of Economic Relations & Development
CMEA	Council of Mutual Economic Assistance	MOF	Ministry of Finance
CO_2	Carbon Bioxide	N.A.	Not Applicable
CPI	Consumer Price Index	NEAP	National Environmental Protection Program
CSCC	Central Securities Clearing Corporation	NEO	National Employment Office
CSL	Cooperative Savings and Loans	NKBM	Nova Kreditna Banka Maribor
DAE	Department of European Affairs	PAYG	Pay-as-you-go
DISAE	Development of the Implementation Strategies for Approximation in Environment	NLB	Nova Ljubljanska Banka
		NO_2	Nitrogen Bioxide
DM	German Mark	NO_X	Nitrogen Oxide
EAs	Europe Agreements	NPP	Nuclear Power Plant
EAA	Europe Association Agreement	NPV	Net Present Value
EAGGF	European Agricultural Guidance & Guarantee Fund	O_3	Ozone
EBRD	European Bank for Reconstruction and Development	O&M	Operation and Maintenance
EC	European Commission	OECD	Organization for Economic Cooperation & Development
ECoFund	Environmental Development Fund		
ECU	European Currency Unit	ODS	Ozone Depleting Substance
EEC	European Economic Community	PHARE	Poland Hungary Assistance for Economic Reconstruction
EFTA	European Free Trade Agreement		
EMAS	Eco-Management & Auditing Scheme	PIFs	Privatization Investment Funds
Ent.	Enterprise	PSE	Producer Subsidy Equivalent
EPACT	Environmental Protection Act	QRs	Quantitative Restrictions
EPA	Environmental Protection Agency	R&D	Research and Development
ER	Exchange Rate	RCA	Revealed Comparative Advantage
ERM	Exchange Rate Mechanism	REC	Regional Environmental Center for Central and Eastern Europe
EMU	Economic and Monetary Union		
EU	European Union	SA	Social Assistance
FDI	Foreign Direct Investment	SBI	Slovenia Bourse Index
FGD	First Desulphurization Unit	SDC	Slovene Development Corporation
FIAS	Foreign Investment Advisory Service	SEC	Securities Exchange Commission
FSU	Former Soviet Union	SFRY	Socialist Federal Republic of Yugoslavia
FTA	Free Trade Agreement	SIT	Slovene Tolar
GATT	General Agreement of Tariffs and Trade	SITC	Standard International Trade Classification
GDP	Gross Domestic Product	SLO	Slovenia

GEF	Global Environment Facility	SME	Small and Medium-Sized Enterprises
GNFS	Goods and non-factor services	SO₂	Sulfur Oxide
GOS	Government of Slovenia	TAIEX	Technical Assistance Information Exchange Office
GS	Goods and Services	TOM	Base Interest Rate
Ha	Hectare	TORs	Terms of Reference
HH	Household	UCITS	Undertakings for Collective Investment in Transferable Securities
ILO	International Labor Organization		
ISA	Insurance Supervisory Authority	UHT	Ultra High Temperature
ISP	Index of Speculative Pressure	ULC	Unit Labor Cost
IMAD	Institute of Macroeconomic Analysis & Development	UN	United Nations
IMF	International Monetary Fund	US	United States
IPOs	Initial Public Offerings	VAT	Value Added Tax
IPPC	Integrated Pollution Prevention and Control	VOCs	Volatile Organic Compounds
ISO	International Standard Office	WTO	World Trade Organization
KBM	Kreditna Banka Maribor	Yr.	Year

FISCAL YEAR

January 1 to December 31

Vice President:	Johannes Linn
Country Director:	Roger Grawe
Sector Director:	Pradeep Mitra
Sector Leader:	Hafez Ghanem
Team Leader:	Carlos Silva-Jauregui

Economic Performance in the Transition

Introduction

Following its declaration of independence in June of 1991 and its subsequent international recognition in early 1992, Slovenia moved quickly to establish macroeconomic stability, to launch the systemic transformation of the economy, and to normalize relationships with the international financial community. This was achieved despite the disruption of trade flows and despite regional instability associated with the breakup of the former Socialist Federal Republic of Yugoslavia (SFRY). As a result, Slovenia, which was already the most prosperous among the republics of the former Yugoslavia, now enjoys the highest per capita income level among transition economies and access to international capital markets at relatively favorable terms.

This good performance notwithstanding, Slovenia's economy still suffers from persistent structural weaknesses. The large share of the State in the economy, the limited role of the financial sector in resource intermediation, and the low share of the private sector in manufacturing and infrastructure, have all resulted in lower growth relative to other leading economies in Central and Eastern Europe (CEE). The country's public finances are coming under increasing pressure from high and rising social security expenditures, mainly pension and health expenditures as well as from relatively high public sector wage increases in the early years of the transition.

With the signing of the European Association Agreement (EAA) in June 1996, Slovenia needs to achieve faster, sustainable growth and to complete the systemic transformation of its economy and achieve membership in the European Union (EU) by the turn of the century. The authorities have mapped a program of reform in strategy paper for accession to the (EU). If the program of reforms envisaged by the authorities is fully implemented, Slovenia would emerge as an economy largely dominated largely by the private sector, and one with a smaller, more efficient State. This would set the stage for Slovenia's successful accession and membership in an enlarged EU, not only in terms of its high income per capita level, but more importantly in terms of having substantially completed its systemic transformation. Slovenia would by then be ready to take on the opportunities and challenges of the single European market.

The purpose of this chapter is to evaluate Slovenia's experience in stabilizing its economy, implementing the structural reform agenda and in launching the task to become a member in the enlarged EU. Macroeconomic stabilization has been the backbone of Slovenia's fast recovery; nonetheless, the traditional Slovenian consensus-building approach to policy reform has slowed the pace of needed structural reforms. As Slovenia sets its sights on accession to the EU, the overarching development objective is to achieve faster, sustainable growth and enhance the welfare of its population. There is a large coincidence between the policies and institutional reforms that are conducive to rapid and sustainable growth, and the adoption of the EU's *acquis communautaire*. This coincidence should give Slovenia the incentives to adopt win-win policies that contribute to achieving both objectives.

Stabilization and Recovery

During the second half of the 1980s, the deterioration of the economic and political situation in Yugoslavia accelerated. Declining output growth and hyperinflation marked the end of the decade and precipitated the disintegration of the federation. At the time, Slovenia had a privileged position relative comparison to the other members of the former federation. It was the wealthiest and most western-oriented member of Yugoslavia. It generated 18 percent of the social product and 20 percent of the industrial production of Yugoslavia with only 8 percent of the population of the federation. It had about one fifth of Yugoslavia's unemployment (3.2 percent versus 14.9 percent) and a productivity at least twice as much as the national average. Slovenia was also Yugoslavia's window to the West. The crisis in the federation, however, had a significant impact in Slovenia's production capacity. The loss of markets, both in the Council of Mutual Economic Assistance (CMEA) and with the other former Yugoslav republics aggravated the recession of the late 1980s and early 1990s.

The Initial Response

Slovenia responded to the challenges of transition and independence with a strong adjustment program aimed at retaking command of the economy. The implementation of the stabilization program was the most important economic task of the newly established state. A new currency, the tolar, was introduced on October 8, 1991; this aimed at de-linking Slovenia's monetary policy from that of the federation, thus breaking the links with the hyperinflation trends of the past. The impact of this program was remarkable, and the beginning of the turnaround was visible already by early 1993.

A gradual approach of economic policy was typically used in the area of cutting inflation. The Bank of Slovenia together with the government was lowering inflation over a period of several years under a managed floating exchange rate regime. Such an unorthodox stabilization policy eventually proved to be efficient. Inflation, which reached 1,306 percent annually in the last quarter of 1989, was reduced to 201.3 percent in 1992 (average annual rate) and then gradually to the upper single digits (8.6 percent) by the end of 1995. This level of inflation was the lowest in Slovenia since the mid-1970s. Output declined in the early years of the transition, 1991-92, by 8.9 and 5.5 percent respectively, but output growth resumed in 1993, making Slovenia the second CEE economy, following Poland, to turnaround from the initial shock of the transition. International reserves were built from virtually

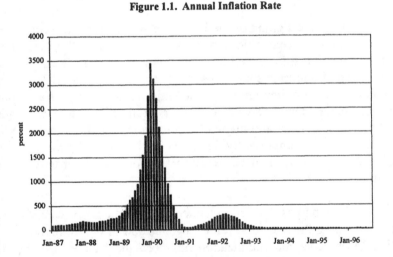

Figure 1.1. Annual Inflation Rate

zero to a comfortable US$4.2 billion by 1996, that is, to about 4.5 months of imports. This was the result of current account surpluses until 1994 and capital inflows thereafter. During the same early transition period, the general government fiscal budget was kept virtually balanced. Comprehensive foreign trade liberalization, integration into the international community, and major advances towards resolving its foreign debt problems -all put Slovenia at the forefront of transition economies in the search for membership in the enlarged EU.

Macroeconomic stabilization was followed by structural reforms that slowly began to redefine the roles of the private and public sectors, and to reorient the economy towards a market-based export-led growth and international integration. Nonetheless the reforms moved slowly; they did not deliver the expected rapid growth in private sector participation or in output recovery that can be seen in other leading transition economies from CEE. Paradoxically, while Slovenia was a forerunner at the beginning of the transition, it pursued a more gradualist approach to systemic transformation relative to other transition economies. By 1996, private sector participation in GDP reached only about 40 percent, well below the levels observed in Poland, Hungary, Czech Republic or

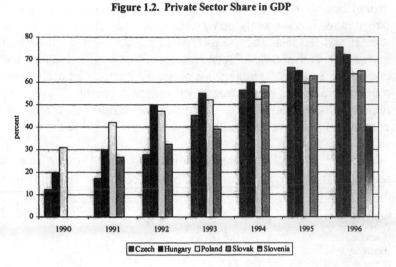

Figure 1.2. Private Sector Share in GDP

Slovakia, which were already over 60 percent of GDP in 1996. Even today Slovenia's private sector generates only about 50-55 percent of GDP.[1]

Fast Turnaround but the Recovery Slows Down

Slovenia's economic turnaround began in 1993 and its economic performance continued to improve during 1994 and 1995. After a 2.8 percent real GDP growth in 1993, favorable economic trends in Western

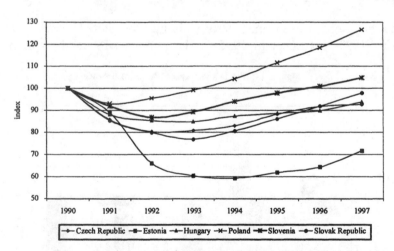

Figure 1.3. GDP Recovery in Selected CEE Countries

Europe contributed to a 5.3 percent real GDP growth in 1994. The growth in Europe provided the room for further expansion of exports to western markets. Slovenia is a small open economy where exports and imports of goods and non-factor services account jointly for over 100 percent of GDP. The economy is therefore vulnerable to external economic fluctuations. The lull in Europe's economic growth in the second half of 1995 affected Slovenia's economic performance, slowing the pace of its economic recovery. Output growth waned to 4.1 percent in 1995 and to 3.1 percent during 1996. In spite of this decline in output growth, over the period 1993-95 Slovenia was able to recover most of the ground lost during the initial phase of its economic transformation.

---

[1] Measuring the size of the private sector in GDP is difficult in Slovenia due to the mixed ownership structure still available. The State, however, is still the single most important shareholder in newly privatized firms (old socially-owned enterprises); it also maintains almost complete ownership in the so-called state-owned enterprises (public utilities, large banks, etc.).

Domestic factors also contributed to the slowdown of the economy. On the one hand, real wage pressures (due to failed wage agreements), the rise of domestic costs of production (due to price adjustments in the energy sector), and the appreciation of the tolar until the first half of 1995 (due in part to sizable capital flows), reduced competitiveness abroad and turned around the trade accounts. On the other hand, structural reforms, namely privatization, advanced but at a slow pace, lagging behind other reforms. This was in part the result of the method of privatization chosen by the authorities, which held back private investment and reduced incentives for foreign participation and FDI. Privatization of state owned enterprises and banks remains one of the most important unfinished structural reform agendas in Slovenia's transformation to a private sector led market economy. By the second half of 1995, the tolar started to depreciate -until mid-1996- improving the conditions for the export sector. Nevertheless, production continued to decline especially in enterprises oriented to the domestic market.

Table 1.1. Annual Inflation and GDP Growth in Selected CEE Countries, 1992-97

	1992	1993	1994	1995	1996	1997
			Inflation (CPI average)			
Czech Republic	11.1	20.8	10.1	9.1	8.8	8.5
Estonia	1069.0	89.0	47.7	28.9	23.1	11.2
Hungary	23.0	22.5	18.8	28.2	23.6	18.3
Poland	43.0	35.3	32.2	27.8	19.9	14.8
Slovak Republic	10.0	23.2	13.4	9.9	5.8	6.2
Slovenia*	201.3	32.9	19.8	12.6	9.7	9.1
			GDP growth (percent)			
Czech Republic	-6.4	0.6	2.7	6.4	3.9	1.0
Estonia	-25.8	-8.5	-1.8	4.3	4.0	11.4
Hungary	-3.1	-0.6	2.9	1.5	1.3	4.4
Poland	2.6	3.8	5.2	7.0	6.1	6.9
Slovak Republic	-6.5	-3.7	4.9	6.8	6.6	6.5
Slovenia	-5.5	2.8	5.3	4.1	3.3	3.8

Source: National sources.
* Retail prices as measure of inflation until 1998, after 1998 CPI.

On the external side, the current account remained strong during the initial years after independence, recording surpluses during 1992-96 (except in 1995). The improvement in the current account between 1993 and 1994 reflected a revival in exports of goods and services, especially tourism. In 1995, however, exports of goods slowed down while imports rose significantly, producing a larger than expected trade deficit. An important component of the import boom, however, was capital goods. This behavior of exports and imports was consistent with the almost one-and-a-half-year real appreciation of the tolar which, combined with an increase in labor costs in real terms, resulted in a decline in the competitiveness of Slovene exporters in 1995.

Figure 1.4. Trade and Current Account Balance

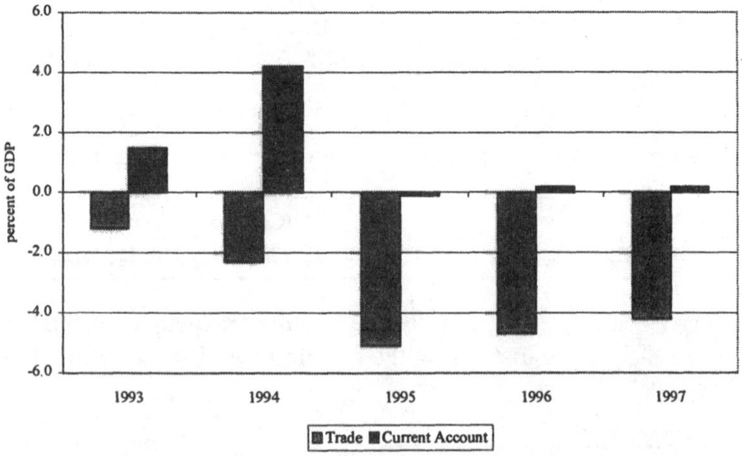

Significant capital inflows began in 1993 and continued through 1995. Together with the current account results, this helped Slovenia increase its international reserves in 1995 to about US$3.4 billion, or

3.8 months of imports of goods and services. During the first half of 1996 capital flows intensified (especially credits to banks and enterprises), putting pressure on monetary and exchange rate policies. Consequently, the Central Bank implemented several measures to slow these flows.

Table 1.2. Selected Economic Indicators, 1992-98[1]

	1992	1993	1994	1995	1996	1997	1998[2]
Real Economy (change in percent)							
Real GDP	-5.5	2.8	5.3	4.1	3.3	3.8	4.0
Domestic Demand	-5.1	5.4	5.1	6.2	3.4	4.4	4.0
CPI (period average) 2/	201.3	32.3	19.8	12.6	9.7	9.1	7.9
Registered Unemployment Rate (in percent)	11.5	14.4	14.5	14.0	13.9	14.4	14.4
LFS Unemployment Rate (in percent)	8.3	9.1	9.1	7.4	7.3	7.4	7.7
Gross National Saving (in percent of GDP)	24.9	21.5	24.8	23.3	23.6	23.8	24.3
Gross Domestic Investment (in percent of GDP)	17.6	19.3	20.9	23.4	23.4	23.7	24.3
Public Finance (percent of GDP) 3/							
Central Government Balance	-0.9	-0.3	0.4	1.0	0.6	-1.1	-0.9
General Government Balance	0.2	0.3	-0.2	0.0	0.3	-1.1	-1.0
Gross Public Debt		21.0	18.6	27.9	28.8	27.3	
Money and Credit (end of year, percent change)							
Real Credit to the Private Sector	3.2	8.8	11.5	31.0	9.6	2.8	14.4
Broad Money (M3)	127.0	63.7	42.4	27.9	21.4	24.0	24.3
Interest Rates (percent)							
Nominal Interbank Interest Rate (percent, overnight)		38.5	28.7	12.0	13.8	9.6	6.3
Real Lending Rates (percent)	18-24	19-20	16-17	13-14	11-12	10-11	5.9
Real Deposit Rates (percent)	6-10	8-11	8-11	7-10	5-7	3-5	0.9
Balance of Payments							
Trade Balance (percent of GDP)	6.3	-1.2	-2.3	-5.1	-4.7	-4.2	-3.7
Exports of Goods & Services (percent of GDP)	63.1	58.8	60.0	55.2	55.6	57.1	55.2
Imports of Goods & Services (percent of GDP)	56.2	57.7	57.8	56.8	56.6	58.3	56.5
Current Account Balance (percent of GDP)	7.4	1.5	4.2	-0.1	0.2	0.2	0.0
Capital and Financial Account (percent of GDP)	-2.3	-0.6	0.3	1.4	2.9	6.9	0.4
Official Reserves (US$ million)	716	770	1,480	1,802	2,279	3,297	3,501
Reserve Cover (months of imports of GS)	1.2	1.3	2.1	2.0	2.6	3.7	3.8
External Debt (US$ million)	1,741	1,873	2,258	2,970	4,010	4,176	4,745
(percent of exports of GS)	22.0	25.1	26.2	28.6	38.2	40.0	43.8
External Debt Service (US$ million)	418	414	480	739	936	960	1,289
(percent of exports of GS)	5.3	5.5	5.6	7.1	8.9	9.2	11.9
Exchange Rates							
Nominal Exchange Rate (SIT per US$, average)	81.3	113.2	128.8	118.5	135.4	159.7	166.5
Nominal Exchange Rate (SIT per DM, average)	61.2	76.4	81.6	87.9	91.0	94.4	94.5[4]
Nominal Effective Exchange Rate (1995=100)	145.7	114.5	100.4	100.0	90.2	85.4	83.3[4]
Real Effective Exchange Rate (ULC, 1995=100)	82.1	91.3	91.9	100.0	97.7	100.3	101.8[4]
Real Effective Exchange Rate (CPI, 1995=100)	87.6	87.5	90.7	100.0	97.1	97.8	101.3[4]
Real Effective Exchange Rate (PPI, 1995=100)	93.7	89.7	91.7	100.0	95.9	95.8	98.7[4]
Memo							
Gross Domestic Product (US$ billion)		12.52	14.39	18.74	18.86	18.20	19.63
Per Capita Income (US$)	6,275	6,366	7,233	9,431	9,471	9,161	9,899

Notes: 1/ IMF projections.
2/ Retail price index 1992-97; consumer price index as of 1998.
3/ Privatization revenues from state and socially-owned enterprises are placed below the line.
4/ As of end-August, real effective exchange rate (ULC based) as of July.
5/ Preliminary.

Source: IMF, Bank of Slovenia, Ministry of Finance and Statistical Office of the Republic of Slovenia.

Starting in 1994 with a ban on short-term bank borrowing abroad, restrictions on capital inflows were progressively tightened. This has involved imposing an unremunerated 40 percent deposit requirement against foreign non-trade-related loans with a maturity of up to 5 years in February 1995 (extended to up to 7 years in July 1996). It entailed raising foreign exchange cover requirements against foreign currency deposits in April 1995 (to 100 percent in the case of sight deposits). Another tightening policy involved requiring banks to increase their foreign assets pari passu with increases in their foreign liabilities in July 1996 as well as subjecting financial loans with a maturity in excess of 7 years to a 10 percent deposit requirement in December 1996. Finally, tightening also required nonresidents to conduct their inward portfolio investments through custody accounts with a fully licensed bank in February 1997. The last measure was relaxed in July 1997 by exempting portfolio investments committed for more than 7 years from the custody account requirement and again in 1999.

The Central Bank is moving to eliminate some of the capital account restriction. On February 1, 1999 it made significant changes to the legislation regulating capital movements. The restriction on short-term borrowing by Banks was eliminated. Banks are required -since November 1998- to limit their monthly foreign exchange exposure to 10 percent of their capital. The non-interest bearing deposit requirement on foreign financial loans -imposed since 1995- was lifted. However, the Bank of Slovenia (hereafter referred to as BOS) retains the discretion to impose a non-interest bearing deposit of up to 30 percent -held at the BOS- for a period of two years from the date of disbursement of the loan. Also eliminated is the freeze of the net foreign indebtedness position of commercial banks -beyond the position at July 31, 1996.

Regulations concerning portfolio investments by non-residents and the use of custody accounts have also been changed in February 1999. Except for the purchases of shares representing non-residents' participation in voting power or capital of domestic firms of more than 10 percent, as well as, purchases of shares issued in primary markets, custody accounts established with licensed domestic banks have to be used to conduct operations in securities and derivatives traded in the secondary market. The custody accounts can be held in domestic or foreign currency. Commercial banks, however, are obliged to pay a premium in relation to the balances held in custody accounts. The premium is to be set quarterly by the BOS and will not be charged if the foreign investors held their balances for four years or more.

The 1997-98 Revival and EU Accession

The slow-down in Slovenia's economic performance lasted for about a year. In the second half of 1996 economic activity began to show signs of recovery, in line with the revival of economic activity in the EU. Inflation resumed its downward trend, although it remained stubbornly high in the upper single digits until mid-1998. Real GDP growth accelerated to 3.8 percent in 1997 and is expected to reach 4 percent in 1998. The rebound in 1997 was mainly due to increasing foreign demand, with exports of goods, growing in volume by 6.5 percent. Domestic demand,

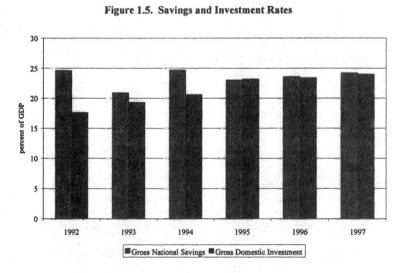

Figure 1.5. Savings and Investment Rates

however, also contributed to the 1997-98 recovery. Investment rose by 11.2 percent in 1997, and a looser fiscal policy boosted public consumption. By contrast, the growth of private consumption was bridled by increasing wage restraint and by stagnating employment. Export growth has slowed in 1998 while domestic demand strengthened further, led by investment and private consumption. Due to late-year expenditure cuts, the growth contribution of public consumption is expected to be somewhat reduced.

Although Slovenia's economy was capable of a fast output turnaround, this has not led to employment growth. The labor force declined by 2 percent during the transition (1992-97); employment declined by 5 percent, real output increased by 21 percent during the same period. This output growth, without employment recovery, essentially reflects productivity gains. Unemployment, as measured by the ILO-survey definition, has remained stable since 1995 at around 7.4 percent -- low in comparison with other transition economies (except Czech Republic) and the EU. The labor shed in manufacturing has been partially absorbed by the services sector, which now accounts for more than half of GDP. In spite of the low unemployment rate, large regional disparities and a high concentration of unemployment among unskilled and older workers still persist. Moreover, unemployment duration has been increasing, suggesting that the bulk of unemployment is structural.

In the early years of the transition, real wages grew above agreed social partners' targets (and productivity increases). This was particularly true for the government sector, which then spilled over the wage demands into the entire economy. The outcome of wage pressures affected competitiveness in the real sector, it affected social expenditures linked to wage increases, like pension payments. The need to establish wage discipline in the government sector was reflected in new wage adjustment law (enacted in mid-1997) that helped moderate real wage growth, helped ease wage indexation and helped reverse the trends of real wage increases exceeding productivity gains. As a result of these policies, unit labor costs started to fall. Although real gross wage growth moderated from 5.1 percent in 1996 to 2.4 percent in 1997 and 1.3 percent in the first eight months of 1998, wage growth in the government sector continued to outpace that in the private sector. Further efforts are thus required to avoid wage escalation in the future that may damage the prospects for growth and integration.

Table 1.3. Index of Real Net Wages and Productivity, 1992-97

	1992	1993	1994	1995	1996	1997
Real Net Wage	100	116.4	123.3	129.1	134.8	138.7
Productivity	100	106.4	119.9	127.7	139.7	141.9

Source: Statistical Office and Agency for Payments of the Republic of Slovenia.

Fiscal Sustainability and the Transition

Slovenia was able to keep its general government budget virtually balanced during the first five years of independence. The policy of maintaining an overall fiscal balance was one of the corner stones of Slovenia's transition and an important support to its monetary policy during the initial macroeconomic stabilization efforts. In 1997, however, the general government slipped into a deficit of 1.1 percent of GDP -small in comparison with other transition economies but large for Slovenia's standards (see Figure 1.6).

Most CEECs in transition undertook price liberalization and privatization reforms, albeit at different paces and using a variety of methods. As a result, all went through cycles of sharp recession followed, in most cases, by private sector-induced recovery. A central feature of the liberalization packages was a set of policies intended to affect fiscal accounts that, in many cases, led to fiscal crises-a rare phenomenon in these previous socialists economies. Unlike many other transition economies,

Slovenia's public finances did not deteriorate during the initial states of the transition. Its fiscal budget was kept virtually balanced most of the time, and its public debt remained below 25 percent of GDP.

The widening of the fiscal gap in 1997 was mainly the result of: (i) reductions on social security contributions, (ii) diminished border trade and lower customs duties in accordance with EU and CEFTA agreements, and (iii) higher social transfers, wages, and subsidies. The size of the fiscal deficit does not, in itself, raise concerns. Nevertheless the size of the 1996-97 deterioration of the fiscal stand reflects a changing trend in Slovenia's fiscal position. The deterioration of the fiscal stand raises concerns about the consistency between the current fiscal position and the government's macroeconomic targets, especially in light of the expenditure demands coming from the EU accession process.

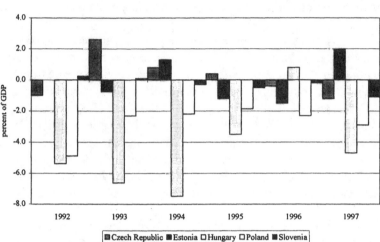

Figure 1.6. Fiscal Balance in Selected CEE Countries

Table 1.4. Summary of General Government Operations, 1993-98

	1993	1994	1995	1996	1997	1998 Budget
	(In percent of GDP)					
Total revenues 1/	46.8	45.8	45.2	44.7	44.6	45.1
Central government	22.3	22.7	23.4	24.0	25.0	25.8
Pension Fund	12.9	12.2	11.9	10.1	9.2	9.2
Health Fund	7.4	6.5	6.3	6.7	6.6	6.5
Local governments	3.4	3.2	2.4	3.0	2.9	2.9
Other revenues	0.7	1.1	1.1	0.9	0.9	0.7
Total expenditure 1/	46.7	46.1	45.7	44.9	45.7	46.1
Central government	21.1	20.3	20.7	20.1	21.0	21.4
Pension Fund	11.9	12.3	12.6	12.3	12.3	13.3
Health Fund	7.3	6.9	6.7	6.6	6.6	6.7
Local governments	5.2	5.4	4.7	4.9	4.9	4.8
Other revenues	1.1	1.1	1.1	1.0	1.0	1.0
Overall balance	0.1	-0.3	-0.5	-0.2	-1.1	-1.1
Central government	1.1	2.4	2.8	3.9	3.3	4.4
Pension Fund	1.0	-0.2	-0.6	-2.2	-3.0	-4.1
Health Fund	0.2	-0.4	-0.3	0.1	0.0	-0.2
Local governments	-1.9	-2.1	-2.3	-2.0	-2.0	-1.9
Other revenues	-0.4	-0.1	0.0	-0.1	-0.1	-0.3
Foreign financing (net)	0.6	0.3	0.3	0.9	0.7	0.5
Domestic financing (net)	-0.2	-0.4	-0.5	-0.5	0.3	0.5

Notes: 1/ Transfers between different levels of government and the funds are netted out.
Source: Ministry of Finance and IMF.

Sustainable economic growth is possible only with a sound macroeconomic framework in which coordinated fiscal and monetary policies play complementary roles. Considering the government budget constraint, it is important to assess the implication of the current policies on Slovenia's fiscal sustainability. To perform such an exercise, it is necessary to evaluate the government's availability to finance its fiscal deficit in the long-term. Table 1.5 summarizes the results of the level of sustainable fiscal deficit under alternative assumptions of inflation, domestic and foreign debt, interest rates, degree of monetization in the economy and output growth. Both overall and primary sustainable deficits are computed for this exercise.[2]

The fiscal sustainability simulations show that under 1997 conditions of inflation, domestic and foreign debt, interest rate level and output growth, Slovenia is capable of sustaining an overall fiscal deficit of a magnitude not larger than 2.4 percent of GDP. Moreover, the results also imply that the sustainable primary deficit is of the order of 0.7 percent of GDP. At current lower levels of inflation (7 percent), the sustainable deficit is just 2.1 percent of GDP (0.5 percent of GDP for the primary deficit). Sensitivity analysis shows that the sustainable fiscal deficit under current condition assumptions ranges from 1.3 percent of GDP up to 2.9 percent of GDP. The latter, however, requires an inflation rate of 10 percent and an output growth rate of 6 percent per annum.

Table 1.5. Sustainable Fiscal Deficit – 1997 Conditions

Inflation Rate		GDP Growth Rate				
		3.8	4.0	4.5	5.0	6.0
2.9	Primary Deficit	0.23	0.26	0.35	0.44	0.61
	Overall Deficit	1.26	1.30	1.39	1.47	1.65
5.0	Primary Deficit	0.37	0.41	0.50	0.58	0.75
	Overall Deficit	1.66	1.69	1.78	1.87	2.04
7.0	Primary Deficit	0.50	0.54	0.63	0.71	0.88
	Overall Deficit	2.02	2.06	2.15	2.23	2.40
8.0	Primary Deficit	0.57	0.60	0.69	0.77	0.94
	Overall Deficit	2.21	2.24	2.31	2.42	2.59
9.0	Primary Deficit	0.63	**0.66**	0.75	0.84	1.01
	Overall Deficit	2.39	**2.42**	2.51	2.60	2.77
10.0	Primary Deficit	0.69	0.72	0.81	0.90	1.07
	Overall Deficit	2.57	2.60	2.69	2.77	2.94
Assumptions:	Domestic Real interest rate	5.0				
	Foreign Real interest rate	2.5				
	Domestic Debt Stock/GDP	11.3				
	Foreign Debt Stock/GDP	11.4				
	Foreign Reserves/GDP	8.9				
	Base Money/GDP	5.0				

Source: World Bank estimates.

The above exercise is useful to get a sense of the degree of freedom available to the government, particularly in light of the expenditure demands that EU accession will bring. Assuming current conditions of inflation (7 percent) and output growth (4 percent), an expansion of domestic debt to 20 percent of GDP increases the overall sustainable deficit by 1 percent to 3.1 percent of GDP, but reduces the sustainable primary deficit to 0.45 percent of GDP. Alternatively, an increase in the monetary base to 7 percent of GDP increases the sustainable deficit to 2.3 percent of GDP. As these results

_____

[2] As with any exercise of fiscal sustainability, the results should be taken with caution. Because of the simplifying assumptions, the exercise is sensitive to the assumptions used on the key variables.

indicate, Slovenia's fiscal stand has limited room for maneuvering with respect to domestic debt increases and monetization. On the other hand, Slovenia has a relatively small level of net foreign debt (government debt minus government foreign reserves). An increase of foreign debt to 20 percent (net foreign debt to 11 percent of GDP) increases the sustainable deficit to 3 percent, but it increases the vulnerability of the country to external shocks.

An additional exercise based on the Maastricht criteria parameters shows that, if the inflation rate is reduced to 2.9 percent (the current Maastricht criteria level) and if growth rate of GDP remains at 4 percent, then the sustainable overall fiscal deficit declines to 1.3 percent of GDP (and the primary to 0.26 percent).

Overall, the fiscal sustainability exercise indicates the need for fiscal discipline. If Slovenia is to maintain current low levels of public debt, it needs to sustain its fiscal prudence of past years and return to a balanced budget. This requires the government to rationalize its expenditures and implement needed reforms of the tax system, including both the VAT, and the social security, particularly that related to the pension system.

The Size of the Public Sector

With the EU accession process providing additional spending pressures and the government slow to reform the pension and tax system, and reduce the scope of government functions, expenditures have surpassed 46 percent of GDP, deviating from both the declining trend of other leading CEECs and Slovenia's own objectives (see Figure 1.7). The 1998 budget envisages a general government fiscal deficit equivalent to 1 percent of GDP. It features higher capital spending, mostly for highways to advance the European corridor structure, and revenue gains from higher gasoline taxation and the new tax on bank assets. Despite tight budget execution, lagging tax collections (especially from wages, retail sales, and imports) have been jeopardizing the 1998 deficit target, prompting the authorities in late September to announce a three percent across-the-board cut in

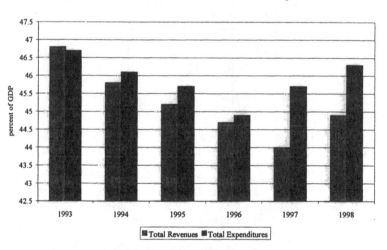

Figure 1.7. General Government Revenues and Expenditures

expenditures. The 1999 budget envisages an expenditure envelope of SIT 960.7 billion and revenues of SIT 931 billion -- implying a general government fiscal deficit around 0.8 percent of GDP.

At its current level, the size of the public sector puts Slovenia in the neighborhood of some advanced OECD countries, but well above countries with similar per-capita incomes such as Portugal and Spain. This raises the question of the adequacy and sustainability of its spending patterns. One way of assessing the adequacy and sustainability of the size of the public sector is to evaluate whether Slovenia's public expenditure ratios over GDP are in line with comparable indicators predicted from structural characteristics. The size of the state in a market economy is the result of those public policy choices made regarding the public/private split in the provision of goods and services, coupled with other factors such as demographic and structural parameters that characterize that economy. Among the factors that can be identified as government spending determinants are the age structure and growth rate of the population, income levels and financial constraints, such as public debt ratio to GDP.[3]

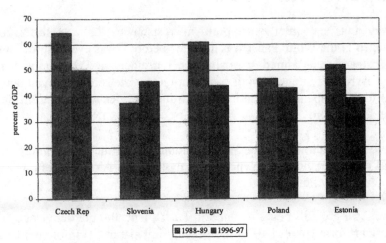

Figure 1.8 General Government Expenditures in Selected CEECs

Based on results from a model that explains cross-country differences in ratios of general government spending to GDP,[4] the predicted expenditure ratio to GDP is calculated for Slovenia. According to these results, Slovenia's expenditure level in 1997 should have been of the order of 41.6 percent of GDP, that is, 4.1 percent of GDP lower. Slovenia is the only member of the leading accession candidates where the size of the State, as measured by public expenditures, has increased during the transition (see Figure 1.8). This is due, in part, to need to establish government institutions.

The Need for Pension Reform

The largest single government program in Slovenia is the pay-as-you-go pension scheme. One in every four Slovenes receives a pension at levels, which are among the highest in Europe relative to the average income in the population. This generosity, along with a sudden surge in the number of pensioners due to permissive early retirement programs, led to one of the highest ratios of pension spending to GDP in Europe at around 14 percent. High payroll tax rates of one quarter of gross wages are earmarked for pensions, yet the scheme required transfers from the central budget of around 3.5 percent of GDP in 1997. Medium and long-term actuarial projections show a sharp deterioration due to demographic factors during the next decade. Unless the current system is reformed, pension deficits are expected to grow to more than 10 percent of GDP by the time today's younger workers retire.

As a result of a deteriorating pay-as-you-go (PAYG) pension system, Slovenia's pension fund deficit has been growing since 1994. The already large pension fund deficit would be substantially larger if its under-reimbursement for services provided to pensioners by the health fund is taken into account. Without a comprehensive pension reform, fiscal balance is unlikely in the medium and long-terms.

A recent White Paper issued in October of 1997 listed the key elements for a comprehensive reform. The first set of measures was designed to reduce projected expenditures to affordable levels. These included a shift away from the current wage indexation formula and toward a combined wage and price indexation. Most countries in Europe have already moved toward price indexation, as this method maintains pensioners' purchasing power while allowing the tax base to outgrow the pension bill. The second measure was the gradual increase in the effective retirement age achieved through the introduction

---

[3] With the help of the IMF the government is currently revising its budgetary classification system. The process is expected to be completed in 1999. Under the new budget classification the size of the government, as measured by the ratio of expenditures (revenues) over GDP is expected to decline by as much as 2 percent of GDP, but the upward trend in expenditures (revenues) will remain the same.

[4] See Barbone, L. and R. Polastri, *Hungary's Public Finances in an International Context*, in Public Finance Reform during the Transition, The World Bank, Washington D.C., 1998.

of actuarial penalties for early retirement along with a gradual increase in the normal retirement age. Other measures included a gradual reduction in the "accrual rate" and an extension of the period over which the pensionable wage base was determined. Both measures would lead to a gradual reduction in initial benefit levels. The Government proposal was originally expected to go beyond the pay-as-you-go reforms and would privatize roughly one fourth of the current scheme.

Reform plans were under way but encounter stiff political resistance. As a result, the government's three-pillar proposal envisaged in the White Paper was defeated before it was even a draft law presented to Parliament for approval. Instead, steps aimed at raising the retirement age, lessening the degree of indexation, thereby penalizing early retirement, raising contributions by the self-employed, and raising the cost of buying pension rights for time spent in education and military service will represent the core amendments to the existing pension legislation.

In view of fierce opposition to a mandatory defined-contribution pillar, the government is formulating a two-pillar reform proposal with a financially balanced pay-as-you-go (PAYG) system as its principal pillar, supplemented by a voluntary fully funded system.

While the details of the new proposal are still being debated in Parliament, the plan envisages a well-regulated environment. The proposed reform solves half of the pension imbalance. If implemented, the pension system will be in better shape for the next 10-15 years, however, Slovenia will continue to have one of the most imbalanced pension system in the region. The reform cuts the expected pension deficit by year 2050 from 12 percent of GDP to 6 percent of GDP -the Hungarian three-pillar reform, in comparison, cuts the deficit from 6 percent to 1 percent of GDP.

The proposed two-pillar reform, however, falls short in not addressing entirely a number of important areas. For instance, it does not produce the level of positive effects anticipated for the development of domestic capital markets, or the potential for higher returns for younger workers, which could reduce labor market distortions and encourage formal sector employment. It would also not alleviate the intergenerational burden of paying off existing pension obligations, a cost that falls disproportionately on younger generations of workers.

External Balance and Capital Inflows

Slovenia has maintained its current account virtually in equilibrium since 1995. The balance of payments pressures in recent years have thus been the result of capital inflows. Despite capital inflow restrictions (introduced sequentially between 1994-97 and, recently relaxed in early 1999), net inflows have been growing during 1994-97, reaching on aggregate around 11 percent of GDP. In 1997 they reached approximately 7 percent of GDP. Inward direct foreign investment has been low, at about 1 percent of GDP per annum, but rose to 1.8 percent of GDP in 1997, its highest level since independence, as prospects for early EU membership brightened with the reaching of an association agreement. In addition, relatively high domestic interest rates, and therefore high interest rate differentials, encouraged foreign borrowing, partly in circumvention of existing BOS restrictions.[5] Capital inflows contracted sharply in 1998 as the interest rate differentials narrowed and as the appetite for emerging market investments dwindled, especially after the Russian crisis. This showed that a correction on fundamentals produces a better response than any form of capital controls. Moreover, direct investment also lost its momentum and returned to its low pre-1997 level.

---

[5] One way to evade the restrictions is through the cash foreign exchange market -- estimated to handle about 40 percent of all foreign exchange transactions.

Table 1.6. Selective External Balance Accounts, 1993-98

	1993	1994	1995	1996	1997	1998*
	(In percent of GDP)					
Trade balance	-1.2	-2.3	-5.1	-4.7	-4.2	-3.7
Exports of goods and services	59.0	60.0	55.3	55.7	57.4	56.3
Imports of goods and services	57.2	57.7	57.1	56.6	58.4	57.3
Current account	1.5	4.2	-0.1	0.2	0.2	0.0
Trade Balance	-1.2	-2.3	-5.1	-4.7	-4.2	-3.7
Service Balance	3.0	4.7	3.4	3.7	3.2	2.7
Capital and financial account	-1.6	-3.6	0.9	-0.2	0.6	1.0
Foreign Direct Investment, net	0.9	0.9	0.9	1.0	1.6	0.9
Portfolio Investment, net	0.0	-0.2	0.0	3.4	1.3	0.7
Government Operations, gross	--	--	--	4.2	1.3	2.9
Change in official reserves	0.9	4.5	1.3	3.1	7.1	1.1

Note: * IMF projections.
Source: Bank of Slovenia.

In 1997, the capital account reflected large capital inflows with a surplus of US$1,217, equivalent to 6 percent of GDP. Although the magnitude of the capital account surplus seems high, a substantial amount of inflows (US$600 million) consisted of transfers of commercial banks deposits abroad to Slovenia. These transfers were converted into BOS foreign exchange bills. In February of 1997, the Bank of Slovenia increased the minimum investment of foreign currency holdings reserve requirement in Bank of Slovenia bills to 60 percent. Consequently, banks had to lower their deposits abroad. Once this operation is accounted for, the *net amount of capital inflows* is equivalent to US$645 million or 3.6 percent of GDP.

The critical question for the Slovene authorities is how to deal with capital account liberalization. With the ratification of the EAA in October 1998, Slovenia will have four years to remove the capital restrictions. Capital account and financial liberalization are inevitable for countries that wish to take advantage of the substantial benefits from participating in the open world economic system. As recent international events have demonstrated, financial liberalization also has its dangers. These dangers rise from imprudent risks of individuals, enterprises or financial institutions that can create systemic disturbances. The risks cannot be completely suppressed, but they can be limited with sound macroeconomic policies aimed at containing aggregate financial imbalances. Proper private sector incentives for risk management in the financial sector are critical. With these safeguards, orderly and properly sequenced capital account and financial liberalization can be clearly beneficial.

Coping with a Volatile External Environment

Slovenia is a small open economy, and therefore vulnerable to external economic fluctuations. The business cycle of Slovenia's major trading partners in the EU (Germany, Italy, France and Austria) substantially affects its output growth. The weak pace of expansion in Slovenia's economic performance during 1995-96 was, in part due to the slowdown in Europe. Slovenia, as with rest of the world, today faces an exceptionally volatile international environment. What was at most an Asian regional crisis in 1997 has since turned into a global crisis. The world faces today unsustainable economic conditions in key emerging market countries in Asia, Latin America and the Former Soviet Union (FSU).

The impact of the Russian crisis on transition economies in CEE has so far been relatively contained, albeit to different degrees.[6] As a result of the various capital inflow restrictions imposed by

---

[6] On August 17, faced with unsustainable market pressure, decreasing international reserves and a sizable amount of short-term debt payments, the Russian government abandoned its pegged exchange rate regime, the anchor of its

the BOS and the virtual absence of short-term foreign capital in Slovenia, recent developments in Asia and Russia have not had an appreciable long-term effect on its financial markets. There were, however, sizable short term effects. Slovenia's spreads in the Eurobond market rose sharply and become volatile during August–October. The spreads of Slovenia's thinly traded Eurobonds declined to 70–120 basis points in November -within manageable margins but still above pre-crisis levels.[7]

The world financial crisis has served to highlight the relative strengths and weaknesses of the region's economies. Although the leading acceding countries have seen their equity markets decline sharply, pressure on their exchange rates, interest rates and external spreads has been quite moderate. Despite some recent weakening of the Ljubljana stock market (see Figure 1.9), the performance of the market remained strong with the twelve-month growth (October 1997–October 1998) of the Slovenian Stock Exchange Index amounting to about 19 percent. The

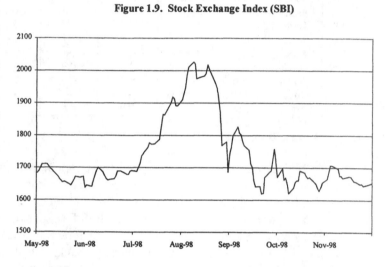

Figure 1.9. Stock Exchange Index (SBI)

banking sector's exposure to Russia is negligible (about 1 percent of on- and off-balance sheet).

The recent financial crises, however, have raised concern among policy makers regarding macroeconomic and financial sector vulnerabilities that could lead to disruption of growth, to pressure on its currency regime, or that could hinder the capacity of the real and financial sectors to operate. Nonetheless Slovenia, has coped remarkably well with the current global financial crisis. External vulnerability indicators do not suggest any imminent danger to Slovenia's stability. Although the current account has deteriorated during the transition from strong surpluses, it remained virtually balanced in the last four years, in contrast with most CEECs that have accumulated large current account deficits.

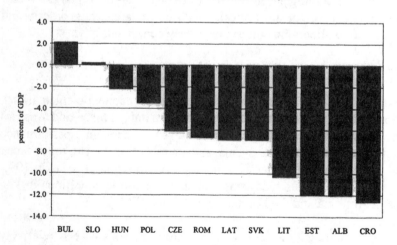

Figure 1.10. Current Account Balance, 1997

The buildup in Slovenia's external debt in the last few years was, in part, a consequence of the country's assuming specified portions of the debt of the former Yugoslavia. External indebtedness continues to be moderate, with total external debt (public and publicly guaranteed and private non-guaranteed) at end-1997 amounting to US$4.2 billion, about 23 percent of GDP. Slovenia's

stabilization policy over the preceding 3 years. Simultaneously, it announced a 90-day moratorium on private external obligations, a restructuring of domestic government debt, and the imposition of foreign exchange controls.
[7] Most of the bonds have been placed with long-term institutional investors.

external debt service ratio (in percent of export of goods and services) is only 9.2 percent. Moreover, short-term foreign debt is negligible, amounting to 0.3 percent of GDP.

Slovenia's relative low degree of external vulnerability to external shocks is also supported by a formal measure. An index that quantifies periods of unusual market volatility and macroeconomic vulnerability was computed. When the index exceeds a defined threshold value and when there is persistence for certain period, this is interpreted as a "warning signal". The indicator is called *Index of Speculative Pressure (ISP)*, and is constructed as follows:[8]

$$ISP_t = \Delta\%\text{exchange rate}_t + \Delta\%\ \text{interest rates}_t - \Delta\%\ \text{international reserves}_t$$

Figure 1.11. Index of Speculative Pressure

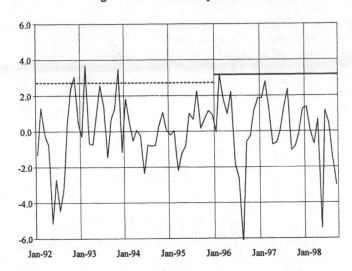

Each variable is calculated in monthly percentage changes and is standardized to have mean zero and unit variance. The threshold is defined as the mean plus 1.5 times the variance of ISP. If the index is larger than this threshold then it is taken as a signal that there is excessive market volatility. Figure 1.11 shows the index and the threshold, which were calculated for two sub-samples, January 1992 to December 1995, and January 1996 to September 1998 (see Figure 1.11). There are few episodes of *"excessive market volatility"* according to the index. The most important ones for the first sub-sample occurred in February and November of 1993. Both cases were primarily due to increases in interest rates, but nonetheless the index did not show any persistence. For the second sub-sample, the index peaks around the time the BOS introduced the custody accounts for portfolio investments by foreigners. Overall, the index reveals no systemic problem with speculative pressures on the tolar.

On the whole, Slovenia's external vulnerabilities are low. Capital inflow pressure eased substantially in 1998, mostly because of lower domestic interest rates, lower net government foreign borrowing, as well as foreign direct investment, and the external borrowing of enterprises.[9] Notwithstanding this development, the large stock of foreign currency denominated instruments issued by the BOS (to moderate the costs of sterilization of capital inflows) continues to be a concern. While these instruments are domestically owned, their already large volume has grown considerably in recent years. These liabilities represented 34 percent of gross foreign reserves of the BOS in 1997. By 1998, this ratio has increased to 50 percent, thus further weakening the foreign currency position of the BOS.

---

[8] See Herrera, Santiago and Conrado Garcia (1998), "A User's Guide to an Early Warning System of Macroeconomic Vulnerability for LAC Countries, mimeo.

[9] The cumulative volume of enterprise borrowing during 1994–97 amounted to about US$1.2 billion. However, changes in the international financial environment combined with lower domestic interest rates resulted in a decline in enterprise borrowing in 1998.

The Challenges of the Pre-Accession Period

The extensive agenda of reforms for the pre-accession period will require a concentrated effort by all levels of government. The implementation period has already been determined by the government's EU accession strategy paper. The growing legislative backlog of recent years is due to both, time-consuming parliamentary procedures and the coalition's political heterogeneity (see Box 1.1). The accession process, however, will not wait for Slovenia as it moves forward. Other leading transition economies are likely to position themselves at the front of the pack unless Slovenia moves forcefully to advance the legislative agenda and the implied structural reforms that it defines. Implementing these reforms will help Slovenia maximize the benefit from accession while minimizing the costs of transposing and applying the *acquis*.

Box 1.1. Status of Main Economic Reform Legislation

Since 1993, the Slovene government has drafted several laws to reduce structural rigidities in the labor market, to speed up privatization of socially- and state-owned enterprises, to improve competition and prudential guidelines in the financial sector, to reform the tax system, and to reduce the deficit of the pension system. Besides updating the current legislation to EU norms and directives, these laws are critical in completing the transformation to a competitive and functioning market economy. However, various impediments, in both the drafting and the parliamentary process, have slowed the approval of these laws since 1996. The following is a status report on this legislation, with the time of submission to parliament in parentheses (when available).

Labor Market Reform

	Status
1. Labor Relations Law (October 1997)	In preparation for 1st reading
2. Amendments to the Law on Labor Inspection	Adopted in June 1997
3. Law on Employment and Insurance in Cases of Unemployment	Adopted in September 1998
4. Law on Safety and Health at Work (March 1995)	In preparation for 2nd reading
5. Law on Wages in the Public Sector	Adopted in 1994
6. Law on Collective Agreements (March 1994)	In preparation for 2nd reading
7. Law on Minimum Wage	Amended in January 1998

Privatization

8. Law on the Completion of Ownership Transformation and Privatization of Legal Entities Owned by the SDC	Adopted in April 1998
9. Law on Privatization of State Assets (1994, revised October 1998)	In preparation for 1st reading
10. Law on Ownership Transformation of Insurance Companies (November 1993)	Prepared for 3rd reading

Financial Market Reform

11. Banking Law (June 1996)	Adopted in January 1999
12. Foreign Exchange Law (May 1997)	Prepared for 2nd reading
13. Securities Markets Law (July 1998)	Prepared for 1st reading
14. Insurance Companies Law	Draft
15. Law on Dematerialized Securities	Prepared for 2nd reading
16. Law on Special Tax on Bank Assets	Adopted in December 1997

Fiscal Reform

17. Value Added Tax Law (June 1996)	Adopted in December 1998
18. Law on Excise Duties (June 1996)	Adopted in December 1998
19. Personal Income Tax Law (March 1997)	Draft
20. Corporate Income Tax Law (March 1997)	Draft
21. Law on Pension and Disability Insurance (August 1998)	In preparation for 1st reading
22. Law on Public Funds (July 1998)	In preparation for 1st reading
23. Amendment to the Municipal Financing Law (July 1998)	Adopted in July 1998

Source: IMF, Ministry of Finance, Ministry of Labor and Social Affairs, and European Commission.

Sustainable Growth and Income Convergence

Introduction

Former applicants to the EU, such as Spain, Portugal and Ireland, had market economies and had been extensively exposed to competition in the Europe-wide economic arena prior to seeking accession. By contrast, Slovenia faces a twofold challenge: complete the transition from a command to a market economy, and concurrently prepare for integration into the EU. Since independence in 1991, Slovenia has made substantial progress in stabilizing its economy and advancing the systemic transformation, but the process is far from complete and does not approach the situation of earlier entrants.[1] The overarching aim of this transformation process is to improve the living standards and the quality of life of its almost two million citizens but also of future generations of Slovenes. A crucial element for Slovenia's development agenda is thus the accession to the EU at the earliest possible date. Accession to the EU is thus not merely an objective in itself, but rather the means to create the momentum necessary to accelerate the reform agenda and to implement needed structural changes to strengthen Slovenia's economic growth prospects.

There are two important reasons to believe that the income gap with the EU can be reduced sharply over the next decade. First, economic history[2] has shown that those countries with lower income per capita that are closely integrated with richer countries tend to grow more rapidly than the richer countries, thereby tending to reduce the gap in per capita income. The divergence in per capita income between member states of the European Union has indeed been significantly reduced during the last decade. Second, Slovenia's income per capita is already relatively high relative to other leading accession countries; it is very close to the income level of Portugal and Greece, both on the lower end of the EU member spectrum. The number of years that it will take Slovenia to converge to average EU income levels depends, to a great extent, on the policy framework and its impact on output growth rates.

This chapter analyzes strategy options for Slovenia to achieve sustained economic growth that will facilitate its economic convergence with the EU, focusing on EU requirements that will provide benchmarks for Slovenia's reforms. While Slovenia has recovered the output growth momentum of 1997-98, it has the potential to attain even higher sustainable growth rates, thereby further differentiating itself from other leading accession candidates. At its current output growth rates, the growth accounting model estimates that Slovenia will reach the average income level of the EU in 21 years. This is essentially at the same time as Poland, which has an income per capita 38 percent below that of Slovenia. Nonetheless, the time to close Slovenia's income gap, however, could be dramatically reduced. If Slovenia increases its GDP growth rate by just one percent, it will reduce the time to achieve EU average income by a third. Moreover, based on results from a growth model assuming diminishing returns on factors of production, Slovenia could cut the time to reach EU average income by two thirds if growth is further accelerated through structural reforms. Paradoxically, Slovenia -the wealthiest among the candidates for EU membership- has been lagging behind other leading candidate countries when it comes to the speed and depth of key structural reforms. Consequently, Slovenia has room for introducing

---

[1] Joining the EU has become a much more complicated process since the *acquis* has been substantially expanded by the Single Market Program and the plans for Economic and Monetary Union (EMU) contained in the Maastricht Treaty (the Treaty on European Union signed at the Maastricht summit). Under the EU Single Market, the EU becomes a space where laws, regulations, standards, and institutions are approximated, harmonized and/or mutually recognized in order to ensure a leveled play field and free competition on an EU scale.

[2] Neoclassical growth theory predicts that within a group of economies with roughly similar tastes, technologies and political institutions, those with lower per capita income will tend to grow faster.

reforms that will boost economic growth and help the country avoid loosing ground to other applicant countries.

European Integration: The Experience of Ireland, Greece, Spain and Portugal

The benefits from economic integration are many, but perhaps the most important one is raising the welfare of the population by increasing the growth capacity of the country. The two main channels through which economic integration can affect growth are accumulation of physical and human capital on one hand and technology or knowledge creation on the other.[3] Economic integration has the advantage of improving the investment climate by reducing the risk premium. For both domestic and foreign investors, confidence is boosted by many factors. In particular, joining the EU makes the country potentially less risky: EU membership assures well-defined property rights, levels of competition, and state-aids policy. Through the four freedoms, the EU promotes the efficient allocation of resources; if securing market contestability as well as trade and capital account liberalization. On the technology side, integration brings the benefits of international spillovers of knowledge through foreign direct investment. This reduces the duplication of innovation efforts and increases competition, thereby bringing efficiency gains and welfare.

The growth effects of economic integration with the EU can be illustrated through the experience of Ireland, Greece, Portugal and Spain. It is relevant to look at the experience of these four countries for at least two reasons. First, because they are among the countries that joined the EU during the enlargements of the 1970s-80s and indeed are countries with an income per capita relative to the EU similar of that of Slovenia. As such, their performance can provide some information about income convergence.[4] Second, sufficient time has passed since they joined the EU to derive conclusions about the medium-run growth effects of economic integration. Accordingly, Table 2.1 shows that the income gap between the EU and these four countries has narrowed.

Table 2.1. Income Convergence of Ireland, Greece, Spain and Portugal

	1960	1973	1980	1985	1990	1993	1997	Index 1997*
GDP per capita (EU average=100)								
Ireland *(1973)*	61	59	64	65	71	77	96	163
Greece *(1981)*	39	57	58	51	47	49	69	119
Spain *(1986)*	60	79	74	71	75	76	78	110
Portugal *(1986)*	39	56	55	51	56	61	71	138
GDP growth rate								
Ireland *(1973)*	5.2	6.2	3.1	3.1	7.8	3.1	7.0	
Greece *(1981)*	4.4	7.3	1.7	3.1	3.7	-1.0	3.1	
Spain *(1986)*	2.4	7.8	1.3	2.6	3.7	-1.2	3.0	
Portugal *(1986)*	..	11.2	4.8	3.0	4.1	0.3	3.4	

Note: ***:** The index measures the improvement between the year of accession and 1997 of the respective country vis-à-vis the EU average.
Source: European Commission Annual Report (1994) for years 1960-93, EUROSTAT and World Bank.

---

[3] Baldwin, R. and E. Seghezza (1996), "Growth and European Integration: Towards an Empirical Assessment," Centre for Economic Policy Research, No.1393.
[4] Ireland joined the EU in 1973, Greece in 1981, and Spain and Portugal in 1986. By the time Greece, Ireland and Portugal joined the EU, their income per capital was around 60 percent of the EU average, while Spain's income per capita was just over 70 percent at accession.

The pattern of income convergence has been sensitive to the policy framework implemented by the individual countries. Although Ireland's income per capita convergence started after accession, if accelerated in the mid-1990, that is, 20 years after entry. Spain and Portugal have been more or less converging at the same pace. Greece's income gap widened after entry, and it was not until the late 1990s that it started catching up.

Except for Greece, these countries experienced investment booms upon accession to the EU. Capital formation was boosted in three of the entrants, Ireland, Portugal and Spain, while Greece experienced instead a consumption boom. There is also evidence that these countries (with the exception of Greece) experienced a stock market boom.[5] The investment boom was driven primarily by the reduced political risk, by the restructuring of the capital stock in view of new production patterns and by the introduction of new technologies accompanied by increased FDI. The opening of the capital account also played an important role; for these countries entry was generally accompanied by an increase in capital inflows.

In summary, the income gap of the countries that joined the EU in the enlargement of the 1970s-80s has been reduced, yet, the benefits on growth from accession were by no means automatic. Gains from economic integration have been contingent on the choices made by policy makers. The commitment and implementation of reforms played a key role in the relative performance of the acceding countries -- a reason why Greece lagged behind the others.[6] Income convergence has not been the artifice of exchange rate valuation, but of real output growth rates that have exceeded those of the richest members of the EU.

Bridging the Income Gap with the EU

The capacity to bridge the income gap with the EU depends, not only on achieving higher growth rates than the EU, but on the ability to sustain these rates of output growth for long periods of time without generating macroeconomic imbalances through domestic (fiscal) or external sources.

Slovenia is today the most affluent country among the group of those Central and Eastern European Countries (CEECs) seeking EU membership. At current exchange rates, Slovenia has a per capita income of US$9,161 -- around 1.8 times that of the Czech Republic, more than twice of that of the Poland and Hungary, and almost three times that of Estonia. Nonetheless, Slovenia only has 40 percent of the EU average income per capita. For international comparisons, these relationships are more informative if income is measured in purchasing parity power terms (PPP).

When measured in PPP terms Slovenia's income per capita rises relative to the EU average. At the same time, the difference in income per capita among transition economies declines markedly. Table 2.2 shows the 1997 GDP per capita, both, at current exchange rates and at PPP[7] levels for EU countries as well as for the leading five CEECs seeking EU accession. Although Slovenia remains the

---

[5] Baldwin, J. Francois and R. Portes (1997), "The Costs and Benefits of eastern enlargement: the impact on the EU and Central Europe," *Economic Policy: A European Forum*, No.24, 127-76, April.

[6] Baldwin and Seghezza (1996) found that, for three period averages (1971-90, 1971-74, and 1975-90), European countries experienced higher total factor productivity growth than the sample average that included non-European countries. Another important finding is that European countries that resisted deep integration had systematically worse productivity growth than the EU members. They argue that, because European integration has substantially liberalized trade, it has promoted growth.

[7] The PPP calculations in Table 2 are based on a major price survey covering and a basket of goods and services, which are both comparable and representative for the countries included in the comparison (EU-15 countries and the candidate countries). The survey was conducted by EUROSTAT in 1996; the other years' PPP were extrapolated using 1996 results.

country with the highest per capita income among the candidates, its gap with the average EU is significantly reduced. According to these estimations, Slovenia's per capita income is 68 percent of the EU average -- only 0.7 percent below of Greece, followed by the Czech Republic with 63 percent of the EU average per capita income. Another observable feature is that the dispersion between Slovenia's income at current exchange rates and that at PPP is considerably less than that of the other candidate countries; it is about the same as Portugal. Given that most of the candidate countries have made significant progress in liberalization, this could imply that the differences in non-tradable prices between Slovenia and the EU is less acute than in the other countries.

Table 2.2. Per Capita Income Level in Europe, 1997

	Per capita GDP		Per capita GDP - PPP		Ratio of US$ GDP to PPP
	1997 US$	% of EU avg.	1997 US$	% of EU avg.	
Austria	25,555	112	21,300	112	120
Belgium	23,799	105	21,500	113	111
Denmark	32,143	141	21,800	115	147
Finland	23,314	102	18,700	98	125
France	23,787	104	19,800	104	120
Germany	25,605	112	20,900	110	123
Greece	11,402	50	13,100	69	87
Ireland	19,981	88	18,300	96	119
Italy	20,294	89	19,200	101	106
Netherlands	23,108	101	19,800	104	117
Luxembourg	40,791	179	31,500	166	129
Portugal	10,422	46	13,400	71	78
Spain	13,512	59	14,800	78	91
Sweden	25,735	113	18,700	98	138
United Kingdom	22,118	97	18,900	99	117
EU Average	22,771	100	19,000	100	120
Czech Republic	5,169	23	12,000	63	43
Estonia	3,168	14	7,000	37	45
Hungary	4,305	19	8,900	47	48
Poland	5,169	23	7,500	39	69
Slovenia	**9,161**	**40**	**13,000**	**68**	**70**

Source: EUROSTAT, Statistical Office of the European Communities.

Loosing Ground in the Transition

In the coming years, both during the remaining pre-accession period and well into EU membership, a key economic issue facing Slovenia will be the speed of income convergence, more than convergence *per se*. Slovenia's output growth during the transition has been moderate, reaching an average 4 percent during 1994-97. Other leading accession countries have performed better in this respect, thereby reducing their income gap with Slovenia and the EU to a significant degree. By growing at rates of 6 and 5 percent on average in the last four years, Poland and Estonia in 1997 reached a per capita income that was equivalent to 58 and 54 percent of Slovenia's, respectively. The per capita income of both countries was 53 and 49 percent of Slovenia's in 1994. Although Slovenia's per capita income levels give the country room for maneuvering, the authorities should not loose focus on implementing a reform agenda that will bring efficiency and boost growth.

Simulating Alternative Growth-Accounting Scenarios

The differential growth rate between Slovenia and the EU will play a key role in closing the income gap. If Slovenia grows only slightly faster than the EU, income convergence could take several decades, whereas high sustainable growth rates will close the income gap in much shorter time. To appreciate the consequences of apparently small differences in growth rates when compounded over long periods of time, we have calculated the per capita income path of the first five countries, assuming slightly different growth rates. Table 2.3 shows the results of these simulations.[8] We assume that per capita income in the EU grows on average at 2 percent per year -- a reasonable assumption given the average output growth of the EU in the previous decades. For the applicant countries, we assume two scenarios: in one, the country grows at the average rate of the last four years, whereas in the other, we assume that the country grows at 5 percent. The latter implies a 3 percent differential in income per capita growth rate with the EU.

Table 2.3. Years Required to close Per Capita Income Gap with the European Union[1]

	Average Growth Rate	EU Average		75% of EU Average		Low End EU Average	
		Scenario 1	Scenario 2	Scenario 1	Scenario 2	Scenario 1	Scenario 2
	μ	Avg. μ	$\mu = 5\%$	Avg. μ	$\mu = 5\%$	Avg. μ	$\mu = 5\%$
Czech Republic	3.5	58	16	21	6	18	5
Estonia	4.5	41	34	29	24	28	28
Hungary	2.5	154	26	95	16	89	15
Poland	6.3	22	32	15	22	15	21
Slovenia	4.1	21	13	5	3	3	2

Note: 1/ Assumes EU per capita growth rate at 2 percent. Low End EU is the average of Greece, Portugal and Spain.

Source: EUROSTAT and own calculations.

If Slovenia's per capita income grows at a sustained rate of 4.1 percent, it would take 21 years to bridge the income gap with the EU average. In other words, by growing at its average rate it takes Slovenia about the same number of years as Poland, which has about half the per capita income of Slovenia but in the last four years has been growing at an average rate of 6.3 percent. On the other hand, if Slovenia manages to grow at 5 percent, this is 3 percent above the EU, then the time to close the gap would be cut by a third, to 13 years, i.e. by 2010. Note that Slovenia, at

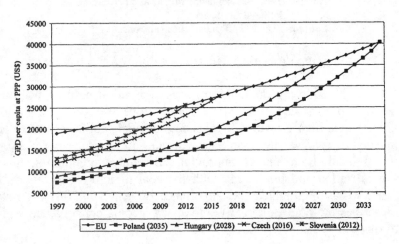

Figure 2.1. Convergence in Per Capita Income
(Growth Rates: EU=2%; CEE=4.5%)

---

[8] All the calculations are done with per capita income measured in PPP terms.

current growth rates, will reach 75 percent of the EU average in 3-5 years and will reach the lower end of the EU (Spain, Portugal and Greece) in just 2-3 years.[9] By comparison, the Czech Republic will require 18 years, Estonia 28 years, Hungary 15 years and Poland 15 years to bridge the gap with the low-end EU at their current average growth rates.[10]

Another way of looking at income convergence times is to set a target date and find out the required growth rate for closing the income gap. Table 2.4 below summarizes these simulations. By growing at a constant rate of 5.9 percent per year over a 10 year period, Slovenia will achieve parity with the EU average. It will take only 3 years to reach 75 percent of EU average at this growth rate. Notice that this growth rate is below Poland's average for the last four years, and is thus easily achievable by Slovenia under a reinvigorated structural reform agenda.

For Slovenia, the growth rates required to catch up with 75 percent of the EU average income per capita are quite reasonable; this is not the case for the other leading candidate countries. Of course, Slovenia should set its objectives higher since it is starting with a privileged position relative to other acceding countries. It should not miss the opportunity to bridge its income gap with the EU by implementing a sustainable growth strategy that enhances efficiency through microeconomic reforms, thus allowing Slovenia to fully benefit from a successful integration into the EU. A key issue for Slovenia is therefore to identify and implement the policies that generate higher growth rates than the current trend thus far.

Table 2.4. Growth Rate Required to Achieve EU Parity[1]

	EU Average		75% of EU Average		Low End EU Average	
	Scenario 1	Scenario 2	Scenario 1	Scenario 2	Scenario 1	Scenario 2
	10 years	20 years	10 years	20 years	10 years	20 years
Czech Republic	6.7	4.3	3.7	1.4	3.4	2.7
Estonia	12.7	7.2	9.5	4.2	9.1	5.5
Hungary	10.0	5.9	6.9	2.9	6.5	4.2
Poland	11.9	6.8	8.7	3.8	8.4	5.1
Slovenia	**5.9**	**3.9**	**2.9**	**1.0**	**2.6**	**2.3**

Note: 1/ EU per capita growth rate at 2 percent. Low End EU is the average of Greece, Portugal and Spain.
Source: EUROSTAT and own calculations.

Sustainable Growth: Alternative Policy Reform Scenarios

Meeting the challenges of accession and benefiting from membership in the EU are among the most important tasks that Slovene authorities are now facing and will continue to face in the future. Sustainable high growth will enhance Slovenia's ability to meet these two challenges. Both the policies needed to achieve sustainable growth rates and those required by the EU accession process are closely interrelated: both aim at improving efficiency, maintaining macroeconomic balance and promoting liberalization and integration with the goal of improving the welfare of the population. The previous section has highlighted the importance of achieving faster growth rates for Slovenia. This section describes the policy alternatives to speed income convergence with the EU through long-term balanced growth.

---

[9] The threshold of 75 percent of the EU average per capita income is important because a number of development fund transfers from the EU budget to its members countries are directed to regions with incomes per capita below that threshold.

[10] Hungary's growth rate has been increasing in recent years as its reform process advances. At current GDP growth rates, just over 5 percent -or twice as much as the four-year average used in the exercise- income convergence to the EU will be dramatically accelerated.

In recent years, a large number of empirical studies aimed at providing policy advice and at identifying the correlation between growth, endowments, initial conditions, and the role of the government policy regime.[11] These studies have identified key features that distinguish countries with high and low rates of economic growth. Most of the studies have been based on the neoclassical growth model which predicts that, within a group of economies with roughly similar tastes, technologies, political institutions and policies, those with lower per capita income will tend to grow faster. This is known as the *absolute convergence* hypothesis, and is based on the assumption of diminishing returns to reproducible capital. [12]

A less strict version of convergence, which assumes that all countries are not equal and indeed differ in many aspects, is the so-called *conditional convergence*, also known as σ convergence.[13] This type of convergence implies declining cross-sectional dispersion of per capita income across units, as measured by the coefficient of variation or other measures of dispersion. The basic difference between the two definitions is that, while absolute convergence relates to the relationship with initial levels of income and subsequent growth rates, conditional convergence implies that each country has its own steady state level of income and will grow faster the farther away it is from this level. Growth is thus affected by a number of things, including the policy framework a country chooses to implement.

Box 2.1. Equation and Parameters used for Convergence Simulation

The model produces an estimate of the long-run (steady state) annual growth rate using a growth equation. The equation is estimated by using a large cross-section of countries over the period 1965-89. The reduced form growth equation is the following:

$$Y = b0 + b1\ X1 + b2\ X2 + b3\ X3 + b4\ X4 + b5\ X5$$

where X1 is the logarithm of the initial income per capita of the country, X2 is the logarithm of the average level of fixed investment over GDP, X3 is a proxy of the level of human capital measured as the logarithm of the level of educational attainment, X4 is the logarithm of a quality adjusted labor force growth rate and X5 is the logarithm of a policy index that summarizes the existing policy framework. In the equation above, b0 to b5 are the parameters of the model. The estimated reduced form equation is given by:

$$Y = 0.0879 - 0.0190\ X1 + 0.0170\ X2 + 0.0098\ X3 - 0.0267\ X4 + 0.0250\ X5$$

The index of liberalization (X5) is composed of ten different indicators reflecting the current state of policies in the economy. It includes, among other variables, indicators of monetary policy, fiscal policy, trade liberalization, and other factors that strengthen the enabling business environment of an economy. The Index of Economic Freedom is used as a proxy for this policy index, modified to incorporate a broader definition of trade liberalization.[14] This index is based on ten different indicators, namely; (i) the degree to which tariffs and quotas hinder the free flow of commerce; (ii) the extent to which taxes burden economic activities; (iii) the share of government consumption in output; (iv) the rate of inflation as a proxy for monetary policy; (v) the degree to which a country is receptive to FDI; (vi) the extent of government involvement and level of distortions in the financial sector; (vii) the importance of market forces in determining prices and wages; (viii) the degree to which property rights and rule of law are perceived to be supportive of an enabling business environment; (ix) the role that government regulations might play in hindering private sector development; and (x) an estimate of the size and importance of the underground economy. Its scale goes from one, reflecting a low degree of liberalization, to five, reflecting full liberalization. Some of these indicators are measurable whereas others are not measurable. In the latter case, Johnson and Sheehy assign values according to scales based on non-quantifiable criteria.

---

[11] See Barro, R. (1997), "*Determinants of Economic Growth, A Cross-Country Empirical Study,*" The MIT Press, Cambridge Massachusetts.

[12] Known in the neoclassical growth literature as *β convergence*.

[13] Barro, R and X. Sala-i-Martin (1995), *Economic Growth*, New York: McGraw-Hill Inc.

[14] Johnson, B. and T. Sheehy (1996), *Index of Economic Freedom*, The Heritage Foundation, Washington, DC.

We base the analysis on the simulation of different policy scenarios and their impact on the growth prospects of Slovenia. To measure the impact on the long-term growth of the economy, we used the estimation results of a cross-section growth model.[15] Investigating the growth performance of a large number of countries over a long period of time allows the assessment of any country's long-term growth potential under key assumptions about the levels of capital, both physical and human, endowments and policy variables. The model enables us to make comparisons between Slovenia's future growth rates relative to those of the EU under different policy scenarios.

The growth determinants for Slovenia and the other candidate countries are presented in Table 2.5. According to these determinants of growth, Slovenia ranks first in the initial level of income per capita, third in the level of investment as ratio of GDP (behind the Estonia and the Czech Republic), last in the policy index of market reforms and third in the adjusted labor force growth rate (behind the Czech Republic and Poland). Slovenia's average income growth rate (over 1994-97) has been 4.1 percent; although good by EU growth standards, it is much slower than in countries such as Estonia or Poland. According to the model, the higher per capita income -- which Slovenia enjoyed when it became independent -- explains part of this development. On the other hand, market reforms have been slower in Slovenia than in other countries. In Hungary, for example, the economy has become more open and market-oriented, as reflected in the policy framework index of 3.1 against 2.65 for Slovenia.

Table 2.5. Growth Determinants for EU Candidate Countries

	Average Growth Rates 1994-97	GDP per capita 1997 PPP level	Average Investment as % of GDP	Human Capital Stock 1985	Structural Framework Index, 1996	Adjusted Labor Index 1984-89
Czech Republic	3.5	12,000	26	N/A	4.00	5.4
Estonia	4.5	7,000	27	N/A	4.00	5.3
Hungary	2.5	8,900	22	10.75	3.10	4.9
Poland	6.3	7,500	17	8.41	2.95	5.6
Slovenia	4.1	13,000	24	N/A	2.65	5.3

Source: Barbone and Zalduendo (1997), EUROSTAT and World bank staff estimates.

The simulations were conducted by using some modifications to the original model to reflect the current state of the Slovene economy. The policy framework index is increased to 3.0 to reflect the advances of the last two years in economic liberalization -- mainly import tariffs reductions and reforms associated with the accession process itself, including the transposition of certain parts of the *acquis communautaire*. For simplicity, Slovenia's human capital stock was assumed as the average of Hungary and Poland (9.58), comparable with EU levels.

We analyzed two policy scenarios. The first scenario assumes no further policy reform, hereafter referred as current status. The second scenario assumes that Slovenia accelerates its structural reform agenda and adopts policies that replicate those of fast growing economies. Under this second scenario, we evaluate both the impact of independent changes of the key policy variables and the joint effects. In addition, we assume that Slovenia's convergence (steady-state) income per capita level is the EU average. Furthermore, we assume that the EU income per capita level will grow at a steady 2 percent per annum. The results are presented in Table 2.6.

---

[15] Barbone L. and J. Zalduendo (1997), "EU Accession of Central and Eastern Europe: Bridging the Income Gap," Policy Research Working Paper No.1721, The World Bank. This growth model is an extension of Sachs, J. and A. Wagner (1996), "Achieving Rapid Growth in the Transition Economies of Central Europe," Harvard Institute for International Development, Cambridge.

Table 2.6. Years to Close Income Gap Under Alternative Policy Scenarios

	Current Status 1996/97	Policy Index of Fastest Growing	High Investment Rate	Human Capital Candidate Highest	Combination GDI & Policy Index	Combination of all Reforms
Slovenia						
EU Average	37	18	24	32	15	14
80% EU average	11	7	8	10	5	5
75% EU Average	6	4	5	6	3	3
Germany's level	42	22	29	37	18	17
Austria's level	41	21	27	35	17	16
Memorandum						
Czech Republic	29	22	26	26	21	20
Estonia	29	20	26	31	18	17
Hungary	66	28	37	66	22	24
Poland	N/C	50	103	N/C	34	28

Notes: For the simulations, the policy index is set at 4.22; the investment rate is set at 30 percent; and the human capital index is set at 10.75. N/C means no convergence.

Source: World Bank staff estimates.

The model predicts that the reforms implemented in Slovenia to date are sufficient to generate convergence with the EU average income per capita, but not sufficient to generate rapid convergence. Under the current policy framework it would take 37 years to converge to the EU average, 11 years to 80 percent of EU average and 6 years to 75 percent of EU average. If we hold all the other variables constant and assume that the policy liberalization index takes the value of the fastest growing economies (4.22), then the time period to converge to EU average income per capita is cut in half, to 18 years. To reach 80 percent of the income per capita of the EU average -- the level of income that corresponds to Spain's current income per capita[16] -- it takes 7 years.

We also estimate the number of years required for Slovenia to converge to the income per capita of its two major trade partners, Austria and Germany. If Slovenia is to converge to these levels of per capita income then, under the current policy stand, it would take more than four decades to bridge the income gap. However, by accelerating the structural reform agenda through increased liberalization the model predicts that the period of time is reduced by half, to 22 years.

When we assess the individual impact of other growth determinants -either the ratio of investment to GDP or the human capital stock- the results are also important, although not as important as the advancement of structural reforms. By increasing the human capital stock by 12 percent, the number of years needed to reach the average EU income per capita is reduced by 5 years or 14 percent. This is the result of an already high level of human capital in Slovenia. On the other hand, increasing the investment rate to 30 percent of GDP, from the current level of 24 percent, reduces the time to bridge the income gap with the EU by a third. The combination of policy improvements generates interactions and accelerates growth performance.

The Challenge Ahead: Accelerating the Structural Reform Agenda

The strategy for sustainable growth in the pre-accession period and early membership in the EU has been identified by the Government. The strategy covers macroeconomic issues, structural issues, and their interactions. To develop a strong economy well prepared to absorb shocks and to adhere to the aims

_____

[16] The relative lower speed of convergence in is due to the implicit assumption of diminishing returns.

of the EMU macroeconomic policies aimed at stabilizing the economy during the transition, Slovenia must implement a wide range of structural reforms. Such structural reforms must aim at increasing the international competitiveness of the Slovenian economy while also promoting long-term growth that is socially and environmentally sustainable.

Table 2.7 summarizes the major components of the government's pre-accession strategy for Slovenia and its timetable. These reforms constitute the critical mass of Slovenia transition and EU accession strategies. Their completion conditions the success of the development agenda that Slovenia has chosen to follow. Delaying these reforms will inevitably postpone the date at which Slovenia will be in a position to join the EU and benefit from its membership in an enlarged Union.

Table 2.7 Major Components of the Slovene Pre-accession Reform Agenda					
	1997	1998	1999	2000	2001
Monetary policy and capital flows					
Reduction of interest rates to approach EMU members' level	■	■	■	■	■
Maintaining of flexible exchange rates	■	■	■	■	■
Reduction of inflation rates to 3-5 percent, by end 2001	■	■	■	■	■
Liberalization of capital flows		■	■	■	■
Reform of the tax system					
Approbation of legislation (VAT and excise) by Parliament		■			
Preparation of implementation of VAT and excise tax	■	■			
Implementation of VAT and excise tax			■	■	■
Reform of the pension system					
Prepare a White Paper on pension reform	■				
Discuss White Paper		■			
Submit proposed legislation to Parliament		■			
Adoption of the legislation by the Parliament		■			
Preparation of the reform	■	■			
Start implementation of first phase of reform			■		
Continue implementation of successive phases			■	■	■
Financial sector reform					
Opening market to branch offices of foreign banks		■			
Abolish inter-bank agreement on max. deposit rates			■		
Privatization of NLB & NKBM					
Adopt legislation on bank privatization			■		
Preparation of privatization and divestiture			■	■	
Introduce new payment system					■
Complete ownership transformation of insurance companies			■		
Rehabilitation and privatization of insurance companies			■	■	■
Opening of insurance market to foreign capital			■	■	■
Broaden and deepen capital market	■	■	■	■	■
Develop/ improve legal/regulatory framework (all financial sectors)	■	■	■	■	■
Harmonize with EU essential legislation in the sector	■	■	■	■	■
Reform of public utilities					
Price liberalization	■	■	■	■	■
Liberalization and competition, including privatization	■	■	■	■	■
Regulation, incl. introduction of public procurement system	■	■	■	■	■
Price liberalization of the remaining administrated prices					
Announce full program of price liberalization with dates		■			
Implementation according to announced plan	■	■	■	■	■
Enterprise sector reform					
Rehabilitation & privatization via Slovene Development. Corp.		■	■	■	■
Replace distortive subsidies with transparent measures		■	■	■	■
Bringing state aids in line with EU rules		■	■	■	■
Develop horizontal mechanisms to stimulate competitiveness		■	■	■	■
Develop institutional and legal framework (take-over etc.)		■	■	■	■
Stimulate FDI and capital restructuring in privatized sectors		■	■	■	■

The requirements for successful accession to the EU, as identified in the strategy paper for Slovenia, include the achievement of sustainable growth in the context of the single market as well as the adoption of the *acquis communautaire* at the least cost. The sequence of reforms that can be characterized in three stages: (i) macroeconomic stabilization; (ii) macro- and microeconomic transformation, including the proper definition of property rights and achievement of the structural reforms needed for the efficient operation of a market economy; and (iii) the adoption of those rules and regulations needed to achieve the required degree of compatibility with the EU members.

Slovenia needs to accelerate its transition process to achieve the status of a modern market economy and to become a viable member in the EU internal market. The requirements for a successful accession include the implementation of sustainable growth policy and the adoption of the *acquis communautaire*. To achieve these objectives, Slovenia needs to implement a set of macroeconomic policies to maintain the macroeconomic stability achieved so far, and to provide the growth framework for economic convergence with the EU.

Macroeconomic stability is an absolute prerequisite. Slovenia needs sustainable foreign (BOP) and fiscal balances; it needs a declining rate of inflation that converges to EU levels. Moreover, Slovenia needs to enhance its environment for the development of the private sector and the accomplishment of structural reforms. These objectives are essential whether or not Slovenia joins the EU. Macro stability requires (i) monetary policy compatible with the goal of reducing inflation and real interest rates, (ii) fiscal policy aimed at maintaining stable public finances, (iii) income policy which is compatible with macroeconomic stability, and (iv) further opening of the economy to foreign competition, thereby creating the proper framework for integrating Slovenia's enterprises into the international economy.

Slovenia also needs to complete its microeconomic transition by accelerating its structural reform agenda to address structural weaknesses from the former regime of market-socialism. The major objective of structural reform is to make the Slovenian economy efficient in the allocation of resources, thus making it a viable and competitive actor in the internal market of the EU. Macroeconomic reforms alone will not lead automatically to supply responses needed for a comprehensive transformation.

To address structural weaknesses, a clearly defined set of reforms is needed. They will help to develop a strong economy, better prepared to absorb shocks, and will contribute towards achieving macroeconomic objectives. Within this general framework, structural reforms should aim at: (i) creating conditions conducive to high and sustainable economic growth; (ii) increasing international competitiveness of the economy by improving the efficiency of factor markets; and (iii) designing policies and measures which make the transition process socially and environmentally sustainable.

Slovenia has already fully or nearly completed a number of reforms, such as the transformation of social ownership, bank rehabilitation and trade liberalization. The completion of the remaining structural reforms, together with adequate macroeconomic policies, represents the country's medium-term economic policy priorities. The agenda has already been set by the government strategy for EU accession. The most crucial reforms for the coming years include:

- the completion of the reform of the tax system, with focus on the introduction of VAT and excise taxes;
- the completion of the reform of the social security system, with focus on pension reform;
- the completion of the reform of the financial sector, with focus on further liberalization of the capital account, foreign competition and privatization of the remaining two state banks and the insurance sector;

- the development of a proper regulatory framework in the area of public utilities aimed at liberalizing and strengthening competition, and privatization of public utilities;
- the completion of price liberalization and the enhancement of competition;
- the completion of the reform of the enterprise sector, with focus on restructuring and privatization or liquidation of non privatized enterprises, thus setting the conditions for profitable performance of privatized enterprises, including adjustment of subsidies and other forms of state aid, in line with the Europe Association Agreement (EAA).

The development of a performing enterprise and financial sector is precisely what economic transition is about. Although substantial progress has already been realized in Slovenia, it still remains an area of concern. The process of formal transformation of ownership of socially-owned enterprises has been virtually completed. Bank rehabilitation has taken place. As such, the major ingredients for a well functioning market economy capable to stand the pressures of the single market in the medium term –as recognized in the Agenda 2000– are present. Nonetheless a fundamental requirement for sustainable growth in a market economy, i.e., a profitable enterprise sector is not yet fully realized.

This situation conveys an important message needed to complete the transition process and to pave the way for a successful integration in the EU: (i) the need for the enterprise sector, especially the externally and internally privatised enterprises, which form the core economic tissue of the country, to be profitable; (ii) the need for a rapid reduction of the large loss making non privatised sector in a way that is socially and financially viable; and (iii) the need to establish a business environment that boosts the creation of new and foreign entries.

Finally, the third dimension of the overall growth strategy is the transposition and adoption of EU rules and regulations known as the *acquis*. This is an accession requirement that supports the macro stabilization effort. It sets the proper incentives to accelerate the structural reform agenda, thereby promoting sustainable and balanced growth. The authorities should not underestimate the effort required to adopt the *acquis*. Indeed, transposing and implementing the *acquis* is one of the most demanding tasks of the accession process. It requires not only the modification of a number of laws and regulations in many sectors of the economy, but also the modernization of the administrative and judicial capacity of the state to efficiently apply the *acquis*. The outcome, however, is a growth enhancement environment where Slovenia can develop and prosper, to fully benefit from EU membership.

Complying with the European Union Environmental Directives

Introduction

Environmental protection has an extremely high priority for the EU. The 1987 Single European Act specifies powers to act on all environmental matters. Furthermore, in the 1997 Amsterdam Treaty, the EU raised environmental protection to a guiding objective-a status not accorded to other crosscutting objectives such as social protection. The body of EU environmental directives is wide, comprising some seventy directives, supplemented with "daughter" directives and regulations. However, EU does not assume that Slovenia or any of the other acceding countries will have implemented all of the environmental *acquis* before joining. Indeed, the EU recognizes extended transition periods will be necessary. The Commission stated in a recent communication on Environment and Accession that it expects each country to address its own national priorities and problems as well as the economic constraints of accession.

Accordingly, joining the EU will require Slovenia to (gradually) adopt and implement the whole body of EU legislation and standards (the *acquis communautaire*) pertaining to the environmental field. This paper reviews the issues that this challenge raises. First, the status of institutional development in the Slovene environmental sector will be presented, accompanied by the EU environmental requirements. Second, the paper aims to assess the implications of the EU accession efforts for institutional arrangements, the cost of the required investment program, the scope for managing investments as efficiently as possible, and the implications of these changes in households. In this section, the paper will focus on the priority areas, such as water supply and treatment, waste management, industrial pollution and air pollution. A final section lists Recommendations for an Implementation Strategy.

Slovene Environmental Policy and the EU Accession

Adopting the EU environmental legislation and practices presents particular challenges for Slovenia due to several reasons. First, the scale and scope of the EU legislation concerning environment is broad, by its very nature it touches on all sectors of the economy and all sections of society. Such compliance requires substantial investment. The acceding countries would choose to make these or similar investments at some stage in the future, even without the imperative of EU directives since most of the investments also bring direct benefits to the population. Accession, however, accelerates the investment program and reduces the opportunity for Slovenia to adopt different implementation policies.

Second, while the benefits of the needed investments will only be seen in the very long term, the costs will affect each Slovenian household now. Government at all levels will need to engage in systematic public consultations and to invest in awareness-raising campaigns. In the short term, environmental investment may have to be considered the price tag of joining the EU.

Third, the requirements of EU directives do not always correspond with Slovenia's immediate national priorities at this stage in its development. The challenge is to identify actions that will have both domestic and transboundary benefits and, where this is not possible, to be clear about tradeoffs. Fourth, the investment programs required to upgrade infrastructure could exacerbate regional disparities in income and employment. Therefore investment programs should be examined carefully for their local and regional as well as their national financial, economic and social impacts, and appropriate transfer mechanisms should be implemented where necessary.

Currently, the Slovene environmental legislation comprises a framework of the Environmental Protection Act (EPAct) of 1993 and various regulations and decrees covering individual aspects of environmental protection. Under the EPAct, the Ministry of Environment and Physical Planning (MEPP) is responsible for environmental monitoring and the operations/maintenance of an environmental information system. Although staff and financial resource are limited, the infrastructure is in place to ensure the effective enforcement/monitoring of legislative and regulatory regimes (Environmental Inspectorate was established). In July 1993, the MEPP founded the EcoFund (See Box 3.1) to provide favorable interest rate funding for environmental protection projects. Funding is focused on projects involving air pollution abatement, phasing out of ozone-depleting substances, municipal infrastructure development, and the reduction of industrial pollution.

Box 3.1. Environmental Development Fund

The Environmental Development Fund of the Republic of Slovenia (EcoFund) was established under the EPAct in 1993 as a public legal entity and organized as a join stock company. The EcoFund is a non-profit financial organization, which engages in channeling assets for crediting environmental investment projects. The basic goal of the fund is to provide loans on preferential terms for investment activities in the field of environmental protection from its own capital and from capital obtained from other sources. The interest rate on loans should secure the maintenance of the real value of capital as well as the operational costs of the fund without profit.

The Fund provides loans on the basis of a public announcement, i.e., tendering procedures for the purposes defined as priorities in the EPAct and the forthcoming National Environmental Protection Program (NEAP).

The capital of the Fund is supposed to be used to support investment projects related to:
- State services on environmental protection in the public sector;
- Compulsory local environmental protection public services;
- Purchase and development of equipment and technologies for environmental protection;
- Introduction of environmentally friendly technologies and products;
- Support polluters in the implementation of rehabilitation programs.

Apart from supporting investment projects in the above areas, the resources of the EcoFund can be allocated to provide additional resource for the implementation of forthcoming NEAP. The EcoFund may also provide services in terms of assistance in financial transactions or financial engineering.

In 1995 the Eco Fund and the World Bank have started the Air Pollution Abatement Program providing soft loans for household and boilerhouse conversions from dirty fuels, such as wood, coal or heavy oil to cleaner fuels like NG, LPG, gasoil as well as renewable energy sources. Four thousand household loans and 50 boilerhouse loans have been approved until mid 1998 and over DM30 million have been disbursed of the DM40 million available. The Fund has gained important experience in dealing with multi borrower projects and financing.

Funding through EcoFund to private and public sector projects has totaled approximately 4.3 billion SIT (94 SIT/DEM) in 1995 through 1997. The budget for 1998 is SIT 4.3 billion. The emerging systems of charges for the use of natural resources and special taxes will increase the EcoFund's current financing from the State budget. Some of the current programs include:

Carbon Dioxide Emission Tax (1997): tax on liquid, gaseous, and solid fuels based on CO_2 released in the burning process, usually about 2 percent of the selling price of the fuel.

Tax for Water Pollution Prevention (1995): tax based on level of pollution and set at rates to encourage municipalities to construct water treatment plants.

Slovenia has already undertaken several activities with respect to the approximation of Slovene legislation to the EU environmental legislation (see Box 3.2). In January 1997 the MEPP established a Department of European Affairs (DAE). The DAE coordinates all EU accession approximation activities in the MEPP, coordinates with other ministries, the Governmental Office for European Affairs, and EU institutions/programs. The United Nations Committee on Environmental Policy completed an Environmental Performance Review in May 1997. The recommendations of the report were used for the development of National Environmental Action Plan, which is currently in the preparation for the first reading in the parliament, and the development of the EU approximation activities.

Box 3.2. Environmental Accession Strategy

The activities undertaken by the Ministry of Environment and Physical Planning (MEPP) in matters related to the Environmental Accession Strategy of Slovenia include:

A. Inception Phase (completed Feb/Mar, 1997):
- Establishment of the Department of European Affairs within the MEPP as a co-ordination unit for the accession activities of the MEPP,
- development of the inception plan for the preparation of an accession Strategy.

B. Strategic Planning Phase (completed July 1997):
- preparation of the Accession Strategy, and National Environmental Protection Program,
- first comprehensive review of current and proposed EU legislation,
- first compliance assessment of the current status of national environmental legislation relative to EU legislation (gap analysis)
- through PHARE support, completed the development of the Implementation Strategies for Approximation in Environment (DISAE) and effectively utilized Phare's Technical Assistance Information Exchange Office (TAIEX),
- preparation of a gradually phased work plan resulting from the "gap analysis".

C. Implementation Phase (July 1997 through present):
- political commitment for the Environmental Accession Strategy,
- work program, implementation costs, key personnel allocations, and timetable for the transposition of the environmental *acquis* (EU legislation),
- preparation of environmental implementation scenarios based on available financial and other resources. The TORs and priorities of these scenarios have been prepared,
- preparation of a timetable for environmental accession activities has been completed, and
- implementation of the accession activities beginning in early 1999.

PHARE has a role as an accession vehicle and focuses on assisting Slovenia on the restructuring of economy through technical assistance programs and projects. It has identified the environmental sector as a priority sector for assistance in approximation and integration. Effective Jan. 1, 1998, 70 percent of PHARE funds are devoted to major infrastructure projects and institution building. PHARE also funded 5 other MEPP Projects ranging from urban wastewater treatment to municipal services programs.

In 1996, the Regional Environmental Center for Central and Eastern Europe (REC) found that approximately 55 percent of the content of the Slovenia's environmental provisions were compatible with EU environmental legislation[1]. Since then, the government has made considerable efforts to update the state environmental policy to include full transposition of the framework directives dealing with air, water and soil, and to fill the gaps in sectoral legislation.

During the past years most of the environmental spending has focussed mainly in controlling and abating air pollution. In 1994-95, for example, air pollution control programs accounted for 70 percent of total investments for environmental protection.

In terms of implementation, the country has also made modest progress since the early 1990s. Figure 3.1 shows the level of environmental expenditures from 1990 to 1997.[2] During this period, the level of environmental expenditures as a share of GDP has been kept at a much lower level than the current level of environmental spending in the EU member states, which is around 1-2 percent of GDP.

---

[1] Since the Republic of Slovenia has been adapting its legislation to that of the EU for the past few years, it is difficult to estimate the costs above the level Slovenia would have done in the absence of plans to join the EU.

[2] This represents both investment (80 percent) and recurrent expenditures (20 percent). Because of the lack of transparency in the allocation of public funds for environmental protection activities, it is not possible to estimate the true level of environmental expenditures.

It is then a requirement for Slovenia to gradually adjust its environmental expenditure levels to the existing EU levels. The issue of estimated investment costs is addressed in the next section.

Figure 3.1. Overall Expenditure on Environmental Protection

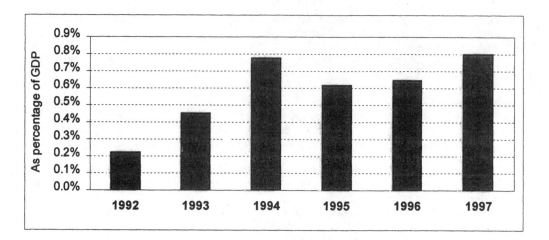

Institutional Changes and Investment Costs

Costing has been undertaken on an Environmental Sector Basis rather than on an EU legislative/directive basis. This method addresses situations where the legislation/directives apply to several sectors. It should also be noted that the Industrial Pollution Sector has been included in other sectors (i.e., wastewater, quality water, waste management, etc.) resulting in some costs being passed over to these sectors. Cost analysis is based on the achievement of EU compliance with only major directives representing around 93 percent to 95 percent of the total cost. In the interest of brevity, this report does not provide the results of the complete gap analysis. Only EU legislation and directives that are associated with major compliance costs have been identified in this report.

The high impact sectors summarized in Table 3.1 contribute 92 percent of the projected environmental approximation capital costs. The balance is in the medium, small, and insignificant categories. The average cost per capita is 1300 ECU. All costs are presented in millions of ECUs.

As the table shows, total envisaged investment costs amount to almost ECU 3 billion. If the government commits itself to full compliance by 2005, this will involve investing around ECU 450 million per year,[3] which represents a fourfold increase over current investment level. An investment program of this magnitude clearly represents an enormous additional cost for Slovenian population. The key will be to develop a credible program that clearly identifies priority investments for the early stages of compliance.

The public sector, and the MEPP in particular, will play an important role in implementing, managing and financing investments driven by the environmental *acquis*. The public sector will finance on average two-thirds of the overall investment needs in drinking water, sewerage, wastewater treatment, and improvement of ambient air quality. The central government will have two important roles: first, development of strategic sectoral plans and operational programs integrating sectoral economic,

---

[3] Without counting the additional costs associated with O&M of current and new infrastructure or ongoing investments or cost of capital.

financial, spatial, social and environmental considerations; and second, assistance to the local authorities to adopt and implement the national operational programs for specific areas or sites.

Table 3.1. Total Estimated Investment Costs, 1998-2005
(million of ECUs)

Environmental Costs	Total Investment Cost	O&M Annual Cost	Present Value of Cost Stream	Total Annualized Cost	% Public Sector 1998-2005	% Private Sector 1998-2005
High Impact Sectors						
Water Quality	1,183	65	1,079	87	73	27
Waste Management	1,118	6	1,006	81	68	43
Industrial Pollution	50	3	44	4	0	100
Air Quality	241	12	336	30	70	30
Medium Impact Sectors						
Horizontal EU	10	0	7	1	50	50
legislation	120	1	106	8	100	0
Nature Protection	0	3	0	0	61	39
Chemical and GMOs						
Nuclear Safety & Radiation Protection	1	17	1	0	100	0
Total	2,723	106	2,578	210	70	30

Source: Assembled with information contained in "EU Accession Strategy Complying with EU Environmental Legislation, Associated Costs and Financing Instruments," and World Bank estimates for O&M in wastewater and waste sectors.

The role of the central government will be different in the various environmental sectors. In the water sector, local governments are responsible for exploiting and developing water resources and for delivering and expanding water supply services. Water services, in turn, can be provided either through public or private companies. The central government should help coordinate between municipalities to manage and protect overall water resources. Allocation of needed financial resources can play a significant role in this regard.

Municipal governments and local authorities have the responsibility for collection, removal and disposal of solid household waste. Municipalities' waste management obligations are performed by 50 local public enterprises, which are governed by the 1993 Law on Commercial Public Services. Apart from developing operational programs, the central government also provides funds for the implementation of waste management programs, and promotes the efforts of local communities to work together. In the case of air protection, the local authorities implement the national Government's decisions for a specific area or site. They have their own local regulations and specific activities to solve local air pollution problems, i.e., installing a central heating network. All these activities of local authorities are partially subsidized by the local environmental taxes, state budget, and donors' contributions, however, they will still place an important burden on municipal finances and municipal capacity.

Compliance with the EU environmental directives requires changes in two areas that fall exclusively within the state administration: harmonization of national legal acts[4] and institutional improvements, such as adapting institutional structures, changing procedures and increasing management capacity. Over the past years, Slovenian authorities have made considerable efforts to harmonize national environmental legislation with EU standards, but still much needs to be done to fill

---

[4] Which in the case of the Republic of Slovenia doesn't mean complete uniformity with EU legislation, but rather to establish common environmental aims and targets.

existing gaps in sectoral and enforcement legislation. The major task ahead is, however, to adapt and reshuffle existing institutions. The environmental administration will have to make changes in many of its several agencies including possibly creating some new bodies.[5] Agencies will need to have systems in place and staff with sufficient training and experience to enforce the new environmental legislation and standards, implement effective policies, monitor environmental quality accurately, report and disseminate information. Public agencies will also see their roles changing. Drafting primary legislation will become less important, whereas assessing and commenting on draft legislation from Brussels and representing the interests of the Republic of Slovenia will become an important role.

Enforcement is key to the whole endeavor, wherever the investment costs are incurred, and will call for an increased cooperation between ministries, departments, regional and local authorities. Successful enforcement of legislation also requires well-designed monitoring system.

In financial terms, incremental expenditures for administration, monitoring and enforcement associated with the EU environmental approximation have been tentatively estimated at ECU 23 million or ECU 11 per capita per year or 0.8 percent of total capital investments associated with approximation. These estimates, however, underestimate the true institutional cost of approximation since they do not include expenditures associated with training of staff. Nevertheless, the financial costs of public sector change are relatively low. Experience elsewhere, however, suggests that efforts in this area are administratively extremely difficult to achieve and require long lead times. As the effectiveness of the whole investment program depends on credible and effective institutions, serious early and sustained efforts in this area are an important priority.

Main Environmental Areas

The 1995 EU White Paper on accession identifies the essential measures relevant to the internal market that the accession countries must adopt before they enter the Union. It covers legislation affecting the free movement of goods and services, which in the environment field covers only around 20 percent of the whole *acquis*. The major environmental areas are:

- Chemical substances (administrative procedures, risk assessments, classification, labeling, packaging, notification, transport, import and export);

- Waste management (waste oils, PCBs, PCTs, sewage sludge, batteries, packaging materials, incineration, landfills, recycling, and shipment);

- Air pollution (lead and benzene content of petrol and sulfur content of diesel fuel and gas oil, VOCs and ozone depleting substances); and

- Radioactive contamination of food stuffs and radiation protection.

Significant elements of the White Paper related to the internal market have already been adopted, although institutional capacity and enforcement require further development. Since all measures stated in the White Paper must be adopted by the time of accession, there are few strategic options.

Formal adoption of White Paper measures relating to specific products such as chemical substance will have little financial cost to the public sector, since producers and users will bear most of

---

[5] Management of chemical and preparations, management of genetically modified organisms, integrated prevention and limitation of industrial pollution, are a few areas that require the establishment of new state administration.

the cost. Producers, in turn, are likely to welcome the changes since the adoption of EU standards will ease their access to the EU internal market. In the case of air pollution, remarkable progress has been made over recent years, but still more efforts are required in air pollution management. Improvements in urban air quality will be seen soon as a result of implementing new regulations pertaining to fuel standards, the introduction of a CO_2 tax, and the accelerated turnover of the car fleet, as a result of growth in income levels.

Compliance with the waste management legislation by leading Slovene industrial companies is also progressing well as a result of having incorporated cleaner production targets into their development policies. Non-exporting companies, however, lack the incentives to cut pollution. The compliance of the Slovene legislation with the EU legislation and the estimated investment costs in each of these environmental areas are addressed below in more detail.

Water Supply and Treatment

Background Information. There are 84 water quality sampling points in 18 different aquifers. Data shows that water quality in the eastern part of Slovenia is directly influenced by agricultural activity with NO_2 concentrations of between 11 and 115 mg/l and some pesticide concentrations. This exceeds EU standards for drinking water. The ground water in western Slovenia is relatively good and is in compliance with EU Standards.

Surface water monitoring follows the US Environmental Protection Agency (US/EPA) Standards. In intense agricultural areas comparisons between nitrogen inputs and harvested output point to serious fertilizer, organic manure, and nitrogen leaching problems. Generally, industry is responsible for 60 percent of pollution of toxic substances (metals, pesticides, and organic compounds), municipal discharges account for 10 percent, and agricultural sources for 30 percent. Pollution by industry has decreased over recent years.

The water supply system is very scattered with 77 percent distributed from public networks, 14 percent from private wells, and the rest from other sources. 47 percent of the total drinking water supplied by public networks is used by households, 39 percent by industry/manufacturing, and 8 percent by livestock farms. An ECU 120 million project to build waste water treatment facilities in Ljubljana, Maribor, and Rogaska Slatina for treatment prior to discharge in rivers has been started. Pending projects include (i) an ECU 10 million waste disposal project at iron factories, (ii) ECU 2.2 million WW Plant for the paper industry, and an ECU 45 million second phase WW Plant in Ljubljana. 70 percent of the funding is provided by the State and the balance provided by the Danube Environmental Program.

First Findings. The quality level of drinking, surface, and groundwater is the highest priority in the MEPP legislative program. EU legislation and directive not covered in the existing Law on Water (1981) are included in the new draft Law on Water and the new Law on Fishing. The waste water strategy, based on long term EU directives, includes the installation of waste water treatment plants in important areas.

Costing Assessment. Current drinking water quality analysis suggests that the majority (90 percent) of drinking water meets EU quality and microbiological standards. Under the directive, sensitive urban and coastal regions will require pre-treatment resulting in an increased water cost of approximately 1 percent. EU directives on urban waste water systems are expressed in absolute values rather than relative values. The specifications range from settlement size of under 2,000 (requiring no connection to a sewer and no secondary or advanced treatment) to greater than 150,000 (requiring connection to sewer, secondary treatment and advanced treatment). Settlement of over 5,000 require connection to a sewer and often some form of secondary treatment. Slovenia has approximately 90 communities with over 5,000 inhabitants that have no waste water treatment facilities. Compliance requires upgrades to 9 systems and the construction of 137 new systems (13 of which require secondary treatment). No tertiary treatment is required in Slovenia at this time. Costs are based on a standard primary treatment plant and an activated sludge plant. Full compliance is estimated at 20 years.

Industrial waste water generally requires the same treatment as urban waste water. In some cases, pre-treatment is required (toxic matter, and biodegradable waste water). Appropriate industrial waste is added to the municipal systems. Table 3.2 itemizes the specific priority Water Quality Sector EU Compliance Projects and the associated projected costs (millions of ECUs).

Table 3.2. Investment Costs – Water Quality Sector EU Compliance, 1998-2005
(million of ECUs)

Projects	Directives	Investment Cost[a]	O&M Cost[b]	NPV[c]	Annual Cost[d]
Municipal Waste Water Treatment Plants and sewage network to comply with EU legislation	Urban waste water 91/277/EEC	889	63	811	65
Industrial Waste Water Treatment Plants to comply with EU legislation	Dangerous Substances to the Aquatic environment 76/464/EEC	25	0	25	2
Compliance of existing installations to EU legislation	Drinking water 80/778/EEC	235	0	181	15
Additional investment around Koper and Bled	Bathing water 76/160/EEC	30	0.5	31	2.5
Administration, monitoring, and enforcement	All directives in the field	4	1.5	31	2.5
Total: Public Sector 73%, Private Sector 27%		**1,183**	**65**	**1,079**	**87**

Source: Project Identification and Costing based on "Development of a Costing Assessment for the Slovenian Environmental Approximation Strategy", April 1998, Agriconsulting Europe S.A., Brussels.

Notes:

  a/ Investment cost: Full costs of meeting the EC directives, starting from the current situation. This leads to overestimation as it does not consider work that would be undertaken in the absence of accession to the EU. Full cost is the same as "least cost" unless otherwise noted.

  b/ Operations and Maintenance costs for the life of the facilities/project.

  c/ Present Value of Cost Stream: lifetime is based on current engineering best practices and guidelines (civil work 20+ yr., equipment 15 yr. Max., vehicles etc., 7 yr.) and a 5 percent discount rate on straight line depreciation.

  d/ Annualized Costs based on the NPV algorithm.

Major Issues. All drinking water is obtained from ground water sources. Although the quality is generally acceptable by EU standards in most regions, these sources are being contaminated by industrial, agricultural, and municipal contaminates.

Generally, there is little or no treatment of waste water prior to discharging to rivers, evaporation beds, or the Adriatic Sea. In 1995, about 40 percent of the wastewater discharge into the public system did not receive any treatment. Of the volume wastewater that received treatment, about 60 percent was mechanical only. There is minimal data available on the pollution load or on the pollution eliminated by existing waste water treatment facility. There are no secondary treatment (biological) facilities in Slovenia. The cost of building treatment facilities is very substantial. Slovenia now has approximately 160 municipalities, many of which are too small to even contemplate addressing treatment facilities. Under current law, municipalities cannot borrow more than 10 percent of their operating budget for capital acquisitions (changes pending).

Strategy and Objectives. The objective is to improve water quality, therefore, EU standard emission limit values and the best available technology (BAT) are the guiding principles for the MEPP. There is a need to draft regulations that address economic incentives to encourage compliance with water quality standards. In 1995, a regulation introducing a waste water tax was adopted. The tax is proportional to the pollution loads of the waste water and is set at tax rates that would cover both investment and operating costs of technology to remove that pollution load. This program has proved very effective.

At present, the legislative framework for the management of water resources in the Republic of Slovenia is comprised of the EPAct,[6] the National Water Resources Strategy (under preparation), the Master Plan for Waste Water Sewerage and Treatment (under preparation), and the framework Water Act (under preparation). Once the overall framework legislation is finally completed, it will determine the role of the state, local communities and individuals (concessions) in the management of water resources. Development of all administrative tools, including institutional structure, for the successful implementation of the new framework is perceived as a major challenge.

International cooperation on water management in Slovenia is well established, particularly in terms of bilateral agreements. Slovenia has joined the (i) ECE Convention on the Protection and Use of Transboundary Watercourses and International Lakes, and (ii) the Convention on Cooperation for the Protection and Sustainable Use of the River Danube. These agreements are particularly useful for settling future disputes. For example, the ongoing Slovenian Coastal Management Program will be efficient only if coastal management programs are also developed by Italy and Croatia.

Waste Management

Background Information. There are 54 municipal waste landfills and 50 public service enterprises providing collection/disposal services. Waste collection has grown from 64 percent of the population in 1987 to 76 percent in 1996. These sites are used for all municipal waste and selected industrial waste that complies with a disposal criteria. Waste water sludge is generated from 422 industrial and 100 municipal waste water/sludge treatment facilities. A small amount of this sludge is used in agriculture but the bulk is deposited at the landfills. There are over 6,000 illegal (1 or more cubic meters) disposal sites that are putting additional pressure on the landfill sites. Although not a serious problem, leakage from legal and illegal waste dumps has contaminated the drinking water in some areas.

In 1995 manufacturing and energy generated almost one quarter (2 million tones/yr.) of the total waste: 41 percent, 29 percent, and 16 percent from energy production, manufacturing, and mining, respectively. As the economy expands, quantities of waste are expected to increase. The introduction of FGD units (flue-gas desulfurization) in the energy sector will also create additional solid waste. The bulk of industrial waste is deposited at 13 sites specific to either a single or mixed-waste types. Recent expansion in the construction industry is currently producing 2.3 million tones of waste or about 25 percent of the total waste generated in 1995, whereas mining waste decreased with the closure of mines. The processing/refining of stone aggregates will increase and follow growth in construction activities.

Under the Statute on the Handling of Special Waste (1986), companies are obligated to keep records on hazardous waste and about 40 companies are licensed and monitored. There is one landfill for selected hazardous waste (manufacturing substances, coatings, etc). Other hazardous wastes must be

---

[6] The Environmental Protection Act (EPAct), includes the implementation of regulations on the control of water pollution from point sources. It sets out the principles of (i) control by State bodies, local authorities, and the polluters, (ii) the liabilities for pollution and damage, and (iii) public access to relevant information.

stored on the company's site. About 75 percent of the hazardous waste stem from used lead batteries. Other waste is primarily from mineral oil production, used tires, electro-plating sludge and waste solvents. Slovenia exports roughly 10 percent (about 2000 tones) of hazardous waste and imports about 22,000 tones. Slovenia is currently seeking authorization to import used car batteries (Croatia, Hungary, and Austria) for its recycling plant.

Farming, forestry, and food processing generate 3.5 million tones/yr (measured as dry). The majority of this waste is forestry waste and animal feces/straw at 1.1 and 1.6 million t/y respectively. Small-scale livestock farming is a significant source of effluent waste biomass and constitutes a problem for ground water contamination. The use of fertilizers and other chemicals is not excessive but will require monitoring in terms of ground water and river contamination.[7]

Low and intermediate radioactive waste generated by Slovenia's Krsko Nuclear Power Plant (NPP), the TRIGA M II Research Reactor, hospitals, and research institutes and industry are generally contained in 200 liter drums and stored either on site or at a facility in Podgorica, Slovenia. The NPP generates approximately 750 drums/yr. Spent fuel assemblies (442) are stored in the storage pond at the NPP site. In September, 1994, Slovenia signed the Convention on Nuclear Safety. It is the override agreement among foreign experts that nuclear safety in Slovenia is at EU levels. The NPP will be decommissioned in 2023.

Slovenia has a long tradition of collecting and reusing iron, non-ferrous, metals, glass, paper, fabrics, used car batteries, plastics and waste oil. The Chamber of Economy has established the "Waste Material Stock Exchange" as a trading organization for these materials. Although Slovenia does not have a municipal waste sorting and collection system at this time, this program is detailed in the Strategic Guidelines on Waste Management that is now before the Government for ratification. When implemented, Slovenia will have the needed additional source material to support the existing marketing infrastructure and recycling plants.[8]

First Findings. The primary differences are in (i) licensing for collection/transport, and disposal facilities, (ii) waste management plans, and (iii) regulations for the disposal of PCBs/PCTs and batteries, (iv) packaging of waste, (v) incineration of municipal waste, and (vi) waste landfills. To address the gaps, the MEPP will address items (i) and (ii) through the current DISAE project on the Development of an Implementation Program for the Slovenian Waste Management Strategy and item (iii-vi) through drafts of secondary legislation under the EPAct and the Public Services Trading Act. Over the long term it is expected that the MEPP will develop a specific law for waste management that includes all the EU directives. It is expected that the Phare TAIEX Office would play a role in this transition process.

Costing Assessment. The harmonization of reduction programs involves measures to reduce waste, source separation, recycling, composting, etc. Legislation has to developed that requires the segregation of waste types, the recycling/reuse of waste streams, and the collection/sorting systems for each stream. Costs are assessed in terms of the establishment of recycling and reuse system which are almost entirely absent in Slovenia. Slovenia has only a few small industrial incinerators. Complying with

---

[7] 35.6 kg/ha nitrogen, 20.9 kg/ha phosphates, 23.3. kg/ha Potassium, 1.1 kg/ha pesticides and up to 5.4 tones of solid animal waste.

[8] The waste management goals include reduction of domestic waste by 40 percent in the mid term (60 percent in 15 years) while achieving a 48 percent rate of material and energy recovery (78 percent in 15 years), which includes a recycling strategy; by the year 2000, reuse 35 percent of waste construction materials and 65 percent in the long term; reduction of dumped waste in the construction sector by 30 percent; reduction of dumped industrial waste by 45 percent through a number of ambitious programs; reduction of liquid effluents in agriculture operations by 40 percent to 50 percent; and reduction of hazardous waste through technological measures.

the EU directives requires the construction of several large municipal and industrial incinerators as detailed in the MEPP's Waste Management Strategy. Slovenia will also require two hazardous waste incinerators (and/or export hazardous waste) to comply with EU directives. This represents a very substantial increase in costs over the current methods.

There are currently 53 landfills and they will be full in less than 5 years. Closing existing landfills requires "full compliance" with the directive, which involves leaching control, groundwater monitoring, gas extraction, and fencing. In addition, there are very substantial costs for the development of new landfills (lack of land and very high cost of land). EU compliance on this matter is going to be very costly. Based on the EU Framework Directive, the MEPP's Waste Management Strategy includes measures to deal with agricultural and fisheries waste. It also includes changes in farming practices, establishment of composting facilities and special disposal facilities (i.e., asbestos). The following table itemizes the specific priority Waste Management Sector EU Compliance Projects and the associated projected costs (millions of ECUs).

Major Issue. Total available municipal landfill capacity is 13 million cubic meters, whereas the availability of new sites is limited. Incineration is being seriously investigated as an optional approach.

Table 3.3. Investment Costs – Waste Management Sector EU Compliance, 1998-2005
(million of ECUs)

Projects	Directives	Investment Cost	O&M Cost	NPV	Annual Cost
Introduction of technical systems for recycling, and reuse	Harmonization of reduction programs 92/112/EEC	166	0	128	10
Reconstruction and enlargement in conformity with EU Standards	Municipal water incineration for existing/new facilities 92/429 & 89/396/EEC	311	0	240	19
Construction of two incinerators to comply with EU legislation	Hazardous waste incineration 94/67/EEC	275	0	244	20
Costing of closing present tips reconstruction and upgrading	Proposal for a directive on landfill of waster COM(97)105	321	0	278	22
Wastes from farming and forestry	Waste Framework Directive 75/442/EEC	45	0	35	3
Administration, Monitoring and enforcement	All directives in the field	0	6	81	7
Total: Public Sector 68%, Private Sector 43%	**All directives in the field**	**1,118**	**6**	**1,006**	**81**

Air Quality

Background Information. The situation regarding air pollution in Slovenia has developed positively in recent years, thus no extraordinary measures are required. Slovenia has a country wide 24 hour monitoring system for SO_2 and smoke through 49 stations. In addition, there are 8 automatic monitoring stations in larger cities and 11 monitoring stations in the most polluted areas near power plants. The Hydrometerological Institute operates the system and is currently preparing for accreditation under international standards and quality compliance with western European systems.

Over the past few years, Slovenia has had a decrease in the concentrations of sulfur dioxide (SO_2), and increase in ozone (O_3), nitrogen oxides (NO_x), and volatile organic compounds (VOC).

Fluctuations since the early 1980 is due partly to the implementation of environmental measures and partly to an increased economic activity. Environmental objectives focus primarily on the energy, industry, transport, and agricultural sectors and are in accordance with international conventions and protocols (i.e., Convention on Long-Range Transboundary Air Pollution, Vienna Conventions for the protection of the Ozone Layer, UN Framework Convention on Climatic Change, etc.).

Sulfur emissions. In 1992, the desulfurization of flue gases from thermal power plants was identified as the highest priority and the first desulfurization unit (FGD) was put into operation in April 1995, resulting in a reduction of 40 million tones in 1994 through 1995. Through conversion to natural gas, emissions by households and small enterprises have been reduced by 22 percent based on 1980 levels and air quality in several towns has been improved by a factor of 2 -3. Ljubljana will reduce emissions from 100,000 tones in 1995 to 26,000 tones by 2005. This will be achieved through using imported low sulfur/ash Indonesian coal and the conversion of 10,000 household and 100 large municipal boilers to natural gas.

SO_2 and NO_x Emission from Industrial Sources. emissions have decreased primarily through the conversion to natural gas, the closing of uneconomical technological process units, and the implementation of rehabilitation measures.

Ozone-Depleting Substances. The Montreal Protocol and London Amendments were ratified in 1992 and the Copenhagen Amendments are currently being ratifying. Slovenia was approved a grant in the amount of US$6.2 million by the Global Environment Facility Trust Fund. The grant is approved to 6 Slovenian companies for financing 6 investment projects within the Slovenian ODS project. According to the grant agreement, the EcoFund was determined as the financial intermediary in this project responsible for appropriate procurement and disbursement procedures and implementation monitoring.[9]

Traffic Generated Air Pollution. The transport sector constitutes 30 percent of the CO_2, 90 percent of the CO and 70 percent of the NO_x emissions. It also accounted for 35 percent of all energy consumption versus 32 percent for EU countries. In addition, the current extensive road construction programs will most likely increase transit traffic. By 2005, diesel fuel sulfur content will be limited to 0.05 percent from the 1995 limit of 0.2 percent.

First Findings. The Slovenian legislative and regulatory regimes are in place that meet or exceed the EU framework directive on Air Quality. Legal instruments for the control of volatile organic compounds (VOCs) are in draft form and emissions from heavy duty mobile machinery are not currently covered. The main emphasis is on monitoring and data collection with special attention given to increasing pollution from power plants and urban traffic.

Costing Assessment. The directives require that SO_2 emissions from existing plants be reduced to 1980 levels and new plants comply with emission standards. A desulfurization treatment contract has been let for the Sostanj Power Station which produces ¾ of the total current SO_2 emissions. The second largest contributor are district heating plants. Many of these plants will be replaced by Combined Heat and Power Plants and the remaining coal based systems will be converted to natural gas. The EU compliance target date is 2005. Nitrogen oxide emissions are being reduced through the SO_2 programs at thermal power station and district heating plants. Mobile sources are currently the largest source of NO_x emissions. It is projected that Slovenia will be under the required ceiling before the 2000 compliance date. The main cost will be NO_x reduction at proposed gas fired plants after 2000 (see Table 3.4).

---

[9] GEF funds are disbursed through the state budget's account. The project was completed by the end of June 1998.

Major Issue. In recent years, Slovenia has focused on reducing air pollution and has improved the air quality monitoring system, therefore, no extraordinary efforts are required in air pollution policy and management. Major air pollution sources have been addressed or are in the process of being resolved through either technology upgrades or closing down uneconomic plants. The most noteworthy upcoming future air pollution issue is related to increasing road traffic resulting from Slovenia's extensive road construction programs.

Table 3.4. Investment Costs – Air Quality Sector EU Compliance, 1998-2005
(million of ECUs)

Projects	Directives	Investment Cost	O&M Cost	NPV	Annual Cost
Desulfurization of Sostanj V Power Plant	SO2 and particulates, 80/779/EEC, amended by 81/857, 89/427/EEC	80	3	111	9
Public Heating System – desulfurization and denitrification	Nitrogen Oxide, 85/203/EEC	100	1	83	8
Road to rail shift	Lead, 82/884/EED	40	0	31	4
Additional costs at terminals and service stations, traffic restraint measures	VOC emission from storage & transport of petrol, 94/63/EEC & proposed directive on industrial emission of VOC/Solvents, COM(96)538	21	2	32	2.5
Administration, Monitoring and enforcement	All directives in the field	0	6	79	6.5
Total: Public Sector 70%, Private Sector 30%		**241**	**12**	**33**	**30**

Strategy and Objectives. Ambient air quality standards are based on the forthcoming EU Air Quality Control Directives and WHO Air Quality Guidelines. The ambient air quality is not a problem in many areas of the Slovenia, with 40 percent of the population enjoying acceptable ambient air quality. Air pollution is particularly intense in areas prone to temperature inversion in the winter and near thermal power plants. In addition, Slovenia is not a large CO_2 emitter at 7.1 tones/cap/year (1995) representing about 2/3 of total greenhouse gas emissions. Slovenia ratified the Convention on Climate Change in 1995 that requires greenhouse gas emissions not to exceed 12 tones/cap/year by the year 2000. This would require a decrease of 13 percent over current levels that is being addressed be cutting emissions from power plants and traffic.

The Carbon Dioxide Emission Tax was introduced in January 1997 to reduce greenhouse gas emission and the use of non-renewable natural resources. Users of liquid, gaseous and solid fuels for heating, turbines, and motor vehicles are taxed relative to the amount of CO_2 released in the burning process. The tax per kg. of emitted CO_2 is about 2 percent of the fuel sales prices and is current in force for all liquid fuels. The Coal Tax will be introduced on January 1, 2004.

Several upcoming air pollution issues will require attention including urban air pollution from increased road traffic. However, the EPAct has a sufficient legal basis to develop and enforce an appropriate monitoring and regulatory regime.

Industrial Pollution, Control, and Risk Management

Introduction. Generally, industrial pollution and related matters are addressed under 4.1. Water Supply and Treatment, 4.2. Waste Management, and 4.3. Air Quality.

First Findings. The priority is the legal incorporation of the provisions in the Directive on Integrated Pollution Prevention and Control (IPPC), which encourages industries to prevent or minimize all emissions, rather than considering "end of pipe" solutions. Elements exist in current legislation but are not sufficiently comprehensive. Slovenian air emission regulations are consistent with the EU targets set by the Emissions for Large Combustion Plants Directive and the Air Pollution for Industrial Plants Directive. Slovenia has adapted the ISO 14001 Standard.[10] This program is supported by the Ministry of Science and Technology and the Slovenian Institute for Quality and Metrology. The necessary regulations for eco-labelling and awards for achievements in environment protection aiming at the introduction of Eco-Management and Auditing Scheme (EMAS) are still lacking.[11]

Costing Assessment. The following table itemizes the specific priority Industrial Pollution Sector EU Compliance Projects and the associated projected costs (millions of ECUs).

Table 3.5. Investment Costs - Industrial Pollution Sector EU Compliance, 1998-2005
(million of ECUs)

Projects	Directives	Investment Cost	O&M Cost	NPV	Annual Cost
Industrial waste gas purification and EU compliance for existing large combustion plants	Large combustion plants, 88/609/EEC	50	0	43	4
Industrial site risk management measures	Control of major accident hazards, 96/82/EEC	0	3	1	0
Total: Public Sector 0%, Private Sector 100%		**50**	**3**	**44**	**4**

Major Issue. Pollution from industrial sources has reduced over recent years through the introduction of new technology and operating procedures. In addition, several high pollution sources have been shut down. However, industrial pollution remains a major source of pollution and is a high priority action strategy in terms of air, waste water, and solid/hazardous waste pollution. It is also projected that increased economic development will increase the volume of industrial and manufactured output resulting in potential increased pollution.

Implications for Households

An investment program of the scale outlined above will necessarily involve an increase in the costs to consumers. Some utilities and municipalities may have access to EU grants and/or concessional finance, but many will have to borrow on commercial terms. Furthermore, most of the investments have high operations and maintenance costs, which neither outside sources nor the central government will subsidize. Under any scenario, utilities and municipalities will have to pass a large part of the additional costs onto consumers.

---

[10] Many Slovenian companies have already obtained ISO 9000 quality certificates as their primary efforts are directed toward the demanding markets in the EU.

[11] The Regulation 1836/93/EEC on EMAS encourages the voluntary participation of industrial plants in the development of internal environmental management systems and audit programs as a means to improve their environmental performance.

The ability and affordability to pay will play an integral part in future price increases, and may become a key constraint on the pace in which the Republic of Slovenia complies with EU directives. Figure 3.2, which is intended for illustrative purposes only, shows possible increases in the average household utilities' bill as a result of alternative investment scenarios assuming a 3 percent real income growth per year. The grant financing scheme is assumed at 60 percent of the total investment needs, with the rest being financed through loans, at 7 percent real interest rate and 20 year repayment periods. Even under these conditions, average household utilities' bill will increase in real terms as a result of the investment associated with EU environmental directives. A 20-year investment program allows a smooth increase in the household utilities' bill as a share of household income, reducing the price tag of EU accession.

Figure 3.2. Impacts on Households Income

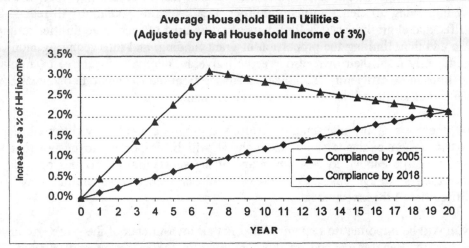

Note: It assumes that investments are shared equally between domestic and non-domestic consumers.

Recommendations

Clearly, an investment program of this magnitude has to be managed carefully. Much of the investment will bring benefits to the consumers, but, by its very nature, much will bring benefits elsewhere. The key will be to develop a credible program that clearly identifies priority investments for the early stages of compliance. The backbone for any successful mechanism will be to strengthen institutional capacity. This will be fundamental to developing policies that bring greatest environmental benefits for a given expenditure or level of effort, and that use public and external funds most wisely, both in terms of maximum environmental benefit and reducing distortions elsewhere in the economy. This will be particularly important, and challenging, because so many of the issues involved cut across sectoral areas of responsibility, and across different levels of government. Furthermore, building up capacity to enforce laws or set incentives for improving compliance will be essential to meeting many of the regulations that affect the private sector.

It will be important to negotiate carefully. Clearly all major sources of pollution will have to comply with relevant standards. There are however many areas of ambiguity in the legislation that allow for national circumstances. Many directives explicitly contain clauses that allow exemptions where environmental benefits are low or where costs are excessive, e.g., the urban wastewater treatment directive which allows exemptions for certain small towns. It will be important to negotiate either derogations where it is agreed that there is no environmental benefit, or very long transition periods for compliance with the most costly aspects of the directives for the smaller or less environmentally significant sources of pollution.

Furthermore, the analysis shows clearly the impacts of different compliance timetables. The government will want to phase investments over a long period so as to let incomes rise sufficiently to be able to absorb the increased tariffs. Planning to comply with the urban wastewater directive, the waste provisions and most of the air legislation by 2005 must be unrealistic. It is unlikely to be acceptable to make investments that affect such a large proportion of household budgets.

The government should use public and EU subsidies to direct investments towards strategic goals, during that long transition period. This is particularly important for wastewater collection and treatment, and for municipal solid waste. This prioritization has various aspects. First, there remains large scope for improving efficiency in many utilities. Realizing this potential will reduce the upward pressure on tariffs, and eligibility criteria for grants could be used to encourage utilities to improve their performance. In addition, limiting the proportion of grant funding, and thus requiring municipalities to contribute significantly from their own resources will give an automatic incentive to municipalities to operate their utilities more efficiently. Technical assistance from the EU and other sources could also be used to help the less efficient utilities improve their performance.

Second, the costs of the investments themselves can be dramatically different, depending on some of the basic design parameters. For example, it will be important to ensure that wastewater treatment plants are large enough to take advantage of the substantial economies of scale, traded-off against the increased sewerage costs, even though multi-municipal co-operation may increase the institutional difficulties of the investments.

Lastly, it will be important to remember that not all investments of the same size have the same environmental benefit. Benefits depend on the conditions in the receiving environment. Developing detailed plans so that authorities know which investments have the greatest environmental impact can be used as a further mechanism to direct investments strategically in the interim period towards full compliance.

Foreign Trade Sector

Introduction

Among those countries seeking membership in the European Union, Slovenia's position seems to be unique. It is the most developed economy among them, with a physical infrastructure suggesting an enormous potential for economic expansion; it has a very favorable geographical location and its economy has suffered less from socialist misdevelopment then the others. Ultimately, taking advantage of these assets hinges critically on acceleration of microeconomic liberalization while consolidating macroeconomic stability.

Slovenia can further prosper by being an open and outward looking economy. As the government's strategy of international economic relations argues, the challenge for Slovenia is to adjust "... its development model and its economic and legal systems to that of developed (European) countries regardless of the outcome of Slovenia's application for full membership in the EU." Reforms establishing a modern market-based regime should indeed lead to improved economic growth performance. A pre-accession strategy for a country like Slovenia -whose GDP *per capita* is the highest of the ten countries seeking EU membership, and just below that of a poorest EU-member- should be fast and sustainable economic growth based on removing barriers to the efficient allocation of resources, thereby generating healthy competitive pressure on domestic markets.

The slow down of the process of microeconomic liberalization has negatively impacted Slovenia's economic development. A loss of the initial dynamism of the trade sector best describes the current state of the Slovenian economy. Although nothing presages an impending crisis, as the economy is growing and as macroeconomic stability does not seem to be in imminent danger, symptoms of declining vigor nonetheless abound. The growth rates of GDP have been moderate. Export penetration to the EU had run out of steam. After a three-year spell of double-digit growth rates over 1993-95, the value of total exports remained flat for the 1996-97 period. In the second half of 1995 and through 1996, export performance was maintained, but maintained in large part due to the depreciation of the domestic currency. Moreover, the slow down in export expansion and the stagnation in net revenues from services could negatively impact the country's capacity to import capital equipment, thus undermining its potential for restructuring and for stronger economic growth. Although the current account has been in surplus since 1995 (when it recorded a negligible deficit), considering Slovenia's modernization requirements this cautionary policy outcome may not be optimal.

From the perspective of foreign trade and foreign investment, the prerequisites of a good pre-accession strategy generating growth, employment and improved microeconomic efficiency include easy entry of goods, services and capital to domestic markets. This should contribute to economic growth through at least two channels: the reduction of barriers to efficient allocation of resources; and the creation of competitive pressures on domestic producers to reduce costs and launch new initiatives and products. The challenge is to get firms to revamp product lines, to streamline marketing efforts, and to cut costs. A business-friendly environment and a reliable supply of services, thereby attracting foreign investment and creating opportunities for participation in global division of labor -- driven today mostly by vertical product differentiation and fragmented technology -- should help attain these goals.

External Equilibrium

Slovenia had long been a gateway for the former Yugoslavia to the European Union. Most Yugoslav exports to EU and EFTA markets originated in Slovenia. In the aftermath of independence, the reorientation of foreign trade patterns was mainly driven by the collapse of import demand in the former Yugoslav republics as well as by changes in Slovenia's economic regime, that is, by opening domestic markets to external competition.

An Impressive Record of Maintaining Macroeconomic Stability

Slovenia appears to have been strongly committed to maintaining macroeconomic and, consequently, external sector stability. Except for 1995, its current account has been in surplus from 1992 to 97, thanks to its net position as an exporter of services, mainly related to revenues from tourism. The value of total revenues from foreign tourism almost doubled between 1992 and 1996 from US$671 million to US$1,230 million, and slightly fell in 1997 to US$1,188 million. The balance had been in surplus, increasing from US$389 million in 1992 to US$688 million in 1996 and contracting in 1997 to US$644 million. Combined with surpluses in construction and merchant services, this has allowed financing of imports exceeding exports. Around three-fourths of imports have been related to either investment or inputs to current production, i.e., intermediate products.[1]

Table 4.1. Slovenia's External Performance, 1992-97
(in US$ million)

	1992	1993	1994	1995	1996	1997
Exports of Goods (FOB)	6,681	6,083	6,828	8,316	8,310	8,369
Share of EU (in %)	61	63	66	67	65	64
Imports of Goods (CIF)	6,141	6,501	7,304	9,492	9,421	9,366
Share of EU (in %)	60	66	69	69	68	67
Trade Balance	540	-418	-476	-1,176	-1,111	-997
Current Account Balance	926	192	600	-23	39	37
Foreign Direct Investment, Net	111	113	128	176	186	321
Portfolio Investment, Net	-9	3	-33	-14	637	236
International Reserves	720	788	1,499	1,821	2,297	3,315

Source: Bank of Slovenia.

Quick Re-adjustment of Foreign Trade Patterns

Slovenia's response to the challenge of the loss of markets in the former Yugoslavia has been impressive. The adjustment thus far has been mainly through, the redirection of trade flows away from the former Yugoslavia towards EU markets. Developments in foreign trade have passed through two phases: the 1992-95 phase including a massive reorientation towards the EU, and the emerging 1996-97 phase characterized by the falling share of the EU in Slovenia's foreign trade turnover. The share of trade with the EU, which had already accounted for the bulk of Slovenia's external trade even before independence, increased on both the export and import side, amounting to more than two-thirds of total

---

[1] The composition of imports by end-use has been remarkably stable since 1993, with intermediate products accounting for 57-59 percent, capital goods for 16 percent and consumption goods for 26-27 percent. Calculated from data in *Bank of Slovenia: Monthly Bulletin*, February 1998.

trade turnover by 1995. Since then, the trade shares with the EU fell on both the export and import sides, while that of former Yugoslavia (only on the export side) and CEFTA increased. Slovenia, however, still trades more with the EU than many EU members' trade among themselves (see Table 4.2).

Table 4.2. Geographic Composition of Slovenia's Exports and Imports, 1992-97

	1992	1993	1994	1995	1996	1997	1995 vs. 1992	1997 vs. 1995
	Exports (in percent)						Percentage change	
EU (15)	60.9	63.2	65.6	67.2	64.6	63.6	+10.3	-5.4
EFTA	1.0	1.0	1.0	1.0	1.0	1.0	0.0	0.0
CEFTA	3.5	4.3	4.5	4.9	5.4	5.7	+40.1	-22.4
Former Yugoslavia	22.6	15.8	15.2	14.5	16.7	16.6	-33.2	-16.1
of which: Croatia	14.2	12.1	10.8	10.7	10.3	10.0	-26.1	-4.8
Other	12.0	15.7	13.7	12.4	12.3	13.1	-4.4	-1.6
	Imports (in percent)						Percentage change	
EU (15)	59.6	65.6	69.2	68.9	67.5	67.4	+15.6	-2.2
EFTA	1.8	2.3	2.5	2.5	2.6	2.1	+4.2	-16.1
CEFTA	4.7	5.1	6.2	6.7	6.5	7.5	+42.6	-11.9
Former Yugoslavia	19.8	10.7	8.0	7.1	7.5	6.3	-61.6	-11.3
of which: Croatia	13.9	9.2	6.8	6.1	6.3	5.0	-56.1	-18.0
Other	14.1	16.3	14.1	14.8	15.2	16.6	0	-12.2

Source: Statistical Office of the Republic of Slovenia.

But Low FDI Inflows

The developments in the current account position suggest potential for a significant increase in foreign investment flows. Considering Slovenia's modernization needs, there would be nothing wrong with Slovenia's running a small current account deficit, provided that foreign direct investors finance it. The development of capital markets, the removal of various legal barriers to the development of the private sector and the convertibility of the Slovenian tolar have all enabled inflows of foreign capital. But foreign investment inflows, although fast growing in 1996-97, remain relatively low in comparison to other leading applicants to the EU.

Considering its superb location and its relatively high level of industrial development, Slovenia has a very high propensity to host FDI and, indeed, should be among its top recipients. One would expect to see more FDI inflows actually occurred during the transition; in fact, other EU candidate countries have attracted remarkably more FDI than Slovenia. On a per capita basis, cumulative FDI for 1990 to 1997 in Slovenia were around one-third of those into Hungary, and half of those into the Czech Republic. Slovenia's were only above Poland, whose population is 20 times larger and where GDP per capita almost three times lower. FDI stock in terms of 1997 GDP is almost seven times lower than in Hungary, four times lower than in Estonia and the Czech Republic, and two and a half times lower than in Poland (see Table 4.3).

Although the breakup of the former Yugoslavia and the circumstances associated with independence could hardly create an environment favorable to foreign investors, the remarkable political stability that has characterized Slovenia since independence was sufficient to compensate for those initial barriers. Nonetheless, except for Renault's investment and the more recent Goodyear Tire & Rubber joint venture with Slovenia's Sava Group, producer of car tires, firms investing in Slovenia have been only small to medium in size. Foreign firms have invested mostly in manufacturing (43 percent of total

FDI stock at the end of 1996), financial institutions (17 percent), electricity production (14 percent), and trade and services (12 percent, or US$239 million). A sector that has increasingly attracted foreign capital is the service sector, specifically the financial sector with the share of total FDI stock rising from a mere 0.2 percent in 1991 to 17 percent in 1996. These flows into services seem to have contributed, in some measure to remedy an important legacy of 'market socialism'--the underdeveloped service sector. With many areas of services still closed to foreign capital, their potential is yet to be fully explored.

Table 4.3. Cumulative Foreign Direct Investment, 1990-97

(per capita US$)										
	1990	1991	1992	1993	Average, 1990-93	1994	1995	1996	1997	Average, 1994-97
Estonia	0	0	55	163	109	305	440	513	620	476
Czech Republic	12	61	153	216	111	301	549	683	809	586
Hungary	29	168	308	531	259	639	1,068	1,256	1,439	1,101
Poland	2	10	27	71	28	119	213	329	411	268
Slovenia	0	0	56	112	84	154	239	328	476	299
(share in GDP)										
Estonia	0.00	0.00	2.17	6.64	3.32	12.20	16.59	18.89	22.03	3.85
Czech Republic	0.38	2.48	5.86	7.97	1.99	10.41	16.15	19.10	21.81	3.46
Hungary	0.98	5.55	9.71	16.01	4.00	18.87	29.40	33.98	38.26	5.56
Poland	0.16	0.56	1.36	3.37	0.84	5.39	8.48	12.06	14.48	2.78
Slovenia	0.00	0.00	0.88	1.77	0.88	2.36	3.27	4.19	5.67	0.98

Note: The average in the early years is calculated over 1992-93 for Estonia and Slovenia and over 1990-93 for the rest.
Source: *Global Development Finance*, The World Bank, Washington D.C., 1998, and *Economic Survey of Europe 1998 No.1*, United Nations Economic Commission for Europe, New York and Geneva, 1998.

All together, FDI should be higher levels, for Slovenia is particularly well endowed to be a host to FDI on all counts. The amount of FDI directed to one country by other countries varies according to four factors -the location, the level of economic development, the structure of *created* and *natural* resource endowments, and the role played by government polices. In terms of a reference group, i.e., other transition economies, Slovenia has a superb location. It is also the most developed country. The structure of *created* and *natural* resource endowments also puts Slovenia ahead of the group. The presence of these factors, combined with the quality of labor, explains why firms do engage in FDI. While each component of *created* assets does not render itself to a straightforward numerical appraisal, Slovenia possesses all the requisites to rank very high on FDI among transition economies.

There are several reasons why Slovenia has attracted less FDI than expected. Although market size and the relative cost of labor matter, its domestic policies may have had a larger impact. On the one hand, Slovenia's structural reform agenda has been slower than in other first-wave EU candidates. On the other hand, the Slovene privatization method -which has played a significant role in attracting FDI in other CEECs[2]- has not been conducive to significant foreign participation. The privatization program favored insider (manager and worker) buyouts over outsiders, both foreign and domestic. Foreign participation was exceptional only during the privatization of socially owned enterprises -amounting to just one percent of the privatization deals. Insider ownership rarely results in the aggressive shedding of excessive employment, and adjustment to increased competition; it does not contribute to better corporate governance, as it retains the old corporate power structure. More significantly, it produces a powerful lobbying group with a strong interest in frustrating attempts by foreign investors to buy into firms.

---

[2] Privatization-driven FDI amounted to 40 percent of all FDI in the region.

Furthermore, the privatization program explicitly reduced the scope for trading, as shares acquired through vouchers in the mass privatization could not be sold for two years.

The existing regulatory framework has also restricted access by foreign firms to some sectors of the economy. The framework has imposed limits on foreign participation in other sectors; it has reduced the rights of investors to select the management of their companies, thus erecting an extra barrier to FDI. The purchase of 25 percent or a controlling share of a company requires prior approval by the government -a requirement that discourages some investors. Limits imposed on foreign participation exist in auditing (49 percent), investment companies dealing with the management of investment funds (20 percent) and stock brokerage firms (24 percent).

Last but not least, regulations governing the foreign exchange regime erected yet another barrier to foreign investment. As part of its policy to restrict capital inflows, the BOS introduced, in February of 1997, restrictions on the acquisition of securities by foreigners. This regulation compels non-residents to use custodian accounts with authorized domestic banks to conduct portfolio investments in Slovenia, thereby increasing the costs of these transactions. The measure was subsequently softened in mid 1997 and again in early 1999, but not eliminated (see Chapter 1). Although the regulation was aimed at reducing Slovenia's vulnerability to short-term capital flows, it segmented the equity market and increased costs for foreign investors.

Thus, low FDI inflows have been partly the result of domestic impediments. With its high technological capabilities, its disciplined and educated workforce, and its well-developed physical infrastructure, Slovenia should have been host to larger inflows of foreign capital. Considering the positive impact that FDI has had in transition economies, including Slovenia[3] (albeit in a more restricted way), on restructuring and integration into international markets, the absence of an active strategy to open Slovenia's economy may have resulted in significant losses in terms of welfare and economic efficiency.

Export Performance in EU Markets

During the first years of the transition, the pattern of Slovenian EU-oriented export growth was strongly reminiscent of patterns experienced by some other rapid reformers -- Hungary and Poland. What set Slovenia apart was a slump in EU-oriented exports over the period 1996-97 and a dramatic slowdown in change in the diversity of its export offer.

Exports to the EU surged by 53 percent in 1993; over the next two years, they sustained a double-digit expansion averaging 22 percent per year over 1993-95. This had provided both a boost to recovery and an expansion in imports. Imports have provided higher quality products, both for consumption and investment. This, combined with competition from imports, stimulated local producers to improve their performance. In both 1996 and 1997, however, the value of EU-oriented exports fell slightly.

Initially, those manufactures redirected from the markets of former Yugoslavia were the driving force behind Slovenian exports to the EU. The initial impulse to growth did not come from capital and transportation equipment, although they did later catch up with other manufactures. It came mainly from products sold to other Yugoslav republics before the demise of Yugoslavia.[4] Their share in EU-oriented

---

[3] See Rojec (1996, 98).

[4] These included footwear, chemicals, textiles, metalworking, and paper. Sales of these products to other Yugoslav republics accounted for more than 40 percent of their respective trade turnover. The growth rates of exports of these

exports rose from 17 percent in 1992 to 19 percent in 1994, but fell to 17 percent in 1997. Thus, it seems that the impulse from redirection of exports has lost its momentum.

Indeed, engineering products and furniture were the only major exportables among major exportables, which registered an increase over 1995-97, there were only engineering products and furniture. The value of machinery and transportation equipment grew by 3 percent; that of furniture by 24 percent. Their respective shares in EU-oriented exports increased from 35 to 38 and 5 to 8 percent between 1995 and 1997. The value of exports of manufactures (excluding machinery and transport equipment and furniture) fell by 15 percent. Exporters from only a few sectors were successful in increasing their presence in EU markets over 1995-97. Ores and minerals increased their share by 14 percent over this period; metal manufactures by 18 percent (from 0.62 to 0.71); transport equipment by 3 percent (from 1.69 to 1.74); furniture by 6 percent (from 5.39 to 5.69). The share of manufactures in EU imports declined by 12 percent.

Diversification in Export Offer: Moderate Change After 1995

In order to assess emerging patterns of specialization in the Slovenian economy as viewed through the lens of EU markets, it is useful to look at the changes in revealed comparative advantage (RCA) – assessed, not against world trade, but that of the EU.[5] In terms of broad product groups, as used in Appendix Table 3, the estimates of RCA confirm an improvement in Slovenia's position in those EU markets where, even before independence, its firms were significant suppliers. Along these broad product groups, there were no significant changes in Slovenia's comparative advantage.

A similar conclusion can be drawn from a less aggregate picture based on estimates for 807 four-digit SITC (Rev.1). Within the top ten products with the largest values of RCA, there were only minor changes in terms of both rank and new entrants.[6] Thus, it seems there was no significant expansion in new specialization in the Slovenian economy between 1993-94 and 1995-97.

Commodity Chains: The Move towards Final Stage Products

While Slovenia's export offer has remained relatively stable, an interesting question is whether there has been a change towards more advanced products in terms of processing. To examine this question, we use a classification developed by the World Bank to analyze different levels of processing of commodities.[7] The classification distinguishes, at a minimum, between two stages: a primary and

---

products in terms of value were 12 percentage points higher in 1993 (65 percent versus 53 percent) and 2 percentage points higher in 1994 (21.7 percent versus 24.4 percent). These exports still grew at a highly respectable rate of 23.4 percent in 1995, but this was 1.4 percentage point less than the total.

[5] A country's "revealed" comparative advantage in a product "j" is defined as the ratio of the share of "j" in the country's exports to the share of the product "j" in world trade. A value for this index below unity indicates a comparative disadvantage. If the index takes a value greater than unity, the country is considered to have a "revealed" comparative advantage in the product. In this particular case, Slovenia has a revealed comparative advantage in a product if its export of that item as a share of its total exports exceeds the EU imports of the item as a share of EU total imports.

[6] There were some rearrangements among leather products: leather belts (6121) moved to the top in 1995-97 while leather articles (6112 and 6119) did not make the top ten; neither did roasted iron (2814) nor builders wood (6324) nor vessels for breakup (7358).

[7] For a discussion of the commodity processing classification, see *Slovenia: Trade Sector Issues*. PREM, The World Bank, Report No. 18456-SLO, Washington D.C. September 1998.

processed stage product. (For instance, the primary stage of vegetable chain consists of fresh vegetables whereas the processed stage includes preserved vegetables) and frequently among three stages including a semi-fabricated or intermediate stage.

The share of 48 commodity-processing chains in Slovenian exports to the EU has been steadily declining, from 24.5 percent in 1992 to 19.7 percent in 1997. Over 1992-97 the Slovenian presence in EU markets for commodity chains increased by 57 percent, primarily because of expansion in exports of processed commodities. Between 1995 and 1997, however, there was a contraction in terms of the share in EU imports (see Table 4.4).

Table 4.4. Changes in Slovenia's Exports to the EU in Individual Commodity Chains, 1992-96

	1992	1995	1997	Index 1995, 1992=100	Index 1997, 1995=100	Index 1997, 1992=100
	in percent of total					
Primary	6.5	3.9	4.0	59.5	104.4	62.1
Intermediate	19.8	18.0	19.3	90.8	107.6	97.7
Final Stage	73.7	78.1	76.6	106.0	98.0	104.0
Share in total EU-destined exports	24.5	21.3	19.7	86.7	92.5	80.1
Memorandum:	Share in EU imports					
Primary	0.04	0.04	0.04	108.3	93.6	101.3
Intermediate	0.57	0.95	0.86	166.6	91.5	152.4
Final Stage	1.02	1.78	1.52	174.6	85.1	148.5
Total chains	0.35	0.62	0.54	177.6	88.3	156.7

Source: Derived from data in United Nations COMTRADE Database as reported by EU.

Factor Content: The Move towards Skilled Labor and Capital Intensive Products

In contrast to other transition economies, where initial expansion has been pulled by unskilled labor intensive products, Slovene export expansion over 1992-95 was driven by technology-intensive and human capital-intensive manufactures. Their aggregate share in EU-oriented exports rapidly increased from 50 percent to in 1992 to 57 percent in 1995. The share of technology intensive products rose from 17 percent in 1992 to 20 percent in 1995; that of human capital intensive products from 33 to 36 percent over this period. Nonetheless, the pace of change declined significantly over 1995-97. The share of technology and human capital intensive products increased from 57 percent in 1995 to just 58 percent in 1997. The share of unskilled labor remained roughly the same, and that of natural resource-intensive products dropped by 1.5 percentage points (see Table 4.5).

Table 4.5. Factor Content of Slovene Exports to EU over 1992-97, in percent

Relative Factor Intensity Groups	1992	1993	1994	1995	1996	1997	Index 1997, 1992=100
Natural Resource Intensive	18.4	16.2	16.7	16.0	14.9	14.5	79
Unskilled Labor Intensive	31.2	31.8	28.5	26.9	27.0	27.0	87
Technology Intensive	16.6	17.6	19.3	20.4	20.4	20.8	125
Human Capital Intensive	33.0	33.5	34.8	36.3	37.2	37.5	114

Source: Own calculations. Data on Slovenia's exports as reported by the EU to UN COMTRADE.

Calculations of Slovenia's RCA in EU markets confirm that human capital-intensive products were at a comparative advantage in trade of these products over 1992-96. Indeed, the revealed comparative advantage index of these products grew from 2.2 in 1992 to 2.7 in 1996-97. This group recorded the largest increase between 1992 and 1997: their share in EU imports more than doubled over this time, increasing from 0.9 percent to 1.98 in 1995 and then falling to 1.82 in 1997.

The factor content of Slovene exports has also undergone some significant changes. Given Slovenia's endowments in factors of production, it should specialize in high skilled labor intensive and technology intensive products. The share of these products in EU imports significantly increased between 1992 and 1994. There are, however, two potentially distressing trends: (i) stagnation of high technology exports in terms of their share in EU imports over 1995-97, and (ii) continuing reliance on unskilled labor intensive products. While a significant share of the latter products in Slovene exports is not surprising, one would expect that its share would fall faster, given the high relative labor costs in Slovenia in comparison with other transition economies. Although there is nothing wrong with Slovenian exports still deriving their competitive strength from specializing in unskilled labor intensive products, one would expect a quicker change towards human capital and technology intensive products.

Comparative Advantage of Pollution-Intensive Sectors

Environmentally dirty industries tend to concentrate in countries where environmental control measures are less stringently applied. Since these affect costs, as more demanding measures impose higher costs of compliance and production, countries with relatively lax environmental regulations tend to specialize in so called "dirty" industries. Less developed countries have less demanding compliance rules and therefore have revealed comparative advantage in markets for dirty products. Indeed, some empirical studies confirm the shift in specialization in these products away from highly developed and toward developing countries. There is nothing inherently bad about it, as less developed countries may have higher pollution assimilative capacities and less-environment biased social preferences.

As one might expect, the share of environmentally dirty products in Slovenia's EU exports increased during the early years of the transition. The share increased from 21 percent in 1992-93 to 24 percent in 1994-95, but it fell in both 1996 and 1997 (see Table 4.6). Exports of pollution-intensive products remain highly concentrated, with the top ten four-digit SITC (Rev 1) industries accounting for around 50 percent of "dirty" exports.[8] The environmentally dirty sectors have been at a comparative advantage in the trade of these products: the value of RCA increased between 1992 and 1994, falling in 1995. Since then, they have remained stable.

Ultimately, Slovenia's exports of environmentally dirty products to the EU remains high considering he country's geography and its potential for development of tourism. The persistence of comparative advantage in "dirty" products should serve as a warning that incentive structures and state policies require adjustment.

---

[8] The most important item has been builders' woodwork (6324) contributing on average around 14 percent to dirty exports to the EU over 1994-96. With a value of exports of US$173 million, this share was 14.1 percent in 1996, down from its peak level of 17 percent in 1992.

Table 4.6. Selected Features of Slovenia's 'Dirty' Exports to the EU, 1992-97[9]

	1992	1993	1994	1995	1996	1997
Exports of "dirty" products (in US$ million)	516	781	1,064	1,376	1,237	1,158
Share in Slovenia's EU oriented exports	21.4	21.1	23.6	24.5	22.5	22.0
Share in EU "dirty" imports	0.66	1.12	1.33	1.29	1.26	1.16
RCA Indices	1.63	1.69	1.82	1.66	1.71	1.70

Source: Own calculations from data in UN COMTRADE database.

Competition in the Single Market

Why has Slovenian export expansion to the EU run out of steam and what does that imply for accession? During the initial phases of transition, the expansion was triggered by the redirection of trade from the former Yugoslav republics to EU markets. By 1995, their initial ability to increase market share in the EU eroded significantly. This seeming decline in competitiveness in EU market appears to be the result of the absence of a significant entry of "second generation" firms, i.e., those which were either newly established or which were successfully restructured. The 1995-97 period also witnessed a "freeze" in both diversity and factor content of the Slovenian export offer in EU markets. There were less of mostly the same products sold to EU consumers. The factor content, which changed dramatically during the expansion phase, displayed little change over 1996-97.

A perceptible stagnation in overall competitiveness of Slovenian exports in EU markets, as measured by its share in EU imports, raises concern about the ability of Slovenia's firms to continue competing with, and gaining share in EU markets from, firms from other applicant members. The fall in the export competitive edge often boils down to real exchange rate appreciation. That is, it boils down to an overvalued domestic currency, as well as to increases in labor costs not fully compensated by productivity changes. If Slovenia succeeds in exporting only if it repeatedly devalues its currency, then its purchasing power over imports, as well as over domestically produced goods, will decline. In 1996-97, Slovenia's average wages in dollar terms were around three-times higher than in other EU applicants. The key to maintaining high wages is productivity growth. Considering the huge share of foreign trade in GDP, such growth must be faster relative to other applicant countries.

Contestability of Domestic Markets

Markets are contestable if there is an easy entry of goods, services, capital and people. There is thus a close relationship between contestability of domestic markets and the EU's four freedoms. From an international perspective, contestability includes issues of market access for foreign products, as embodied in tariffs and narrowly conceived non-tariff barriers. Contestability also includes market access implications of domestic policies and regulations underpinning business activities (e.g., technical standards, environmental standards, phyto-sanitary measures, etc.). Ideally, one would like to see full adherence to the principle of national treatment as well as the absence of differentiation in treatment of imports or foreign investment.

---

[9] The data presented here differ from those in Table 10 (*Slovenia. Trade Sector Issues,* Report No. 18456-SLO, The World Bank, September 29, 1998) because of the change in denominator. In the previous version, data for imports of the EU has included intra-EU imports. These are excluded in Table 4.6 above.

The desired outcome of the transition from central planning is the emergence of competitive and contestable markets. Markets are contestable when relationships among firms are not unduly distorted by anticompetitive governmental or by private action and when there is unencumbered market access for foreign goods, services and investment. Contestability declines with restrictive regulatory regimes; contestability declines with differentiation in treatment of local and foreign competitors, border and nonborder protection, and anticompetitive practices.

The former Yugoslavia had neither an open economy nor a state monopoly over foreign trade. Yugoslav market socialism was based on self-management: firms had considerable autonomy in conducting business transactions, although they were closely monitored by the state. With formal recognition of Slovenia's independence and with accession to the General Agreement on Tariffs and Trade,[10] the process of dismantling those vestiges of market socialism accelerated. By 1996, most QRs have been removed; they affected less than 2 percent of Slovenia's imports in 1996. Export taxes have also been removed. Furthermore, with the introduction of a new customs legislation (Customs Code and Customs Tariff Law) in line with EU regulations, customs entry procedures have been modernized and simplified, thus improving access to domestic markets. Leaving aside the restrictions on access for foreign investors, there are relatively few restrictions in Slovenia that reduce contestability in the trade sector.

Tariff Structure: Diversification in Protection

Slovenia's tariff structure has three major characteristics: it affords high levels of protection to agricultural products; it is biased in favor of final products; it benefits preferential trading partners versus MFN partners. Slovenia's agricultural import regime is reminiscent of that of the EU with perhaps one caveat -- it seems to provide more protection to low value added agricultural products. Consequently, prices of food products are higher than under free trade, and the standard of living is lower. Tariff rates escalate with the level of processing, thus providing incentive to firms that produce more processed goods. While the levels of implied effective rates of protection had fallen, they still seem to distort allocation of resources.

Higher levels of protection to agricultural products and final manufactures, combined with the discrimination due to preferential trading agreements, result in the diversification of the tariff structure. They are both sources of distortions in resource allocation. The biased protection in agriculture ties up resources in subsidized, low value added activities. The biased protection in final products tends to distort production patterns by discriminating against the production of intermediate products and components. The tariff structure also generates inverse discrimination of suppliers from those countries that do not have a free trade agreement (FTA) with Slovenia, as tariff margins enjoyed by preferential suppliers widen. This pattern will intensify in the coming years as tariffs decline under the EAA and other FTAs.

Leaving aside trade liberalizing commitments associated with WTO-membership, Slovenia has opted in favor of bilateral, rather than unilateral, liberalization of its foreign trade policy. Membership in CEFTA (since 1996) and especially its entry into trade component of the Europe Agreement (in 1997)

---

[10] In January of 1992, the EU recognized Slovenia as an independent and sovereign state; in May Slovenia became a member of the United Nations. The process of integration into international economic structures had been slower but persistent: in October of 1994, Slovenia acceded to the GATT and became the member of the WTO in July; in January of 1996, Slovenia became a full member of CEFTA and signed the EAA in June, 1996.

have resulted in a significant fall in applied tariff rates on industrial imports. Imports from preferential partners -- the EU (67.4 percent of the total in 1997), EFTA (2.1 percent), the Baltic states (0.1 percent) and CEFTA countries (7.5 percent) -- accounted for more than three-fourths of Slovenia's total imports in 1997. In addition, Slovenia has signed FTAs with other countries including Croatia, in operation since January 1998, and Israel, signed in May 1998 but still awaiting ratification in Israel. With the FTA signed with Croatia, the share of imports from preferential partners would increase from 75 to 82 percent in terms of Slovenia's 1997 imports. These will be subject to lower tariff rates (zero rates on almost all manufactures) than those from other sources.

Table 4.7. Share of EU Imports in Total Imports and Estimates of Customs Duties, 1994-2001 (excluding inward/outward processing and agriculture basic products and processed foods)

List (number of codes)	1994		1996		1997	1998	1999	2000	2001
	Share in total imports from EU	Customs duties and other charges	Share in total imports from EU	Customs duties and other charges	Customs duties (estimate)	Customs duties (estimate)	Customs duties (estimate)	Customs duties (estimate)	Customs duties (estimate)
A (3964)	41.1	4.6	41.0	2.5	0.0	0.0	0.0	0.0	0.0
B (2337)	28.5	7.6	26.6	6.3	3.2	2.3	1.1	0.0	0.0
C (2092)	30.3	13.1	32.4	10.5	7.2	5.9	2.0	2.1	0.0
TOTAL (8393)	100	8.1	100	6.1	3.2	2.5	0.9	0.7	0.0

Note: Averages duties weighted by 1996 imports; (2) Inward/outward processing, agricultural basic products and processed foods are excluded.

Source: Own estimates based on data in B. Majcen, "Approaching the European Union--Effects on Slovenian Economy," paper presented at the conference *The Economic System of the European Economy and Adjustment of the Republic of Croatia*, Rijeka, April 24-25, 1997.

Consequently, actually applied tariff rates are lower than the average tariff rate: the average tariff was 10.7 percent in 1996, whereas the average applied tariff rate was 5.7 percent.[11] Since the schedule for eliminating various tariff concessions is either the same or longer in the EAA than in other FTAs signed by Slovenia, data in Table 4.7 provide an indication of tariffs on about 80 percent of Slovenian imports. By any standards, they were low already in 1997.

Access to Markets for Agricultural Products

Agriculture accounts for a relatively low share of total employment (7 percent in 1997) and GDP (around 5 percent) in comparison with other EU applicant countries. Indeed, Slovenia's agricultural import regime is reminiscent of the EU. The level of protection is similar, although the tools differ, in that Slovenia relies on administrative micromanagement rather than competitive private markets.[12] Prices of some commodities are kept at high levels through various mechanisms including: market intervention and export subsidies, tariffs and quantitative restrictions on imports, and an administrative pricing system that is still maintained for several crops and animal products. Import levies and specific tariffs for live

---

[11] See *Strategy of the Republic of Slovenia for Accession to the European Union: Economic and Social Part*, Institute for Macroeconomic Analysis and Development, Ljubljana, April 1998.

[12] The European Commission notes: "The main policy measures in sectors with market organizations are similar, or close to, EC policies. However, a number of sectors have very few market intervention mechanisms other than external trade protection." (*Commission Opinion on Slovenia's Application for Membership of the European Union, European Commission*, Bulletin of the European Union, Supplement 15/97, p.55).

animals, meat, dairy products, eggs and wine all erect barriers to external suppliers. In addition, some imports are subject to a system reminiscent of arrangements existing in the past. This concerns pricing practices, the actual management of exports and imports, the allocation of production, buffer stocks and strategic reserves. The focus of protection is on low processed products, whereas processed food products are much less protected; as such, the effective protection rates at various levels of food marketing chains tend to de-escalate, rather than escalate as is the case with most national tariff schedules.

Taking into account the objective of EU membership, Slovenia should change its current system of agricultural protection in line with the EU proposed reform measures of the CAP.[13] This would involve dismantling vestiges of direct administrative controls on wheat, rye and sugar; it would involve shifting from price support to direct payments and developing a coherent rural policy to accompany this process. Nonetheless, this, should not involve moving towards the levels of subsidies provided under the CAP.

MFN and Preferential Rates: Growth in Reverse Discrimination

Preferences and exemptions from uniform treatment of external suppliers may result in economic losses because of reliance on supplies from a higher cost source than otherwise available. Slovenia's import regime (not unlike that of the EU) is characterized by a myriad of preferential arrangements. Maximum tariff rates, as well as average weighted and simple tariff rates, are highly diversified -- reflecting differences in baskets of Slovenian imports from various trading partners, as well as differences due to preferential agreements.

Because of their geographical proximity and because of the economic superpower status of the EU, these countries seem to be Slovenia's natural trading partners. Although the potential for trade diversion seems limited, there is nevertheless one important caveat. The potential for trade diversion has increased since 1997 as a result of the growing divergence between MFN and preferential treatment of imports. This divergence is reflected in the increased difference between duties on imports from the EU, EFTA, Baltic States and CEFTA partners on one hand and those from MFN partners on the other.

These reverse tariff preferences for industrial products will further increase. Annual reductions in tariff rates on imports from the EU and EFTA will lead to the elimination of almost all duties on manufactures in 2000 and with the elimination of duties in manufactures trade with CEFTA. Although MFN rates will also be reduced, the tariff-induced margin for preferred suppliers will increase in comparison with 1997.

It would be difficult to quantitatively assess the welfare cost of discrimination of MFN suppliers. One point, however, is clear -- there is no reason to offer preferential treatment to external suppliers beyond the levels imposed by the policy objective of EU accession. These levels are determined by the EU common external tariff. There are, in fact, two arguments in favor of adopting EU external tariffs. First, it eliminates opportunities for preferential suppliers to obtain rents at the expense of Slovenian import users. Although the EU members are Slovenia's natural trading partners, they do not necessarily produce all products at the lowest cost worldwide. Those that are not at the lowest cost and yet are sold in Slovenia, thanks to high MFN tariffs, obtain rents at the expense of their Slovenian users.

---

[13] For a brief overview of the EU strategy to reform the CAP, see *Agenda 2000. For a stronger and wider Union*, European Commission, Bulletin of the European Union, Supplement 5/97.

Second, lowering MFN rates in Slovenia to the level applied by the EU would not affect the level of protection enjoyed by domestic producers. Slovenian producers --because of FTAs-- are already exposed to competitive pressures from imports from FTA partners, most significantly from the EU. Lowering the MFN rate would merely increase competitive pressures on EU suppliers. In short, no matter how large or how small the welfare gains, there is no reason against aligning Slovenia's MFN trade policy with that of the EU.

Competition Policies

Competition rules impose disciplines on firms, whereas integrationist arrangements such as the European Association Agreement (EAA) extend that discipline to governments. The basic competition rules of the EU have been designed to complement its internal trade policy, i.e., free trade among its members. The goal is to make certain that member-government's actions or those taken by firms and resulting in market segmentation will not hamper the progress of integration. The EAA envisages both a free trade and a free foreign investment posture towards the EU, once the various transition periods are over. Under the EAA, Slovenia must (i) apply the EAA competition rules to cases affecting trade between the EU and Slovenia, and (ii) approximate its competition law with the EC rules. The first obligation is also binding on the EU.

Slovenia's competition policy framework, rules and enforcement capacities, is neither fully harmonized with that of the EU nor does it provide the authorities with an effective instrument to combat monopolistic practices. The competition rules, as laid down in the 1993 Law on Protection of Competition, do not fully comply with EU competition legislation. The main areas "not-harmonized" are substantive rules (restrictive practices, block exemption and merger control) as well as procedural rules. For instance, the Law does not provide satisfactory provisions on the prohibition of restrictive agreements and abuse of the dominant position along the lines of Articles 85 and 86 of the Treaty of Rome. Exclusive and special rights granted by the Law to public utilities (electricity, oil, gas, railways, and telecommunications) are not compatible with the Community's *acquis*.

The capacity to enforce anti-trust legislation continues to be limited. Consider the following: first, procedural rules including investigation procedures of the Competition Office are not spelled out in the Law. The Office also lacks the power to issue fines should the law on the protection of competition have been broken. Second, the Office is understaffed, and its political autonomy remains doubtful, as it is not constitutionally recognized. Third, the power to fine companies rests with Slovenian courts. Weaknesses in legal underpinnings, as well as the lack of judges competent in anti-trust legislation, ultimately undermine the enforcement of the competition rules.

State Aids

Subsidies, or state aids, distort competition. They give some domestic firms an unfair advantage in competing with other firms, domestic or foreign. State aids -in the form of direct transfers of funds, foregone revenues (tax concessions or credits), etc.- continue to be a prominent feature of Slovenian economic policy. Independence has not produced a decisive break with financial practices characteristic of the old economic regime. The government's support to agriculture and industrial sectors actually intensified in the aftermath of independence. That increase in state interventionism had been justified by the harsh economic and financial circumstances of the transition, triggered by the loss of former Yugoslav markets. Consequently, the channels of state aids are multiple and subsidies are designed to bring remedies in a whole array of different situations. These range from subsidies to agriculture, railways, coal mines, social security and export credit refunds to guarantees on loans granted to enterprises and public works.

Table 4.8. Types of State Aids and Their Evolution Over 1993-98

	1993	1994	1995	1996	1997	1998p
1. Subsidies to Enterprises	0.75	0.59	0.80	0.53	0.68	0.78
2. Expenditure on Restructuring Programs Of Banks and Enterprises	1.49	1.37	1.11	1.09	0.98	0.98
3. Expenditure on Active Employment Programs	1.08	0.70	0.56	0.37	0.30	0.36
4. Government Payments for Guarantees on Loans Granted to Enterprises	0.29	0.20	0.40	0.08	0.05	0.09
5. Capital Transfers from State Budget to Enterprise Sector	0.25	0.27	0.15	0.11	0.28	0.13
A. Total State Budget Expenditure on State Aids (1+2+3+4+5)	3.86	3.12	2.65	2.19	2.29	2.33
B. Subsidies and Investment Expenditures of Municipalities	0.29	0.26	0.21	0.29	0.30	0.30
C. Amortization of Debt Paid from the State Budget as a Form of the State Aids	0.26	0.25	0.50	0.39	0.29	0.13
D. Expenditure of Revenues from Privatization as a Part of State Aids	-	-	0.32	0.40	0.42	-
Total State Aid (A+B+C+D)	**4.41**	**3.54**	**3.67**	**3.26**	**3.29**	**2.76**

Note: p = preliminary.
Source: Ministry of Finance.

No clear picture of Slovene industrial policy emerges from state aid data other than a policy to allow the survival of activities that would have been rejected by markets. For one, state aid policy does not target any potential "sunrise" sector. It does not single out national champions, which is always a risky endeavor -particularly so in the case of transition economies where, within industrial sectors, there is enormous variation in economic performance of individual firms. There are signs that direct aid to enterprises, which usually distorts competition, has been on the decline. This conclusion can be drawn from the contraction in government payments of guarantees on loans to enterprises. On the other hand, expenditures of revenues from privatization as part of state aid were quite significant in the 1995-97 period, accounting for more than 10 percent of the total. In the end, Slovenia would have to rationalize its state aid policy in line with the EU accession process, thus the need to make progress in the area of state aid controls.

External Access to Government Procurement

General government spending accounted for 45.7 percent of GDP in 1997. A significant proportion -amounting to around 10 percent, or almost US$2 billion- is spent on procurement of goods and services. A large number of government and public entities funded from the state budget are involved in procurement and outsourcing decisions. As such, the total market for government (public) procurement is quite substantial, and practices governing government policies may significantly alter conditions in the contestability of domestic markets.

Although the Law on Government Procurement does indeed treat all suppliers equal, regardless of country of origin, the practice implicitly favors domestic firms through a provision stipulating that contracts with domestic content exceeding 50 percent automatically receive a 10 percent preference. This type of preference for domestic suppliers is not uncommon.[14]

Transparent tendering procedures exist in Slovenia. In spite of this transparency, foreign firms can hardly compete for goods and services accounting for a sizable percent of total domestic spending. This result, however, does not significantly depart from the situation in other countries: in the EU, most orders are awarded to local suppliers. In Slovenia, only 2 percent of public orders above the SIT 20 million threshold are taken by external suppliers. Similarly to other countries, the award of a public procurement contract to a foreign firm in Slovenia is rare. Foreign bidders usually reach the local public procurement market through a local firm: this helps them overcome language barriers and facilitates the adjustment to domestic legal system governing public procurement.

Implications for a Pre-Accession Strategy

The challenge of a pre-accession strategy is to identify policy measures that would improve allocative efficiency, reduce adjustment cost and strengthen Slovenia's growth potential within the framework of integration into the EU. Ultimately, the prospects for a quick EU membership and, perhaps more importantly, the ability of the Slovene economy to take full advantage of opportunities offered by membership will depend on shifting to an institutional framework enhancing growth, competition and economic efficiency while regaining the lost momentum in export performance in the EU.

Table 4.9. EU Imports from First-Wave EU Applicants, 1989-97

	1989	1990	1991	1992	1993	1994	1995	1996	1997
Value of EU Imports from					*(in millions of US dollars)*				
Czech Republic	2,843	3,476	4,050	5,513	6,498	8,604	11,597	12,368	13,179
Estonia	N/A	N/A	N/A	344	308	739	1,314	1,579	1,870
Hungary	3,705	4,834	5,799	6,537	5,773	7,260	9,974	11,231	13,398
Poland	5,167	7,705	8,781	10,274	9,834	11,934	15,260	15,678	16,049
Slovenia	N/A	N/A	N/A	2,415	3,698	4,502	5,617	5,501	5,276
Rate of Growth of EU imports from:					*(in percent)*				
Czech Republic		22.3	16.5	36.1	17.9	32.4	34.8	6.6	6.6
Estonia		N/A	N/A	N/A	-10.5	139.9	77.9	20.2	18.4
Hungary		30.5	20.0	12.7	-11.7	25.8	37.4	12.6	19.3
Poland		49.1	14.0	17.0	-4.3	21.4	27.9	2.7	2.4
Slovenia		N/A	N/A	N/A	53.1	21.7	24.8	-2.1	-4.1

Note: N/A = not available.
Source: Derived from data in United Nations COMTRADE database as reported by EU.

The vehicle for designing a strategy that would simultaneously accelerate accession and provide a sound basis for sustainable and employment-creating economic growth is the contestability of domestic markets and a business friendly environment. The latter is important, not only for FDI, but also for domestic firms. The competitiveness of Slovene firms, both domestic and foreign-owned, ultimately depends on competition at home from imports and domestic sources alike. This, in turn, hinges critically on a liberal trade and investment regime. Institutional and policy measures that would improve the

---

[14] Poland and Hungary, as an example, use a 20 percent preference level on domestic suppliers.

business climate and improve the performance of Slovenia's economy have, as a common denominator, the liberalization of foreign trade and investment regime. These measures can be summarized as follows:

- to improve competition policy framework, rules and enforcement capacities of competition authorities: one may consider granting anti-trust authority to a single independent institution empowered to assess the competition and welfare impact of important policy decisions as well as actions taken by firms affecting contestability of domestic markets and monitor their impact *ex post*;

- to align MFN tariff rates on industrial products with those levied by the EU: this would not necessarily involve a formal lowering of statutory tariffs but might simply involve the change in applied rates;

- to overhaul the current framework of state aids: it would involve establishing transparent monitoring mechanisms, streamlining and reducing the scope of subsidies. State aids should be also subjected to scrutiny by competition authority once it is reformed;

- to open services to foreign competition: this would involve *inter alia* removing provisions limiting foreign equity, and opening telecommunications and insurance to foreign capital;

- to apply fully the principle of national treatment[15] in the sphere of foreign investment. This would involve removing legal provisions requiring that purchases by foreigners of equity exceeding 25 percent be subject to government clearance;

- to change the rules governing the agricultural regime. This would involve supporting the agricultural sector through direct payments rather than through high agricultural prices and trade policy (external border protection and export subsidies). In addition, since the present structure offers preference to low value added products (which obtain the largest levels of protection), this would entail changing the current structure of incentives to remove the bias against processed agricultural products.

---

[15] A move in this direction has been the recent elimination of the national requirement determining the make up of boards of directors of companies. In its previous wording, the law discriminated against foreigners.

Financial Sector

Introduction

The financial sector in Slovenia has undergone significant restructuring in recent years. In spite of these advances, the sector is still far from being internationally competitive in terms of product variety, soundness and costs; it remains small in both absolute and relative terms. Consequently, the key overall objective in this area is to increase the international competitiveness of the financial sector to a level that will allow its successful integration into the EU single market and, indeed, the global financial market. The general policy measures required to achieve this are increased competition, restructuring, supervision, and legal approximation to EU legislation.

Slovenia's road to financial integration leads to a broad agenda of reforms that includes improving efficiency, enhancing risk management, privatization, reducing distortions, and bridging the regulatory and institutional gaps with the EU in the areas of banking, capital and insurance markets. The reform agendas in the three sectors mentioned above are complementary. While the banking system in Slovenia is well developed, the capital market is shallow and does not yet play its potential role in financial intermediation. Many challenges exist ahead. Financial integration is likely to increase the intricacy and diversity of financial contracts. At the same time, financial integration is likely to reduce the cost of capital, as financial institutions become more efficient and competitive.

Meeting the regulatory and supervisory requirements of the EU will help financial institutions, supervisory and regulatory bodies, substantially upgrade their institutional capacity to both monitor and manage risk. Identifying and addressing the main challenges and risks of the Slovene financial system, and those entailed by financial integration with the EU and the world, will likely form the core Government strategy in this area.

Having an efficient and competitive financial sector is an integral part of the Slovene development agenda. It is also a crucial complement to macroeconomic policy and stabilization strategy, particularly in view of the role that the financial sector plays in the intermediation of resources and in the transmission mechanism of capital flows in a financially integrated world.

This chapter presents an assessment of the Slovene financial sector. The chapter focuses mostly on the banking system, but addresses key issues in the two other blocks of the financial system, namely capital markets and insurance. Since banks dominate the financial sector in Slovenia and since they are nearly the only real source of credit in the economy, the restructuring of the banking sector is the key element of financial reform. Reforms in the banking sector, however, need to be accompanied by reforms aimed at developing and strengthening the other two segments of the financial sector.

The Banking System

Banks within the former Socialist Federal Republic of Yugoslavia (SFRY) were founded, owned and directed almost exclusively by enterprises, with governmental bodies explicitly barred from ownership. Although barriers to entry into the banking sector were removed prior to independence, the Ljubljanska Banka Group nonetheless dominated the system. The group included Ljubljanska Banka (LBdd) and 12 smaller member banks. By the end of 1991, the balance sheet of the LB Group accounted for about 82 percent of the total assets of the banking system. At that time, SKBdd and Abanka participated with around 10 percent of the banking system total assets while none of the remaining 13 banks accounted for more than 0.5 percent of the system's total assets.

Box 5.1. Structure of the Financial Sector in Slovenia, 1997

Banks

28 commercial banks (SIT 2,013 billion assets), 6 savings banks (SIT 6,200 million assets) and 70 cooperatives (mutual banks), of which:
- Two state banks completed the rehabilitation process and are ready for privatization;
- Three largest banks account for more than 50 percent of total assets in the sub-sector; three largest savings banks account for 73 percent of total assets in the sub-sector;
- First 4 banking groups were created in 1997 and some large banks started links with Insurance Companies;
- Nova Ljubljanska Banka Group accounts for 35 percent of total assets.

Ownership:
- 13 banks are domestically owned and 11 are controlled by Slovenian owners;
- 4 banks are wholly-owned or controlled by foreigners;
- All banks have private participation, except for NLB and NKBM which have a 40 percent of total market share;
- Postna Banka Slovenije (Slovenian Post Office Bank) is indirectly state owned;
- Direct or indirect government participation in the banking system accounts for over 50 percent of market share.

Profitability Ratios (1997):
• Risk weighted capital asset ratio	19 percent
• Average pre-tax return on assets	1.1 percent
• Average pre-tax return on equity	10.5 percent
• Interest rate margin	4.9 percent
• Deposit rates	13.9-16.6 percent (3 months – over 1 year)
• Lending rates	8.0-21.6 percent (short term – long term)
• Non-performing loans	6.2 percent of total assets; 12.5 percent of total loans

Insurance
- 10 Insurance companies and 2 re-insurance companies (of which one has 60 percent of total non life insurance and 40 percent of total life insurance premiums);
- 10 insurance companies offer life insurance services; 2 of them account for 74 percent of market;
- Not acting yet as independent investor, resources are channeled to banks and government securities;
- Restricted foreign entry;
- Not restructured;
- Social ownership level in large insurance firms is being challenged.

Securities
- Market capitalization of SIT 399,345 million, or 13.9 percent of GDP, of which banks account for 80 percent.
- The Securities Market Agency is the supervisory agent (investment firms, Ljubljana Stock Exchange, Clearing depository house, investment funds and management companies);
- Number of traded securities:112 mid-June;
- Basically acting as instrument for ownership transformation of enterprises rather than financial intermediator.

Evolution since Independence

At the time of independence, Slovenia's banking sector faced four major problems. First, some 30 to 40 percent of banks loans were non-performing; consequently, the banks operated at excessively high intermediation spreads and real lending rates. Second, there was practically no real competition in the banking sector. Third, the regulatory and supervisory regime was poor, lagging behind international standards. Fourth, Slovene banks lost assets in Yugoslavia as a result of independence, but retained liabilities, especially those with the London Club creditors.

In order to address the most pressing problem of bad debts, the authorities nationalized three banks that were close to bankruptcy -Ljubljanska Banka (LB), Kreditna Banka Maribor (KBM) and

Komercialna Banka Nova Gorica (KBNG)- and launched a rehabilitation plan for the three banks.[1] The process, conducted by the newly created Bank Rehabilitation Agency (BRA), began by writing off current bank losses against their capital and by replacing their non-performing assets for bonds issued by BRA. A total of DM 1.9 billion of bonds was issued for this program –an amount equivalent to just under 10 percent of Slovenia's 1993 GDP. The swap removed two thirds of the bad assets of the banks; the banks retained about 15 percent of their bad loans.

After these initial steps, several other measures were taken. First, the two remaining banks-LB and KBM- were split in two, with the old banks taking over all claims and liabilities to the former SFRY and the new banks Nova Ljubljanska Banka (NLB) and Nova Kreditna Banka Maribor (NKBM), created in mid-1994 retaining all the rest. Second, to cope with the growing concerns over currency and maturity mismatches in the two banks' balance sheets, the original 30-year DM denominated BRA bonds were exchanged, in November of 1995, for tolar denominated government bonds of shorter and variable maturity and lower interest rate. Third, in June of 1996, an agreement between Slovenia and London Club creditors was reached: it released Slovenian banks from the joint and several liability obligations under the 1988 agreement between SFRY's debtors and commercial banks.

The BRA played an important role during the bank rehabilitation process, supervising the process and dealing with bad assets. The Agency acquired claims in the amount of DM 1 billion in more than 100 firms. As part of the rehabilitation process, they engaged in loan rescheduling, debt-equity swaps, debt write-offs and other financial transactions aimed at recovering part of the bad portfolio of the banks. About 32 percent of the bad debts were recovered though these channels, mostly from small size firms. As of the end 1996, the Agency had received DM 151 million in cash, DM 139 million in shares and equity stakes, and DM 58 million was rescheduled. Moreover, the Agency wrote-off bad debt in the amount of DM 319 million. The majority of the bad debt, however, was the result of only a few loans to large enterprises that are still under rehabilitation in the Slovene Development Corporation.[2]

The remaining regional banks were implicitly transferred to their new owners as part of the privatization process of socially-owned enterprises. These regional banks were originally owned by socially-owned enterprises. The degree of ownership was directly related to the amount of lending the bank had with the enterprise. When the socially-owned enterprises were transferred to join stock companies, the associated regional banks were not separated as independent entities. As a result, when a socially-owned enterprise was privatized, the associated bank was also privatized with the firm. Since many firms partially owned regional banks, the degree of ownership concentration in many of the banks was thus limited. In addition, new banks were established, foreign banks were allowed to participate in the Slovene banking system, both through acquisition of shares in Slovene banks, most notably in SKB, and through the opening of new foreign banks in Slovenia. Branches of foreign banks, however, are still prohibited.

The first results of the bank rehabilitation program were visible by 1994 when the two banks, NLB and NKBM, started to show positive cash flows and net incomes. Moreover, their capital adequacy ratio (CAR) exceeded the Bank of Slovenia (BOS) requirement of 8 percent. Progress in rehabilitation continued during the subsequent years. By early 1997, both banks had satisfied all the conditions set by the BOS for ending the rehabilitation process. As a result, they were taken out of rehabilitation by mid-

---

[1] LB and KBM were the first and third largest banks in Slovenia; KBNG was the sixth. These banks comprised over 53 percent of the banking sector in 1993 and had about 45 percent of their loans as non-performing. In January of 1995, KBNG was merged into KBM.

[2] See OECD (1997), *Economic Survey of Slovenia 1997*, Paris.

1997. Successful banking rehabilitation has contributed to the significantly improved financial position of the banking sector as whole.

Structure of the Banking Sector

By the end of 1997, there were 28 commercial banks, 6 savings banks and 70 credit institutions in Slovenia. Of the total number of banks, 15 have full banking license; of these, 7 are for commercial and investment banking, 6 for commercial banking only, and 2 for commercial and limited investment

---

Box 5.2. Public Sector Ownership in the Banking Sector

Paradoxically, public ownership in the banking sector significantly increased during Slovenia's transition to a market economy. Before independence, State ownership was limited to 12 percent of shares in the parent group of Ljubljanska Banka Group, LBdd, which then owned the majority shares in the 12 regional banks. By 1997, however the government of Slovenia was the most important shareholder in the banking sector. Besides having 100 percent ownership of two of the three major banks, NLB and NKBM, it indirectly has majority control over 6 previous LB Group banks through the new NLB Group. NLB also owns between 40-60 percent of each of these banks. The State also owns 100 percent of Postna Banka Slovenije, the post office bank.

Public sector participation is present across the sector through state-owned enterprises, various state-owned funds, and local and municipal authorities. In the second largest bank (also the largest private bank), SKB, the public sector owns close to 13 percent of the shares distributed among the following: the City of Ljubljana (5.1 percent), Slovenian Railways (2.7 percent), Restitution Fund (2 percent), and two public utilities companies (3 percent). The public sector also has holdings in other banks: 2.6 percent of Abanka own by the Restitution Fund; 20 percent of Banka Koper through the state-owned Luka Koper (port) and 19 percent through Istrabenz, which now is owned by state funds and the largest insurance company (partially state-own); 2.2 percent of Krekova Banka own by the Restitution Fund. Moreover, the public sector share in the banking system is also augmented by the holdings of the capitalization fund for pension insurance.

This direct or indirect ownership structure implies that the public sector controls at least 50 percent of the banking sector assets. NLB Group now accounts for 34.6 percent of the market, and NKBM for 11.8 percent. The State market share then amounts to 46.4 percent. With the participation in SKB, Abanka, Banka Koper, and Krekova Banka, and others, the public sector becomes the most important player in the market. Adding the cross ownership of insurance companies, funds and banks, only increases the presence of the public sector in the sector.

---

banking operations. Commercial banks maintain 98 percent of the market share, while savings banks have 0.4 percent and credit institutions (savings co-operatives) 1.6 percent. Given the size of the banking system -roughly US$12 billions of total assets at the end of 1997- it is commonly accepted that Slovenia is overbanked. From 1991 until 1994, the number of banks increased (see Table 5.1). Since then, there have been 5 mergers and one bankruptcy (Komercialna Banka Triglav in 1996). Between 1997-98, four banking groups were established -the first step towards consolidation of the banking system.

Table 5.1. Number of Banks and Saving Banks in Slovenia

	1991	1992	1993	1994	1995	1996	1997
Banks (1)	26	30	32	35	33	29	28
Saving banks	14	15	13	11	10	7	6

Note: (1) From 1994 LB and KBM included.
Source: Bank of Slovenia.

The majority of Slovenian banks (with the exception of banking groups mentioned above) are independent and regionally concentrated. Shareholders in most banks are local or private firms and individuals. The largest bank (NLB) and the third largest (NKBM) are still state owned. Moreover, 12 banks are fully owned by domestic entities while another 4 are either owned or controlled by foreign owners. Of those remaining 12 banks, all had a majority ownership that was domestic (in 8 of them, foreigners have less than 1 per cent ownership share while in one of them, SKB, foreign ownership represented 49 per cent of the capital. This ownership structure, however, masks substantial public sector involvement in the banking system (see Box 5.2).

Market Concentration

By the end of 1997, Slovenia's seven largest banks accounted for nearly 72 percent of the entire banking sector. This market concentration has remained stable since 1995. The market share of each of the seven banks has also remained fairly stable through these years. This situation is the result of limited competition among banks for deposits, the main component of bank liabilities. Lack of competition is partly a result of the prevailing interbank agreement on deposit interest rates[3]. Consequently, the access to their own sources of funds (equity) and international borrowing determine the increase in market share. Not surprisingly, the four foreign owned banks are showing the largest increases in market share.

New Bank Groups and Strategic Alliances

From 1997 to 1998, some progress was made in the consolidation of the banking sector; the four banking groups were established and strategic alliances between banks and insurance companies took shape. According to the law, a banking group is formed when one bank holds a direct or indirect stake of 40 percent or more in the capital of another bank, and controls it directly or indirectly. The Bank of Slovenia (BOS) determined minimum conditions for the banking groups, namely to coordinate current policies and their future development, particularly that of international business, marketing, new products, information technology, ATM networks, credit activity, business risk management, liquidity, accounting standards, internal audit and external audit. Members of the group should also agree on measures in case of solvency problems. The controlling bank heads all such activities within the group.

Table 5.2. Market Share of the Seven Biggest Banks, 1995-97
(in percent)

	1995	1996	1997
NLB	29.7	28.3	26.8
SKB Banka	12.0	11.9	12.0
NKBM	11.2	11.4	11.8
Banka Koper	5.5	5.8	6.0
Banka Celje	4.6	5.2	5.4
Abanka	4.6	5.1	5.1
Gorenjska Banka	4.5	4.2	4.5
Total - top 7 banks	72.1	71.9	71.6
Total - all banks	100.0	100.0	100.0

Source: Bank of Slovenia.

---

[3] A key element of the banking system is the existence of an interbank agreement setting a maximum deposit interest rate. This agreement was first introduced in April of 1995, with the blessing of the BOS. The agreement has been successful in limiting competition among banks and reducing the cost of deposits. According to the BOS, the agreement is to be eliminated in 1999.

The first four banking groups control almost 60 percent of the market share. They include: Nova Ljubljanska Banka Group (NLB Group); SKB Banking Group (SKB Group), which includes SKB bank and UBK bank; Banka Koper Banking Group, which includes Banka Koper and M Banka; and Banka Celje Banking Group, which includes Banka Celje and Hmezad Banka (see Table 5.3).

Table 5.3. Banking Groups, 1997

Banking Group	Market Share
Nova Ljubljanska Banka Group	34.6
SKB Banking Group	12.6
Banka Koper Banking Group	6.6
Banka Celje Banking Group	6.0
Total	59.8

Source: Bank of Slovenia.

Other steps towards consolidation of the banking system in Slovenia have taken place recently. In the first half of 1998, the management of the two largest banks, NLB and SKB, signed a "letter of intent" establishing some mergers initiatives. The initiative, however, received a rather cold response from the Government. It should be noticed that NLB is still state owned and subject to privatization. On the other hand, negotiations between Banka Koper (head of a banking group) and Abanka (the sixth biggest bank), are at a much more advanced stage. If the merger takes place, the group will increase its market size from 6.6 percent to 11.7 percent. Finally, following the merger of the two largest Austrian banks, Bank Austria and Creditanstalt, their banks in Slovenia are undergoing a parallel/similar process of consolidation. On top of these initiatives, some large banks have started a of linking up with insurance companies. This process is driven by two main forces: insurance companies are large depositors and they are also interested in selling their products through bank networks.

Box 5.3. The New Ljubljanska Banka Group

The Slovenian banking sector is still dominated by the presence of the former Ljubljanska Banka Group (LB Group). In the past (1978), the 22 basic banks owned the majority share in the associated bank called LBdd, while the enterprises acted as majority owners of the basic banks. In 1990, all banks in the LB system became joint-stock companies with a majority of their stock owned by the parent bank LBdd, and the rest by the enterprises. At this time, the government of Slovenia held only a minority share (12 percent) in the LBdd. In a year of consolidation, 14 member banks remained in the system. When LBdd merged with LB Gospodarska, the number of banks in the LB Group decreased to 13 by 1991.

During the rehabilitation process, all the regional banks were granted independence; LBdd, Kreditna Banka Maribor (KBM) and later Komercialna Banka Nova Gorica (KBNG) underwent a formal rehabilitation process under the auspices and ownership of the Bank Rehabilitation Agency (BRA). In the process, the Bank Rehabilitation Agency (BRA) took over the majority shares, previously held by the LBdd, in all of the regional banks. By the end of 1994, the BRA sold its majority shares in four of the regional banks: Banka Celje, Banka Koper, Gorenjska Banka, and Dolenjska Banka.

After the "bad assets" had been separated from the LB balance sheet, and after NLB had been established, this "good bank" began to consolidate by acquiring banks which were part of the former LB Group. In 1996, NLB gave LB-Posavska the status of a subsidiary. A year later, NLB acquired the stock of the following banks: Pomurska Banka (40 percent), Koroska Banka (40 percent), Banka Velenje (59.88 percent), LB-Banka Zasavje (40 percent), and LB-Banka Domzale (40 percent). NLB also entered into a strategic alliance with the state-owned insurance company Triglav.

Banking Sector Assets and Balance Sheet

Aggregate assets of the banking system amounted to SIT 2,013 billion at the end of 1997. This means a nominal increase of 16.4 percent over the previous year. In all of the top seven banks, real growth rates were positive (nominal growth rates were the following: NLB - 10 percent; SKB - 17 percent; NKBM - 20 percent; Banka Koper - 20 percent; Banka Celje- 22 percent; Abanka - 17 percent; Gorenjska Banka - 23 percent) while some smaller banks registered negative real growth rates.

The ratio of total assets/GDP of Slovenian banks increased from 64 percent in 1994 to 70 percent in 1997. This positive trend suggests that a process of financial deepening is taking place. Nevertheless, the change in the structure of the banking sector assets shows that an increasing share of bank portfolios is allocated in government securities and Central Bank Bills. As of the end of 1997, they amounted to a 30.5 percent of total bank assets, up from 23.6 percent in 1995. On the contrary, claims to non-monetary sectors have declined from 59.3 percent in 1995 to 57 percent in 1997. In such circumstances, banks operate, to a limited degree, as financial intermediaries. Clearly this is the result of the sterilization policy implemented by the Central Bank – a policy in which banks seem to play a key role in the implementation of BOS foreign exchange rate policy.

A long-term perspective on banking sector asset structure is given in Table 5.4 below. Since 1994-95, banking sector claims to non-monetary sectors, along with foreign assets, have been declining in relative terms, while there has been a continuous increase of banking sector assets in the form of government securities and BOS bills. Indeed, the share of the latter almost doubled in 1997.

Table 5.4. Structure of Banking Sector Assets, Selected Items, 1991-97
(percent of total)

Year	Claims to Non-Monetary Sectors	Foreign Assets	Government Securities	BOS Bills
1991	41.1	13.0	1.1	0.0
1992	42.0	13.8	1.4	5.1
1993	56.5	14.6	19.6	4.1
1994	54.1	19.1	17.4	6.6
1995	59.3	17.5	16.7	6.9
1996	58.1	18.6	15.0	8.9
1997	57.0	13.4	13.9	16.6

Source: Bank of Slovenia and Simoneti, M., B. Jašovic and M. Mrak, *Investments and Long-Term Financing in Slovenia*, CEEPN, 1998.

On the liabilities side, the trend of decreasing the share of liabilities to the banking sector, and conversely increasing the share of liabilities vis-a-vis customers other than banks, continued in 1997. The share of deposits from this group of clients increased from 64 percent in 1996 to 68 percent of total bank liabilities in 1997. The bulk of these deposits came from private individuals; the balance came from the rest contributing corporate and public sector depositors. Finally, banking sector deposits declined from 14 to 11 percent of total liabilities.

A long-term perspective on the structure of banking sector liabilities is presented in Table 5.5. This information for the period 1991-97 reveals that the participation of foreign currency deposits in total banking sector liabilities remained at the constant level of around 20 percent, while the share of tolar deposits has more than doubled. This is a result of the increasing creditworthiness of the Slovene tolar during the transition period. Moreover, tolar deposits have become financially more attractive than foreign currency deposits. Participation of foreign liabilities, as well as liabilities to the monetary system, have declined in the same period.

Table 5.5. Structure of Banking Sector Liabilities, Selected Items, 1991-97
(percent of total)

Year	Tolar Deposits	Foreign Currency Deposits	Foreign Liabilities	Liabilities to the Monetary System	Capital and Reserves
1991	20.3	19.4	22.3	11.5	19.3
1992	25.6	20.5	18.7	12.5	16.5
1993	28.7	22.6	15.0	12.0	15.2
1994	34.9	19.6	12.7	9.1	17.5
1995	35.2	21.0	12.0	7.2	16.9
1996	37.8	21.4	11.5	5.0	15.9
1997	43.8	19.4	9.3	3.9	15.4

Source: Bank of Slovenia and Simoneti, M., B. Jašovic and M. Mrak, *Investments and Long-Term Financing in Slovenia*, CEEPN, 1998.

Efficiency and Profitability

Slovenian banks have been more successful than corporate enterprises in turning around their financial conditions during the transition. Their financial results have slowly improved with the years (see Table 5.6). Nonetheless, bankers are aware that, in the coming years, they will face important challenges. These challenges will come from the privatization of the two largest banks, the consolidation of the banking sector, the elimination of the interbank interest rate agreement, the rationalization to cut costs and improve efficiency, and the further opening of the market to foreign competition. As a consequence, they expect profits to deteriorate as the process of accession to the EU increases contestability in the financial sector.

Between 1994 and 1997 there was some improvement in the profitability of the banking system. This result can be explained by several factors, among them, lending in domestic currency, given the prevailing high intermediation rates. Profits also came from the significant share of sight deposits (almost 14 percent) which implies that banks collect a portion of the inflation tax. The agreement on the deposits interest rates that limits the cost of funds for intermediation, and the increase in the bank's share of government securities, also contributed to boost banking profits. Some of these sources of profitability, however, will tend to vanish in the coming years: the process of the EU accession will increase competition, will reduce the scope of BOS monetary policy instruments and will bring inflation and interest rates down to EU standards. In addition, operating costs in the sector are almost twice as much as international standards and need to be reduced to make banks more competitive. This indicates that the Slovenian banking will have to consolidate, focus on developing core banking operations and new products, as well as reduce its operating costs and increase its efficiency.

Table 5.6. Indicators of Bank Efficiency

	1994	1995	1996	1997
Return on average assets	0.4	1.0	1.1	1.1
Return on average equity	4.0	9.1	10.2	10.5
Net interest margin	3.7	4.9	5.6	4.9
Operating costs/average assets	3.2	3.8	3.6	3.7
Labor costs/average assets	1.7	2.0	1.9	1.8

Source: Bank of Slovenia.

Capitalization and Asset Quality

Although the quality of the credit portfolio of Slovenian banks improved from 1993 to 1995, a small deterioration was noticeable in 1996-97 (see Table 5.7). This is, in part, the result of the BOS tightening the classification of debts in groups A to E, from loose classification defined in 1993 -requirements still in force by the end 1996. Even more stringent criteria were entered into effect on January of 1997. The methodology applied from 1993 until 1996 took into account the assessment of creditworthiness of a customer. It allowed, under certain circumstances, to classify a loan secured by a lien, both on real estate and movable property, as lending in group A. Since January of 1997, however, the loan secured by a lien could be graded one higher class than the credit-standing of that particular borrower.

In spite of these developments, the classified loan portfolio of the banking system (CDE) is low, at 6.2 percent (see Table 5.7). Provided the claims on the Republic of Slovenia and the BOS were subtracted from the total claims classified in category A, the share of these assets, as of June 1997, would be reduced from 88.6 percent to 84.2 percent; the share of claims graded as B-class assets would rise from 5.1 percent to 7.1 percent, while the share of other assets would increase from 6.2 percent to 8.7 percent. The asset quality of Slovenian banks does not represent a problem for the system as a whole, especially taking into account their capital adequacy ratio.

Table 5.7. Classification of Balance and Off Balance Sheet Assets of the Banking Sector, 1993-97

Category	1993	1994	1995	1996	Jun 97
A	81.1	86.1	89.4	89.5	88.6
B	6.6	5.7	4.8	4.2	5.1
C	4.7	2.5	1.9	2.4	2.3
D	3.2	2.6	2.1	2.2	2.2
E	4.3	3.1	1.8	1.6	1.7
DE	7.5	5.7	3.9	3.8	3.9
CDE	12.2	8.2	5.8	6.2	6.2

Note: A = payment on time; B= up to 30 days overdue; C = 31-180 days overdue, D = 181-365 days overdue; E = over 1 year overdue.
Source: Bank of Slovenia and Banking Association.

The capital adequacy of Slovenian banks has remained fairly high and stable at about a 20 percent level. This is clearly a competitive advantage of Slovenian banks, implying that they are able to support a considerable growth (close to 100 percent) in risk assets. This enables banks to manage new risks with their own regulatory capital, with an important protection against potential non-performing assets. As the process of EU accession continues, the banks should be prepared to handle "private" assets. Consequently, they should improve their experience in both credit and risk analysis. Management would have to switch from a "government securities" oriented policy towards corporate and individual business; this point is particularly relevant for the two state-owned banks.

Money and Credit Developments

According to the Law on the Bank of Slovenia (BOS), the Bank's primary responsibility is to maintain the stability of the national currency and to maintain internal and external liquidity. When the tolar was introduced in October of 1991, the BOS adopted both a monetary targeting policy and a managed floating exchange regime. This combination of tight money and flexible exchange rate was an important component of the stabilization program. As the currency gained recognition, the demand for money increased, and the level of foreign currency deposits declined. By the end of 1997, foreign currency deposits accounted for 29 percent of total bank deposits, declining to 25 percent by September

1998. Slovenian residents, however, still maintain a significant share of their assets in the form of foreign currency deposits.

The changes in the banking sector balance sheets discussed above are closely related to the monetary policy carried out by the BOS over the recent years. Between 1993 and 1996, the BOS had a very restrictive monetary policy. The BOS also offered attractive financial instruments to banks in exchange for foreign currency, but this meant less domestic credit to the real sector and higher domestic interest rates. Moreover, the interest rate differentials between Slovenia and Germany stimulated borrowing from abroad. As a result, capital inflows became difficult to manage, especially when credit ratings improved and as privatization progressed. The Central Bank reacted by imposing higher constraints to the free movement of capital (see Chapter I).

While the Slovene financial system has grown quite rapidly since independence, it is still small compared to Western economies. In fact, bank intermediation -- measured as a broad money net of currency in circulation -- has increased by 15 percentage points between 1992-97, reaching 33.5 percent of GDP in 1997. Moreover, Slovenia has a 47 percent ratio of broad money to GDP in 1997; as such, the Slovene financial sector still has room to grow in order to reach ratios of Western economies, or those countries with a per capita income comparable to Slovenia. Compared to other EU accessing countries, however, Slovenia's financial market is relatively deep (see Table 5.8).

Table 5.8. Monetary Aggregates, 1992-97
(millions of tolars)

	1992	1993	1994	1995	1996	1997
Broad Money	314.3	512.9	735.0	939.9	1,135.3	1,410.7
(real increase)	-0.3	0.2	0.2	0.1	9.9	14.8
(% of GDP)	31.3	35.7	39.7	42.3	44.5	46.9
Domestic Money	186.1	302.6	489.6	616.5	750.9	1,006.7
(real increase)	-0.2	0.2	0.3	0.1	10.8	23.9
(% of GDP)	18.5	21.1	26.4	27.8	29.4	33.5
Currency	24.2	32.7	47.3	60.0	66.8	78.1
(real increase)	-0.1	0.0	0.2	0.1	1.3	8.0
Deposits	161.9	269.9	442.3	556.5	684.1	928.6
(real increase)	-0.3	0.3	0.4	0.1	11.8	25.4
Foreign Exchange Deposits	128.2	210.3	245.5	325.4	384.4	404.0
(real increase)	-0.3	0.2	0.0	0.2	7.5	-2.9
Memo Item: Broad money as % of GDP in EU Accessing Countries						
Czech Republic	75.8	69.6	73.1	80.5	75.4	71.2
Estonia	30.2	27.8	26.4	25.5	27.0	30.0
Hungary	51.2	49.6	45.5	42.3	41.7	41.9
Poland	35.8	35.9	36.7	36.5	37.6	39.7

Source: IMF, National Bank of Hungary and Bank of Slovenia.

The ratio of domestic credit to GDP, at around 38 percent, is relatively small when compared to the other leading transition countries, namely the Czech Republic (62 percent) and Hungary (65 percent). Between 1993 and 1996, there was a reorientation of the credit towards the non-government sector, although the government sector still takes about a third of all credit.[4] In 1997, this trend changed slightly, with the share of credit to government increasing by 1.1 percentage points. At 31 percent of total domestic credit, the public sector crowds out a substantial share of resources that could be available for the private sector.

---

[4] This number is a bit misleading since a large portion of the enterprise sector is in State hands.

During 1997, foreign banks granted more than half of the loans taken by enterprises. Although the high relative yield in tolar investment, or the relative cheapness of external finance, was in place since the beginning of the transition, risk and exchange rate expectations counterbalanced the interest rate differentials. Enterprises have only taken advantage of this situation in the last couple of years. In 1997, credit to enterprises accounted for 51 percent of total domestic credit, while households took 21 percent. By September of 1998, the general government took 30 percent of total domestic credit and enterprises, 48 percent.

Table 5.9. Domestic Credit, 1991-97

	1991	1992	1993	1994	1995	1996	1997
Net Domestic Credit							
Millions of Tolars	133.3	261.0	524.5	672.7	921.1	993.9	1,134.7
% of GDP	68.0	26.0	36.5	36.3	41.5	38.9	37.7
Share of Total Credit							
General Government	8.5	9.2	39.5	37.6	33.5	30.6	31.3
Non-Government	91.5	90.7	60.3	62.1	65.7	73.0	71.9
o/w Enterprises	83.7	82.3	49.8	48.4	48.3	52.1	50.7
Households	7.8	8.4	10.5	13.6	17.4	20.8	21.2
Memo Item: Net Domestic Credit as % of GDP - EU Accessing Countries							
Czech Republic	73.6	75.4	75.9	78.7	74.2	72.7	62.1
Hungary	105.8	100.1	101.0	96.9	85.8	76.3	64.5
Poland	34.5	38.1	40.6	39.0	34.3	34.9	35.1

Source: Bank of Slovenia.

Real domestic credit growth from the financial system to the private sector increased to worrisome levels until 1995 when the BOS introduced tighter monetary policy to contain the explosive credit expansion. As a result, real domestic credit growth rates declined The major factor responsible for this was the high yield on securities issued by the BOS, which have been crowding out credit to the real sector.   Domestic   banks   find government securities a safe and sound investment alternative. Since May of 1997, the BOS has reduced its monetary policy tightening, thereby allowing domestic credit to expand. Despite the cut in interest rates during the last quarter of 1997, real domestic interest rates remained high, and as a result, some enterprises could raise funds abroad at cheaper interest rates.[5]

Figure 5.1. Real Interest Rates

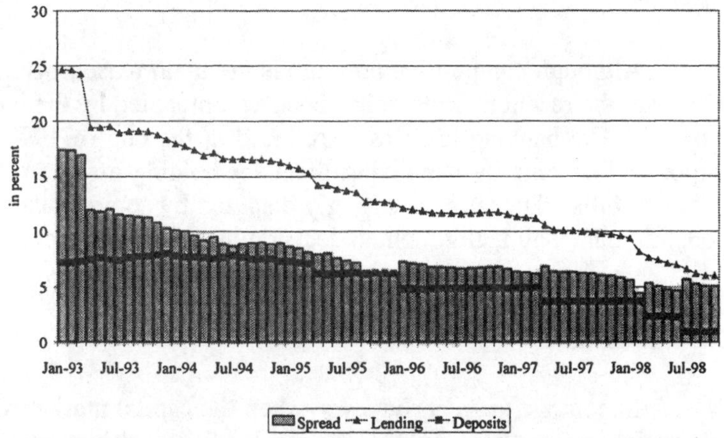

Interest rates have declined in both nominal and real terms since independence, although they remained high in real terms until end-1997. During the period 1992-94, this was mainly due to tight monetary policy, to exchange rate expectations and to the structure of the banking sector. An inter-bank agreement on the highest real deposit rates has been in place since 1995 and has been modified yearly.[6] An additional factor that accounts for the high

---

[5] During 1997 net foreign borrowing by enterprises amounted to approximately SIT 53.8 billion (US$337 million), according to figures reported in the capital account.

[6] In April of 1997, a new amendment to the agreement was introduced. First, the distinction between natural and legal persons was abolished.   Second, the maturity differentiation was increased; third, the real component on

rates of return on Tolar instruments has been the indexation of all financial contracts. The yield of financial contracts has been expressed as a composite real rate, with the indexation based on two revaluation clauses: the retail price index (TOM clause) or to the exchange rate index for DM (DM clause). Several measures have been taken in order to introduce a de-indexation process. Since mid-1995, the BOS has been gradually using nominal rates for monetary policy instruments with less than one-month maturity.

Efforts to reduce interest rates have proven difficult. Interbank market rates have been declining at a much faster rate than commercial real interest rates, and it was not until the end of 1997 that a significant decline in interest rates occurred. Increasingly aware that the current corporate borrowers' preference for credit abroad might be permanent (especially in view of the prospective opening of the sector to branch offices and liberalization of the provision of cross border financial services), domestic banks in Slovenia entered in late 1997 into a strong competition aimed at retaining their first-class clients. As a consequence, real lending interest rates for this group of borrowers began to decline drastically. Real interest rates have declined to 0.9 percent for short-term deposits, and

Figure 5.2. Interbank Market Real Rates

4.2 percent for long-term deposits by September 1998, after and average of 4 percent and 6.4 percent in 1997. Real lending rates consequently declined; they reached 7 percent and 7.2 percent for similar maturities in June 1998. At the same time, the spread remains high at 5.1 percentage points (see Figures 5.1 and 5.2).

Although competitive pressure is the main reason behind the drastic reduction of lending interest rates over the recent months, it has been accompanied by the incentives that the MOF's banking asset tax conveys. The banking tax was introduced at the end of 1997: it aims at stimulating banks to increase corporate financing by penalizing them for holding assets in the form of capital, government securities and BOS bills. The tax was strongly disputed by some bankers. Indeed, the issue was even taken to the Constitutional Court, although no decision has yet been made.

Capital Markets

In contrast to its early years -when the capital market was limited to only a few bonds and shares originating mostly from public offering by financial institutions- the emergence of newly issued shares related to the ownership transformation gave momentum to the capital market in the period 1994–97. Demand for shares have come from domestic investors and, to a lesser degree, from abroad. Securities are traded on the Ljubljana Stock Exchange (LSE), either on exchange quotations A and B or on the open market C. The functioning of the Central Securities Clearing Corporation (CSCC) as a central register of dematerialized papers is fully compatible with the LSE electronic trading system.

---

deposits with a maturity of over two years was set at 7 percent, in addition to the indexation clause TOM (or foreign revaluation clause).

Despite of the rapid growth of the securities market in 1997 and despite impressive institutional development of the LSE over the recent years, this segment of the Slovenian financial sector remains under-developed. Market capitalization on LSE amounted to SIT 399.3 billion at the end of 1997, or about 14 percent of GDP. The volume of trading amounted to SIT 108.3 billion, which was equivalent to around 27 percent of total market capitalization. In addition to being shallow, the Slovenian market, as with other markets in transition economies, is more an instrument for the ownership consolidation process rather than a market for raising new funds.

Table 5.10. Market Capitalization, 1992-97

Year	Market Capitalization (in million SIT)	Market Capitalization (in percent to GDP)	Turnover Ratio (turnover / capitalization)
1992	33,356	3.27	0.253
1993	62,869	4.38	1.132
1994	75,579	4.08	1.143
1995	100,701	4.53	0.675
1996	177,183	6.94	0.453
1997	399,345	13.74	0.248

Source: The Ljubljana Stock Exchange.

Securities Market and Ownership Transformation

In the Slovenian mass privatization program, a large number of companies were privatized in a relatively short time. Regulation determined both eligible groups of owners (employees, the general public, privatization funds, state funds, and foreigners) as well as the means of payment, i.e., ownership certificates, installments and cash payments. As a consequence, many quasi-public companies with potentially tradable shares were created. The legal form of joint stock companies was used to facilitate the privatization process. Many of those companies, however, have no intention of raising additional finances through the capital market and, thus, only a fraction are publicly listed and/or traded in the LSE.

A dominant feature of the mass privatization program was that many shareholders were created through primary distribution of shares, and some of these shareholders desire to sell their shares at the first good opportunity. The situation of many seller relative to few buyers will exist for a long time. As a result, the capital market is not an alternative source of financing to the banking system. In the 1994-97 period, cash public offerings were negligible in terms of total market capitalization, and were actually declining in real terms. Additionally, the issued of securities corresponded mostly to banks, indicating that the capital market had a negligible role as a potential source of corporate finance.

Table 5.11. Initial Public Offerings, 1994-97

	Number of IPOs			Value in billions of tolars	Percent of market capitalization
	Banks	Other	Total		
1994	11	4	15	13.6	18.0
1995	12	6	18	7.5	7.4
1996	9	2	11	10.3	5.8
1997*	3	0	3	5.7	1.4

Note: * January- August 1997.
Source: The Ljubljana Stock Exchange.

Role of Foreign Investment

During the period of 1994 to 1997, market movements were very volatile, influenced by changes in the demand due to incidental and sporadic activities of foreign portfolio investors. The activities of foreign portfolio investors, however, were substantially affected by the imposition of custody accounts for all foreign portfolio investments in early 1997. According to this BOS regulation, commercial banks acting as intermediaries must deposit foreign investors' funds in an external account and must advance a loan to the foreigner at the equivalent value in tolars, with additional interest costs for the foreign investors. As in response to extremely negative investor reactions, the BOS loosened these restrictions. In June of 1997, the regulation was amended, thereby allowing foreign investors to buy Slovenian securities without the requirement that banks balance the foreign exchange position for the amount invested. However, foreign portfolio investors must undertake the obligation not to sell the securities for a period of 7 years. They can sell the securities to another foreign investor if the new foreign owner undertakes the same obligation, while the sale to Slovenian investors is prohibited. The holding period was reduced from 7 years to 4 years in February 1999 (see Chapter I).

Despite relaxed regulations regarding foreign portfolio investments, the evidence on net capital flows shows that this segment of the demand for securities is negligible and volatile. Deducting government Eurobonds in years 1996 and 1997 (US$320 million and US$235 million, respectively), net foreign portfolio investments were either negative in 1996 or slightly positive in 1997 (see Table 5.12). Positive net capital flows from portfolio investments are the result of government placements, which raised capital in the international market for general budgetary purposes. Foreign portfolio investors are probably reluctant to invest in Slovenia because (i) restrictions in force and (ii) the prospects for this segment of the demand for securities to expand are poor until the regulation on custody account will be abandoned.

Table 5.12: Net Capital Flows from Foreign Direct and Portfolio Investments

Year	Foreign Direct Investment		Foreign Portfolio Investment	
	million US$	percent of GDP	million US$	percent of GDP
1992	112.9	0.90	-8.9	-0.07
1993	111.3	0.88	3.1	0.02
1994	131.0	0.91	-32.5	-0.23
1995	170.5	0.91	-13.5	-0.07
1996	177.7	0.94	171.3	0.91
1997	295.3	1.64	235.5	1.31

Source: Bank of Slovenia.

Foreign direct investment (FDI) continues to be a rather modest source of capital. In 1997, Slovenia experienced a substantial rise in FDI because of a small number of large operations. The momentum was again lost in 1998. Slovenia has not attained the level of FDI comparable to other leading transition economies despite a very favorable country risk rating. The main reason for the relatively modest volume of FDI is, in part, the model used for mass privatization programs-a model that made it almost impossible for foreign strategic investors to take part in the first stage of ownership transformation. It is expected, however, that during ownership consolidation process, many strategic alliances in individual companies will take shape, which, in turn, will further boost the volume of FDI.

Concerning liquidity and returns, the performance of the market has been unsatisfactory. From December 1994 to March 1998, the Slovenian Stock Exchange Index increased by just 16 percent in nominal terms -- a return that is well under other investment instruments. Additionally, the liquidity of the market (measured by the turnover ratio) has been constantly decreasing for both shares and bonds.

Although market capitalization has increased rapidly in recent years, due to the listing of some 10 percent of the newly privatized companies, the market is highly concentrated, with 11 companies representing 86 percent of the overall shares market capitalization.

Table 5.13. Market Capitalization by Company, October 1998

Company Name	Market Capitalization	
	US$ million	percent
KRKA	472	21.6
LEK	415	19.0
PETROL	304	13.9
MERCATOR	131	6.0
LUKA KOPER	126	5.7
ISTRABENZ	96	4.4
INTER EUROPA KOPER	84	3.8
RADENSKA	81	3.7
GROGA PORTOROZ	61	2.8
SKB	57	2.6
BTC	56	2.6
Rest of Companies	300	13.9
Total	2,183	100.0

Source: Ljubljana Stock Exchange.

The Bond Market

In addition to the privatization shares, government bonds issued for banking rehabilitation and real sector restructuring dominate the capital market. The total amount of these bonds is approximately DM 3 billion, but only about DM 500 million are listed and traded in the LSE. The bonds were used to carve out bad debts from banking balance sheets or were given to troubled enterprises, which in turn used them to repay debts to their creditors. Either way, the government bonds found their way to banks and other financial institutions that were to intermediate them through the financial system.

The reluctance of the banks to trade more government bonds on the stock exchange stems from the banking rules, which require marketable securities quoted on the stock exchange to be marked at market value. Given the relatively high level of market interest rates and low coupons on government securities, it is very likely that the market price of government bonds would fluctuate below the nominal value. This would entail making additional provisions for the portion of banks portfolio held in bonds, the amount equal to the difference between the nominal value and the market price of the bonds.

Capital Market Development

Several forces could drive the development of the Slovene capital market in the coming years. First, of the approximately 1500 companies that entered the privatization process, about 10 percent went public and are listed in the LSE. Once consolidation takes place, a significant number of additional companies could also access the market, issuing either debt or equity. Second, government bonds in the portfolio of the banks could increase their share in the market. Currently, only 17 percent of these bonds are quoted in the stock exchange. Third, according to the current legislation, about 47 closed-end privatization funds would must go public and be listed in the stock market.

The shares of privatization funds are being gradually listed on the open market segment of the LSE. At the end of 1998, two thirds of the funds were traded in the stock market, accounting (at face value) for approximately 11 percent of capitalization. The reason for the funds' hesitation to be listed in the past is closely related to the fact that, on average, they had only invested 44 percent of the certificates in shares. The funds still hold 56 percent of their assets in ownership certificates. The two main reasons for this are: the delay in the pace of privatization, and the so-called privatization gap. That privatization gap exists because the amount of socially owned assets allocated to the ownership transformation process proved to be insufficient (thus the privatization gap) as compared to the value of ownership certificates issued by the government and collected by privatization funds. The privatization gap is expected to be closed with additional assets owned by the State.

The privatization funds are managed by 23 management companies. These funds are allowed to invest in real state; they can acquire up to 100 percent of a company stock, they are also allowed to invest 10 percent of their assets into shares of a single company. These funds rely on "barter trading" (the exchange of non-listed shares in their portfolios) in order to increase their share size of a company. Only the privatization funds and the pension and restitution fund have access to this special segment of the market.

Privatization funds face many problems that could eventually hinder their development. On average, two thirds of their portfolio consist of investments in closely held companies. These are non-tradable securities and consequently do not have a clear market value. Unused ownership certificates account for 56 percent of total assets of privatization funds. Moreover, the institutional structure and the resulting corporate governance issues of privatization funds are skewed in favor of management companies -- to the detriment of small investors. There is a great dispersion of funds' shares, excessive management fees, and few incentives to facilitate fund expansion. Moreover, investment in a closed-end fund does not hold much appeal to investors; in order to provide for long-term growth, they will have to transform in a more attractive vehicles such as open-end funds.

Other Institutional Investors: Security Brokers and Mutual Funds

Although security brokers are not usually regarded as institutional investors, they have proved to be quite important investors in Slovenia's recent past. Their role as an investor, however, is rapidly declining on the account of growing importance of their intermediary role.

Table 5.14. Structure of Security Brokers Assets

	Own Investments	Assets under Management	Intermediation	Total Assets
	percent of total assets			millions of SIT
1995	47.5	11.8	40.7	77,263
1996 (Sep 30)	37.8	9.0	53.2	101,357
1997	5.4	5.5	89.2	136,676

Source: Bank of Slovenia.

Besides the regular trading on official market, brokers are often engaged in off-market trading (gray market). In the first half of 1997, informal trading amounted to 11.7 billion tolars, in other words, almost 12 percent of total turnover of the official market. Informal trading is rather speculative -driven by asymmetric information and price differentials between informal and formal markets. The participants of this market usually take advantage of arbitrage opportunities, especially before a security is listed and traded on the organized markets and when information on prices and quantities is not yet publicly known.

Mutual funds are not important institutional investors. There are 15 (open-ended) mutual funds operating in Slovenia, with the total net asset value of 3.1 billion tolars (less than 1 percent of total market capitalization). Moreover, mutual funds have not accompanied the growth of the market, because investor confidence was shattered by market volatility because the sudden drop of some of the most traded securities, and because privatization shares came relatively late onto the market. Investment requirements for mutual funds established that, at the minimum, 75 percent of their assets must be invested in securities traded on the LSE. Moreover, the current tax legislation is investment decision bias towards bank deposits, which are not taxed, and against securities which are, more specifically, that transaction tax consists of a 0.1 percent tax the value of each transaction, a dividend tax of 25 percent, and capital gains tax of 25 percent for corporations and 30 percent for individuals.

Insurance Sector

Before 1990, one insurance company with 95 percent market share dominated the insurance sector. In 1991, that company was split into five smaller firms, which were organized as joint stock insurance companies with mixed private and social ownership. By 1997, there were twelve insurance companies operating in Slovenia, five of them with foreign capital. The share of foreign capital is, however, rather small. In addition, a mutual fund, two state funds and an export corporation provide some form of insurance.

The insurance market in Slovenia is under-developed by Western standards, both in terms of concentration and its depth. The three largest insurance agents have a market share of 80 percent. The biggest insurance company, Triglav, accounted for 47 percent of total non-life insurance (the five largest in non-life account for 95 percent); 34 percent of total life insurance (the five largest in life account for 90 percent) premiums in 1996. The market generated gross premiums equivalent to some 5.2 percent of GDP in 1996. The structure of products offered by the market is rather narrow. In most European countries, about half of all insurance premiums is generated by life insurance. In Slovenia, the share of life insurance premiums is growing, but it was just over 15 percent of the total in 1996.

Table 5.15. Development of the Insurance Market, 1991-96

	Premiums in percent of GDP				
	Total	Insurance			Reinsurance
		Total	Non Life	Life	
1991	3.97	3.30	3.07	0.22	0.67
1992	3.82	3.23	2.99	0.24	0.59
1993	3.70	3.30	2.95	0.35	0.40
1994	3.81	3.41	2.92	0.49	0.40
1995	5.05	4.65	3.96	0.69	0.40
1996	5.24	4.85	4.05	0.80	0.39

Source: Slovenian Insurance Association.

The voluntary health insurance generates 21 percent of the gross premiums, followed by life insurance (17 percent), compulsory motor third party liabilities (16 percent), car damage insurance, also called casco (14 percent), fire and natural disaster (8 percent) and accident (8 percent). The reinsurance market accounts for only 7.5 percent of total insurance sector.

The greatest challenge for the life-insurance industry is how to face international competition. With accession to the EU, the insurance market in Slovenia is expected to be fully open to foreign competition. In adjusting to a single market, insurance companies in Slovenia will have to reduce their operational costs, improve their investment policies and, above all, offer transparent and competitive life-insurance products to consumers.

Table 5.16. Insurance Business in the European Union and Slovenia, 1996

Key Figures	EU	Slovenia	Share (%)
Insurance Premiums (ECU million)	455,618	667	0.15
Of which life premiums (ECU million)	232,096	110	0.05
Number of insurance companies	4,836	12	0.25
Number of employees	847,913	3.745	0.44
Premiums/inhabitant (ECU)	1,224	335	27.37
Life premiums/inhabitant (ECU)	623	55	8.83
Non-life premiums/inhabitant (ECU)	600	280	46.67
Premiums/GDP (%)	7.1	4.9	69.01
Average number of employees per company	175	312	180.00
Employees in share of the working population (%)	5.5	5.5	100.00

Note: 1 ECU = SIT 182.66 (August 19, 1997).
Source: Slovenian Insurance Assotiation.

The Legal Framework

The 1994 Insurance Companies Act provides the legal framework for insurance business. It establishes the basic principles for establishing, operating and supervising the sector. According to the Act, insurance activity may be conducted in the form of joint stock companies and mutual insurance companies. There is no branch separation between life and non-life insurance activities, although separate accounting is required. Reinsurance abroad is permitted once domestic capacities are exhausted.

The insurance supervisory function is in the hands of Insurance Supervisory Authority (ISA), incorporated within the Ministry of Finance. The ISA is a relatively weak authority due to the lack of resources, personnel and attributes. It grants licenses subject to the approval of business plans and it may also suspend and revoke licenses. It is authorized to make off-site and on-site inspections, although, due to institutional constraints and insufficient staff, these activities are limited.

The accumulated reserves from life-insurance programs are separated from the assets of the insurance company and cannot be used to cover other liabilities. Although the law on insurance companies provides this basic safeguard, in practice there are still no standards on the size and investment of the reserves. Ideally, such standards would protect the consumers and restrict the costs of the contracts in the first few years. Improving the regulatory framework for the life-insurance industry is as soon as possible is a top priority for Slovenia if it is to avoid a crisis that can easily undermine plans for introducing the privately managed funded pension schemes.

One important problem of the present insurance law is that it does not adequately address the problem of how to deal with troubled insurance companies. Although the law gives to the ISA the power to initiate bankruptcy procedure in an insurance company, it provides no mechanisms for intervention before they reach a critical stage. Indeed, various types of pre-bankruptcy interventions are necessary for the Slovenian insurance industry, as its expansion will inevitably be accompanied with higher risks.

Another issue, which must be addressed in the new insurance company act, refers to the discriminatory treatment of foreign insurance service providers. According to the existing law, foreign establishments may, upon the approval of the ISA, become shareholders in an insurance company; such approval is also required for any further acquisition of shares. The law does not allow those insurers, which have headquarters in other countries to establish business and to sell their insurance products in Slovenia. Moreover, a company in which foreign capital has a majority or controlling share may not handle reinsurance business nor establish an insurance company dealing with reinsurance business.

EU Accession and the Insurance Sector

Insurance companies have, by and large, not yet started the restructuring required to adjust to the competitive pressures accompanying accession to the EU. The most serious problem of the insurance sector is its rather poor financial health; in order to address the problem, a major rehabilitation and an eventual reorganization process must take place. This will be possible only after the Ownership Transformation of Insurance Companies Act is adopted and after transformation of the social into state ownership is complete. The existing conflict between the government and the managers (or the owners) of the biggest insurance company presents one of the main problems complicating this process.

The process of restructuring should include a range of measures aimed both at increasing efficiency of insurance companies and reducing their operational costs. As in the banking sector, insurance companies will have to increase productivity in order to face the EU Accession process. These measures will not be effective unless accompanied by a government policy to open the market to more competition. In this respect, the Europe Agreement provides clear guidelines for gradual elimination of discriminatory clauses in the existing Insurance Companies Act. In addition to the gradual opening of the insurance market to foreign companies, the authorities must prepare a strategy for privatization of the socially-owned share in insurance companies and then to actually privatize them.

Due to imperfect regulation and insufficient supervision, the insurance sector is characterized by a relatively large number of small and poorly capitalized companies. This indicates that there is need to upgrade both the existing insurance legislation and supervision. A priority for the regulator is to adjust legislation to current requirements of the sector. In addition to the required adjustment for eliminating the discrimination against foreigners, improvements of the existing Insurance Companies Act are needed in several other areas, including provisions on clear separation of life from non-life insurance activities, provisions regarding pre-bankruptcy procedures, provisions regulating responsibility of management and governing boards, provisions on the role of the supervisory authority and prudential regulation provisions.

The supervisory capacity for the insurance industry must be enhanced. In addition to off-site inspections, the supervisory institution should more frequently perform on-site inspections. All this implies that the institution must be strengthened in terms of their resources, the number of staff and their expertise. It must be continuously upgraded in order to keep pace with the increasing complexity of the insurance industry and its growing interrelation with other segments of the financial sector.

Legal Harmonization with the EU

Slovenia's accession to the EU requires the transposition and implementation of the *acquis*. In the case of the financial sector, the directives aim at "...coordinating the minimum requirements for the different type of institutions in order to create a minimum standard and a more level playing field as the basis for home country control and the single license".[7] The White Paper proposed to address harmonization in two stages (see Table 5.17). Stage one concerns all those measures (directives) related to fundamental principles and provides the overall framework for more detailed legislation in the financial sector. Stage two consists of measures to reinforce the prudential regulation and are more closely linked with the operation of the internal market.

Slovenia has made progress in transposing the *acquis* in the area of financial services. The process of the transposition, however, has been slow. Gaps still remain in all three areas of the financial

---

[7] See the financial services chapter of the European Commission's White Paper.

sector, namely banking, capital markets and insurance. The government needs to focus on accelerating the legislative agenda and approve a number of laws that are at different stages of development.

Table 5.17. Financial Sector Directives

	Banking Directives		Capital Market Directives		Insurance Directives	
Stage One	First Banking	1977	Stock Exchange Listing	1979	First Non-Life Insurance	1973
	Own Funds	1989	Invest. Funds (UCITS)	1985	First Life Insurance	1979
	Solvency Ratio	1989	Major Holding Notific.	1988	Second Non-Life Insurance	1988
	Money Laundering	1991	Public Offer Prospectus	1989	Insurance Accounts	1991
	Deposit Guarantee	1994	Insider Trading	1989		
Stage Two	Annual Accounts and Consolidated Accounts	1986	Investment Services	1993	Third Non-Life Insurance	1992
	Second Banking	1989	Capital Adequacy	1993	Third Life Insurance	1992
	Large Exposure	1992				
	Consolidated Supervision	1992				
	Capital Adequacy	1993				

Source: European Commission.

Banking Sector

The core EU legislation in this area comprises comprehensive directives -the First Council Directive of 1977 and the Second Council Directive of 1989- and a whole set of directives related to specific aspects of banking operations. While the First Council Directive lays down common standards for the granting of banking licenses and introduces the basic principle of co-operation between the supervisory authorities in different member countries, the Second Council Directive calls for a free movement of capital and free establishment across the EU. Its main provisions are minimum capital requirement for establishment, single banking license and home country control. Related to home country control is the issue of mutual recognition, which means that the supervisory authorities in one country will recognize the prudential equivalence of other bank supervisors. Among the other directives, those addressing banking supervision, financial sector conglomerates issues and deposit protection are highly important.

The new Banking Law was adopted by Parliament in January 1999. With the new Law, Slovenia's banking legislation introduced all Stage One measures in this area (they are aimed at providing the overall legal framework and at addressing fundamental principles and procedures governing the sector). This means that the country's banking legislation is fully harmonized with the First Council Directive as well as with several other directives, including the Own Funds Directive, the Solvency Ratio Directive, the Directive on Deposit-Guarantee Schemes and the Directive on Money Laundering.

The new Banking Law is, however, not be fully compatible with Stage Two measures (they are linked directly to the creation of the EU's internal market) as set in the Second Council Directive. The new Banking law is in line with Large Exposure Directive, the Directive on Supervision of Credit Institutions on a Consolidated Basis, the Directive on Annual Accounts and the Consolidated Accounts of Credit Institutions and Other Financial Institutions. It includes provision related to the single banking license and home country control, but these provisions will only apply at the time of accession. The basic principles of the Capital Adequacy Directive are covered by the new law, although more detailed provisions for implementation shall be determined by BOS decrees in the subsequent years before EU accession.

Capital Markets

The EU has developed several key directives in this area. They have established conditions for admission of securities to the official stock exchange market; they have provided guidelines for information disclosure requirements, supervision, the activities of investment funds, transferability of securities, notification requirements and issues related to capital market operation and development. Two directives are of particular importance. The first one, on investment services in the securities field, is in many ways parallel to the Second Council Directive in the banking sector. It allows investment firms, such as brokers, portfolio managers and professional investment advisors, to offer their services throughout the EU. It therefore establishes the single license rule, mutual recognition and home member state supervision for investment firms. The second directive defines capital adequacy standards; it establishes the possibility of using alternative definitions of capital for both non-bank investment firms and banks in view of their different types of risk.

While Slovenian securities legislation is practically in full compliance with the Stage one measures, its harmonization with EU investment services and capital adequacy directives has yet to be completed. This refers particularly to the discrimination of foreigners in terms of their right of establishment and cross-border supply of services. According to the present Securities Market Act, only stock-brokerage firms and banks can provide services regarding freely transferable securities with a registered office in Slovenia. A 24 percent ceiling is imposed on EU investment firm's stake in stock-brokerage firms. Adjustments are also needed to meet requirements of the capital adequacy directive.

As far as legislation on investment funds is concerned, the existing Slovenian legislation already complies with basic Stage one measures, i.e., depositors, prospectus, designation of authorities responsible for authorization and supervision of funds. However, as the Slovenian securities market is still in the very early stages of development, the provisions in the legislation differ from EU standards.

Insurance Sector

Although there have been fewer EU directives in the insurance sector than in the banking sector, they follow the same principles of free trade and investment, mutual recognition and home country control. The main difference is between life and non-life insurance. As far as the four life insurance directives are concerned, they require the categorization of life insurance instruments, they require the separation of management and accounting of life and non-life insurance, and they provide guidelines for solvency margins and the establishment of a guarantee fund. The non-life insurance directives deal primarily with solvency, supervision and information disclosure on ownership issues.

The 1994 Insurance Companies Act is in accordance with those EU directives related to accounting standards, solvency requirements, supervision rules and risk dispersion. It is also in accordance with other Stage one measures, that are primarily concerned with the EU wide harmonization of conditions allowing one insurance company to establish itself in another member country. The Act is, however, completely incompatible with the Stage two measures which require the introduction of the so-called single passport in insurance and which provide for insurance companies to freely decide whether to sell their insurance products through a company in another country or directly, without being established.

The Pre-Accession Agenda

In the banking sector, increasing the incentive structure, the capacity of banks to compete within Slovenia and to face the pressures of banks abroad are key. Increasing competition is of the highest importance for the Slovenian banking sector, which is characterized by high concentration and a low degree of in-country competition. In order to address these problems, a whole set of policy measures will have to be introduced and implemented. One of the most important ones is to open the sector more widely to foreign competition. The recently approved Banking Law proposes that branches of foreign banks would be permitted; opening the sector to foreign branch offices is also required by the Europe Association Agreement (EAA). Opening the sector to branch offices, in the short-term, and liberalizing the provision of cross border financial services, in the medium-term, is expected to improve the range and sophistication of services that are available, while the additional competition arising from this move is likely to create more pressure for rationalization among small banks.

Another major issue facing the banking sector refers to the privatization of the two big banks, NLB and NKBM, and other banking shares in the hands of the state. The main objectives of the bank privatization strategy have not yet been clearly developed by the government, which needs to focus on this agenda. Privatization of these important banks should involve a transparent process. It should include one or several strategic investors who would strengthen corporate governance in the banks. Moreover, the banks should be sold primarily for cash in order to reduce public debt or to finance key structural reforms. Participation of strategic partners in the privatization of the two banks would, in addition to bringing fresh capital, lead to a more rapid growth in domestic banking services and expertise. It would also accelerate the integration of western standards into the Slovenian banking industry.

The abolition of the inter-bank agreement on the maximum deposit interest rates scheduled for 1999 is also expected to contribute to increased competition among banks. The agreement is not compatible with the needs to strengthen competition in the market. Competition in the deposit market, as in the credit market, is instrumental in forcing banks to identify their areas of comparative advantage and to increase efficiency.

Competition among banks will be improved also by the introduction of a new deposit guarantee scheme. Eligible deposits have been defined in the Banking Law, as well as the ceiling for guaranteed deposits. The banks will seed the deposit guarantee fund; State intervention is not envisaged.

The proposed deposit guarantee scheme solution incorporated in the new Banking Law will improve the degree of competitive neutrality in the banking system. Specifically, this will occur by offsetting the impact of explicit or implicit state guarantee that may be seen to lie behind large banks, either because they are state-owned or/and because they are simply viewed as too big to fail.

Banks will also have to intensify their *internal restructuring* aimed at increasing profitability and, thus, reducing operating cost on the one hand and expanding the range of activities from classical services to more sophisticated products and services on the other. The process involves a whole set of productivity supportive policy measures, including further reduction in the number of bank employees and a consolidation of the banking sector through mergers, particularly of small banks. There is also a need for continuous education and training activities of the bank staff in order to improve its expertise in various areas, particularly in areas such as credit and risk assessment and investment banking.

At present, there are two areas where intensified banking regulation and supervision appears increasingly important in Slovenia. The first one refers to various forms of bank exposure, while the second area covers financial conglomerates and the so-called connected persons. Both areas are going to be addressed in the new Banking Act.

The introduction of the new payment system will open doors for a new line of business activities in the banks. Accordingly, banks have to take all measures necessary to become an efficient partner in the new system.

For banking sector reform to be effective, policy measures within the sector will have to be accompanied by supportive policy measures in many other segments, including in the consumer protection area where a general law has recently been adopted by the Parliament. An enabling legal environment, for example, is instrumental in protecting the rights of lenders. Although legislation regulating bankruptcy procedures, collateral provisions, procedures of execution against a company, execution proceedings and land register regulation have all been put in place, judicial and administrative support must be strengthened in order to speed up its implementation.

In contrast to banking and insurance -which have both been to a certain extent burdened with the legacy from the pre-transition period- capital market development is an entirely new segment of the financial sector. Although the market has experienced sustained growth, especially since 1994, it remains small and depends mainly on privatization related activities.

Further development of the market will require consistent enhancement of all components of the market, including a further increase in market capitalization and improvement of its liquidity, diversification of both individual and institutional investors, and increased opportunities for brokers and other professional participants in the market. The success of this policy depends, to a great extent, on the incentive structure set in place to cope with the excess supply of shares that privatization funds may bring once listed. As a result, it is important to establish the correct policy conditions for increasing domestic and foreign demand for shares of listed companies.

To address these challenges on time, regulatory changes are required. The new draft Securities Market Act puts the emphasis on the development of prudential rules and on the strengthening of supervision mechanisms. Besides increasing the initial capital requirement, the draft law regulates own funds, capital adequacy, large exposure, and liquidity ratios. In the case of an investment firm belonging to a financial group, all prudential rules must be applied on a consolidated basis. All these regulatory changes are expected to lead to increased competition and to greater market stability. The new Securities Market Act will also put the legislation in accordance with the EAA. Specifically, the Act will provide for national treatment of investment firms (there has been a 3-year transition period agreed with regard to brokers' financial services), and will therefore also abolish the 24 percent ceiling on non-resident stakes in investment firms. Adjustments are also needed in the legislation regulating investment funds.

Legislation governing the use of custody accounts in portfolio investments by non-residents has been relaxed in 1999 (see Chapter I). Custody accounts, however, will not be abolished, thus maintaining the market segmentation. This differentiation will have to be eliminated as will the tax treatment differentiation, if the authorities want the securities market to be a savings and investment mechanism.

The changes in the regulatory framework will be accompanied by continuous strengthening of the supervisory institution. It is of utmost importance that the attributes and institutional capabilities of the Securities Exchange Commission (SEC) are enhanced on time, both in terms of the number of staff and in terms of the institution's expertise. To effectively supervise the fast growing securities market industries, there must be enhanced co-operation among supervisory institutions in all three segments of the financial sector.

In contrast to banks, insurance companies have yet to start their restructuring. The process of insurance sector restructuring should include a range of policy measures aimed at increasing the efficiency of insurance companies and at reducing their operational costs. Within this context, each company should clearly identify its comparative advantages, concentrate efforts in those areas and look at potential partners for future co-operation. As in the banking sector, insurance companies will have to boost productivity by increasing efficiency of the staff and/or by expanding the volume of operation. In this respect, training the staff for specific areas of insurance business, as well as the provision of new services offered to potential clients are crucial.

All these measures, carried out within individual insurance companies, will be effective only if accompanied by a government policy to open the market to more external competition. In this respect, the EAA provides clear guidelines for the gradual elimination of discriminatory clauses in existing legislation. In addition to the gradual opening of the insurance market to foreign companies, there is a need to prepare a strategy for the privatization of state holdings in the insurance sector.

A priority for the insurance regulator is to adjust the legislation to the current requirements of the insurance sector. In addition to eliminating discrimination against foreigners, the new draft Insurance Companies Act is expected to address several other key areas, including: (i) provisions on clear separation of life from non-life insurance activities; (ii) provisions regarding pre-bankruptcy procedures; (iii) provisions regulating the responsibilities of management and governing boards; (iv) provisions on the role of the supervisory authority; and (v) prudential regulation provisions.

In addition to improved regulation, enhanced supervision of the insurance industry is necessary. This implies that the institution must be strengthened in terms of the number of staff and their expertise. The staff must be continuously upgraded in order to keep pace with the increasing complexity of the insurance industry and its growing interrelation with other segments of the financial sector.

Enterprise Sector in Transition

Introduction

Transition reforms in Slovenia were determined by its previous economic system, which differed from the socialist economic systems of the rest of the Central Eastern Europe (CEE). The former Yugoslavia adopted the so-called market-socialism -a combination of command and market-based economy, in which state ownership was limited, and the enterprises were socially-owned. This specific ownership structure meant that most enterprises were *de-facto* but not *de-jure* owned by employees. Employees formed workers' councils, which in turn elected the management of the firm. Unlike in a typical command economy, the enterprises had some flexibility regarding inputs, pricing, wages, and investment decisions. There was a significant degree of decentralization. Nevertheless, central or local political authorities influenced certain decisions. As with other CEE economies, the incentive structure in Slovenia was such that the model led to a lack of financial discipline, inefficient production and over-employment, due also to the lack of real hard budget constraints.

Although employees chose the management, the candidates nonetheless required political approval. Moreover, in large and important enterprises, the political elite, not the employees, selected managers. Although in this system of self-management, investment decisions were decentralized, the political agenda, rather than pure economic needs, usually shaped/influenced/conditioned these decisions. This generated enormous deficiencies that were compounded by the limitations of the labor and capital markets.

The structure of this chapter is the following. The second section makes an assessment of the ownership transformation process and describes the present situation after privatization. The third section analyzes enterprise performance in the transition. The final section presents the conclusions and recommendations.

Ownership Transformation

One of the first issues addressed by the authorities upon independence was the process of ownership transformation. The Yugoslav self-management system implied that the firms were legally without owners (although *de-facto* owned by employees). Identifying the owners of the firms thus turned out to be a key element of the transformation process. Constitutional alterations were needed to change the social capital into enterprise specific capital, and then to sell the firms. This process started in the late 1980s. The Foreign Investment Act and the Enterprise Act of October 1988 formally eliminated the existing economic system of self-management; for the first time this allowed for some form of private ownership. According to the law, the socially-owned enterprises could transform themselves into "mixed companies" by accepting additional private capital. Moreover, the 1989 Law on Social Capital granted the workers' councils the right to sell enterprises to private owners. Nonetheless, very few Slovene firms were transformed in this way before independence in 1991.

Privatization Slovenian Style

The process of privatization started after independence. The privatization debate was driven by the need to respect the implicit property rights while at the same time to maintain social justice. Although the population felt that employees were the virtual owners of the firms, the property belonged to society at large. This meant that all segments of society needed to be included in the process. For this purpose, privatization certificates were issued to all Slovene citizens -- the value of the certificates measured according to the citizen's age.[1] The model of privatization, however, went through several heated debates, from a rapid-centralized to a gradual-decentralized concept. The new Slovene authorities provided the legal basis for transformation of ownership, only after a prolonged parliamentary discussion that lasted until November of 1992 (see Box 6.1). In the end, the selected model was a compromise between both proposals.

The Law of Ownership Transformation, approved in late 1992 and amended twice in 1993, was the corner stone of the privatization legislation. It represents a compromise between the two models of privatization under debate. Through this legislation, firms were allowed to select their own privatization plan out of several methods provided by the law. To supervise the process, a government agency for privatization and restructuring was created. The process of ownership transformation in Slovenia included: (a) privatization; (b) restitution; and (c) nationalization of the social capital.

Through the process of ownership transformation, the State nationalized a sizable amount of assets. The agricultural lands and woods previously used by socially-owned firms were nationalized. So were public utilities and three large banks that were put under rehabilitation to avoid bankruptcy.[2] In addition, some insurance companies, mines and steelworks have been rehabilitated under State guidance. The State retained its participation in some strategic enterprises, such as oil and gas companies, and even the famous Lipica horse-farm. Only the remaining socially-owned assets were assigned for privatization. Later on, the State increased its share of assets during the privatization process itself. This was done indirectly, through its holdings of shares in privatized firms in various state-owned funds, namely the pension fund,[3] restitution fund,[4] and the development fund.[5] As a result, it has been estimated that, after the privatization process, only between 50-55 percent of the GDP is produced by the private sector, that is, substantially below the level of other leading transforming economies.[6]

The Law of Ownership Transformation provided a combination of free transfers of capital (mass privatization) and direct privatization methods. The enterprises eligible for privatization (over 1,500 firms or about 2,800, if daughter firms are taken into account) could submit their privatization plans for

---

[1] The certificates had a nominal value between DM 2,000 and DM 4,000. They were non-transferable and could only be used to buy shares in privatized enterprises.

[2] They included (Nova) Ljubljanska Banka, the largest bank in Slovenia, (Nova) Kreditna Banka Maribor, the third largest, and Kreditna Banka Nova Gorica. The last two were merged during the rehabilitation process.

[3] Ten percent of the ordinary shares of every firm were transferred to the Capital Fund of Pension Insurance.

[4] Ten percent of the ordinary shares of every firm were transferred to the Restitution Fund. Restitution to previous owners was part of the ownership transformation process. It could take the form of compensation from the Slovene Restitution Fund, restitution in kind, or restitution through equity stakes in enterprises.

[5] The Slovene Development Fund was transformed into the Slovene Development Corporation in 1997. Since then, the indirect holding of assets by the State through this institution has increased.

[6] See the European Commission's *Agenda 2000*, 1997.

(first) approval to the Agency for Privatization and Restructuring (APR). Once the plan was approved by the APR, the firm went to the legal process of ownership transformation. After an enterprise concluded the privatization according to its original plan, the Agency granted second approval and registered the newly privatized firm in the Court Register.

Box 6.1. A Privatization Bill Dilemma

Privatization of socially-owned enterprises was one of the most controversial economic issues after independence. The advocates of the privatization process were split between a gradual decentralized and a rapid centralized concept. According to the fist concept, the socially-owned enterprises would be sold to workers, managers, creditors, former owners, and domestic and foreign firms. One can identify the benefits and drawbacks of a decentralized privatization process. Among the benefits, this plan would not only minimize the amount of government intervention, but it would also facilitate the emergence of active owners by granting various interested buyers the unlimited right to purchase shares. The opponents, however, were pointing to the drawbacks. Namely, the decentralized process would inherently exclude the privatization of loss-making firms, which would be unlikely find interested buyers. Such firms would become state property. Finally, some skepticism regarding the employees' buyouts reflected the potential abuse of their power to increase their rents to the detriment of the firm's overall performance.

Some political parties within the coalition were afraid that the government and the new political elite would lose the control of the distribution of management positions. Accordingly, they advocated another concept – one based on rapid and centralized privatization with free distribution of shares to the population via investment funds. Advocates of this centralized model emphasized that, in this way, the ownership model would resemble that of Western Europe, while the corporate governance would be improved in a socially just way. Institutional owners would monitor and control the firms, would ensure their efficiency and profitability, and would thereby create pension resources. However, the state presence would intensify since the boards of institutional owners would be nominated by the government, and managers would be nominated by these boards, while a free and massive privatization would create only passive owners, not interested in the firms' restructuring. The centralized plan therefore gave control to the government and new political elite. Its approval in the Parliament was, however, blocked by managers represented in the third chamber of Parliament. After furious debate, the coalition broke down. It was only when new government coalition produced a third draft that the law passed safely through the three chambers of Parliament in November of 1992. This final draft was a compromise between the two proposed concepts.

Reflecting the value of existing social capital, the socially-owned enterprises transformed their ownership by issued shares (or raising new equity) and by choosing among the different ways to transfer them to the new owners. According to the law, the shares were distributed as follows:

- 40 percent were transferred free of charge to public funds,

of which:
  - 10 percent went to the Restitution Fund;
  - 10 percent went to the Capital Fund of Pension Insurance;
  - 20 percent went to the Development Fund, to be exchanged for ownership certificates held by Privatization Investment Funds (PIFs);

- 60 percent were transferred according to the following rules:

  - Internal distribution, up to 20 percent could be exchanged for ownership certificates held by insiders (managers, current, former and relatives of employees). The shares could not be sold for two years from the date the privatization was recorded in the Court Register;

- Internal buyout, up to 40 percent could be sold for cash or exchanged for ownership certificates held by insiders. Managers, employees and former employees received a 50 percent discount on the value of the shares;
- Direct sales, via public offering, public tender or public auction;
- Liquidation, implying the sale of all assets of the firm under bankruptcy, with the Slovene Development Fund assuming all liabilities of the firm;
- Raising additional private equity (if new shares represented more than 10 percent of existing equity); and
- Transferring shares to the Slovene Development Fund.

In the subsequent four years (1993-97), almost 1500 socially-owned enterprises went through the process of ownership transformation. Every Slovene citizen also received an ownership certificate, which altogether represented 40 percent of the book value of social capital as of December 31, 1992.[7] The certificates were used in the internal distribution and buyouts, public sales, or were transferred to the privatization investment funds (PIFs).

Outcome of Privatization

In analyzing the privatization of socially-owned firms, it is important to concentrate on the new ownership structure rather than on the number of enterprises privatized. The Slovene privatization process generated a particular ownership structure in the new enterprise sector. By November of 1998, 1369 companies have registered in the Court Register, and have begun to operate as private companies. Insiders, however, control the majority of firms. More than 90 percent of enterprises chose to transfer ownership via internal distribution/ buyout. Total value of capital held by insiders, however, amounted to only 26 percent

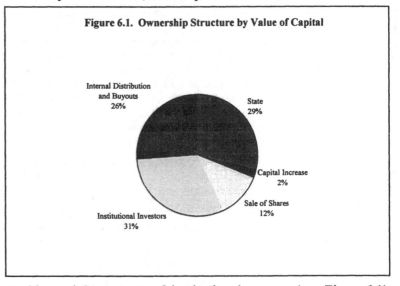

Figure 6.1. Ownership Structure by Value of Capital

Internal Distribution and Buyouts 26%

State 29%

Capital Increase 2%

Sale of Shares 12%

Institutional Investors 31%

-compared to 29 percent of state ownership, and 31 percent of institutional owners (see Figure 6.1). Moreover, foreign investors were practically excluded from the privatization process. As a result, only about 1 percent of the transactions included foreigners.

A strong self-management tradition in Slovenia and a relatively large number of small- and medium-sized firms were two of the most important factors influencing a majority of enterprises to choose management-employee buyouts as a privatization method. This system also maintained the status quo. Insider buyouts were, for the most part, implemented in labor intensive small- and medium-sized firms with a lower value capital. Here many workers could participate with their certificates, whereas in

---

[7] In 1993, about 2,000,900 special ownership certificate accounts were opened in the Social Accounting Service -- one for each citizen of Slovenia. Unlike the privatization model in the Czech and Slovak Republics, the ownership certificates had a nominal value set between SIT 250,000 and SIT 400,000 per person, depending on the age of the citizen. This represented between DM 2,000 and DM 4,000 at the prevailing exchange rate.

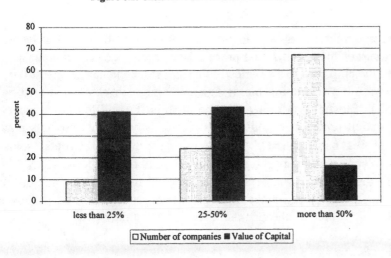

Figure 6.2. Insiders Control after Privatization

□ Number of companies ■ Value of Capital

capital intensive firms, the employees lacked the necessary resources to finance larger buyouts. In 67 percent of approved programs, employees acquired more than half of the enterprise's ownership. Those enterprises with a majority management-employees voting rights accounted only for 16 percent of value of capital. As a result of this transformation, employees can veto key restructuring decisions in the majority of the privatized firms. Moreover, employees have veto power in firms that represent about 59 percent of the value of total capital (see Figure 6.2).

In the case of more capital intensive enterprises, the shares were to be sold in public offerings for either cash or certificates after obtaining the approval from the Slovenian Security and Exchange Commission. Only 12 percent of companies used public sales as their preferred privatization method; by contrast, the share of their capital in total social capital amounted to almost 30 percent. Slovenian citizens had a pre-emptive right to purchase the firms. As a result, public sales to foreign investors were limited. In the case of firms with foreign equity participation, enterprises had to prepare the privatization program with the consent of the foreign partner. While in the case of contractual joint ventures, foreign non-equity was treated as a liability of the company.

Table 6.1. Corporate Ownership Structure after Privatization, 1997

	No. of Firms	Employment	Assets
	(in percent of total)		
New Private	27	8	6
Foreign	8	5	6
Insiders	31	33	17
Outsiders	19	28	27
Non-private	11	13	13
State	5	12	31
TOTAL	100	100	100

Source: IMAD.

The privatization process in Slovenia was not conducive to the participation of foreign investors, who have played a crucial role in the restructuring of the enterprise sector in other leading transition economies, most notably in Hungary. Several times, the Law on Transformation of Ownership refers to the foreign investors, whose participation in the privatization process was regulated in several ways. First, sales of shares with value above ECU 10 million had to be approved by the government (Article 20). Second, common shares issued by enterprises were not allowed to be transferred nor bought by foreign investors during the first three years after enactment of the privatization law (until November 1995), unless approved by the government (Article 22). Moreover, limits to foreign investments were implicit in the privatization model since enterprises were inclined to choose the internal distribution/buyout methods by which the employees and managers could keep the control of the enterprise. As a result, firms with foreign participation represent only about 6 percent of the assets and employ about 8 percent of the labor force.

It is expected, however, that foreign investors will increase their market share in a selected number of enterprises now that the first part of the privatization process has largely been concluded. This process has already started in so-called blue chip, enterprises -mostly through stock exchange operations. With the accession agenda well underway, the remaining biases against foreign investment are to be eliminated. This is likely to boost FDI in Slovenia. Moreover, some of the PIFs and the new owners themselves might be eager to realize implicit profits due to discounts received by internal buyouts now that the moratorium time for those shares has expired.[8] In the case of internal buyouts, some consolidation of ownership has taken place, with managers acquiring dominant positions. This, in conjunction with the need to modernize the production apparatus and the need to pay shares bought in installments from the Development Fund, is likely to induce strategic alliances with foreign partners. This, in turn, will bring to the firm a valuable source of cheaper capital and new technology.

The Unfinished Privatization Agenda

By the end of the privatization of socially-owned enterprises, the private sector is estimated to generate only 50-55 percent of GDP and to employ about 50 percent of the labor force. These figures are among the lowest in leading CEE countries. It has been noted in the European Union *Agenda 2000*, that only eight out of the twenty-seven transition countries have smaller private sectors than Slovenia.[9] The State has thus emerged as a major owner alongside insiders and outsiders. The percent of state ownership in the enterprise sector was determined, in part, by the percent of the state (central or local) financing of enterprise's activities in the past,[10] while the rest of the social capital was open to privatization. Nonetheless, upon independence, the Slovenian state nationalized the socially-owned enterprises thereby providing the following public services: (a) energy supply and distribution; (b) transportation; (c) telecommunications and postal services; (d) water distribution and other municipal public services; and (e) urban and environmental infrastructure. In addition to public utilities, the State also owns two large banks, insurance companies, steelworks and mines.

Paradoxically, for a country where in the past state ownership was non-existent, after privatization, the State became a prime owner of the former socially-owned enterprises, with insiders following closely.[11] In only about 30 percent of the firms, incentives changed in the significant way that one might expect under privatization. Nonetheless, a large share of those privatized firms -over two thirds- possibly face incentives that are not substantially different from those faced when they were self-managed. In effect, the worst performance in terms of profitability is found in companies that are not-yet

---

[8] See Matija Rojec, "Foreign Direct Investment in the Slovenian Economy and its Development Potential," *Delovni Zvezek ZMAR* 5, No. 6 (October 1996). According to the Central Clearing and Depository House report, at the end of February 1998, foreign investors' ownership of shares of Slovene blue-chip companies were as follows: SKB Bank 49 percent, BTC (warehousing) 43.9 percent, Lek (pharmaceuticals) 29.3 percent, Droga Portoroz (food processing industry) 22.8 percent, Kolinska (food processing industry) 13.2 percent and Krka (pharmaceuticals) 6.8 percent.

[9] See Colin Jones, "A Tiny Nation's Giant Recovery," *The Banker*, January 1998: 35.

[10] According to the Law on Public Services (June 17, 1993), the State share was determined as the average percent of enterprise assets acquired through public financing in the last ten years (Article 73).

[11] In terms of the number of firms, insiders are majority shareholders in about 70 percent of all privatized firms, but they control more than 25 percent of the capital in 91 percent of all privatized firms. This gives them veto power. Moreover, in firms with more than 1,000 employees they nominate one half of the Board members.

privatized and those that are in the hands of insiders.[12] In the latter, restructuring is taking place at a much slower pace than is expected; there has been a tendency to "cannibalize" assets (i.e., to survive by depleting capital), thereby setting up the recipe for future bankruptcy. Privatization of socially-owned enterprises was officially completed by the end of 1997, with some enterprises still remaining under indirect government control through the Slovene Development Corporation,[13] and shares of many others are deposited in the Restitution and Pension Funds.

The privatization of socially-owned enterprises is now almost complete. The remaining agenda on ownership transformation consists of the three important items. First, the privatization of state-owned assets, including banks and public utilities. Second, the resolution of the so-called privatization gap problem (see Box 6.2). Third, the sale of remaining government shares in some of the privatized enterprises. That sale has been limited in part by the government's apprehension of losing its position in some Slovenian companies. The recent government reluctance to sell its shares in the oil and gas companies (Petrol and Istrabenz) to strategic investors, and choosing instead state-owned funds and a (partially) state-owned insurance company, demonstrates the continuation of public sector involvement.

Accelerating and completing the privatization process is crucial for at least three major economic reasons. First, privatization of the remaining state banks – Nova Ljubljanska Banka and Kreditna Banka Maribor – and other assets in the financial sector will prove critical in promoting both financial sector competition, and the development of new financial products. It will also impose a higher degree of financial discipline and transparency in the relationship between the State, banks and enterprises. Second, privatization of public utilities is needed to enhance efficiency in production and distribution, and to prepare those public utilities to face competition in the broader EU single market. Third, privatization of large firms, and the remaining shares in already privatized enterprises, will increase the chances for restructuring and enhance the possibilities of these firms to adjust to the new market conditions before they face stricter discipline and stronger competition in the single market.

A secondary financial objective of privatization is the generation of revenue from sales to strategic investors. While the principal justification for privatization is to enhance efficiency in the use of divested assets, almost every government is interested in revenue generated from privatization. The government, however, should focus on the long-term benefits of privatization through efficiency gains and welfare generation, rather than the short-term impact on the state budget. Post privatization efficiency gains generate greater financial returns to the government (over the medium-term) than revenues obtained directly from the sales of state assets.

The infrastructure sector, including public utilities, is going through a period of transformation with a possibility of subsequent privatization. However, the proper regulatory framework still needs to be developed, and legal harmonization with the EU needs to be completed as part of the preparation for EU membership. Inadequate regulation of the relatively autonomous public utility companies has impeded private sector involvement. For the privatization of the infrastructure services and public utilities to be

---

[12] A recent study by the Institute of Macroeconomic Analysis and Development (IMAD) found that, for a sub-sample of 2023 enterprises covering about 80 percent of relevant indicators, internally owned enterprises and non privatized enterprises (firms owned by the Development Fund) are mostly labor intensive and comprise most of the losses in the enterprise sector. State enterprises also had large losses.

[13] As of November 2, 1998, another 27 enterprises have been transferred to the Slovene Development Corporation (SDC). These enterprises did not obtain a second approval due to the unsolved issues under the denationalization act, or difficulties in the agricultural land allotment. The number of enterprises, in the management of the SDC, now amounts to around 360 (from a total of 1500). See Box 3 below on evolution of the SDC's role.

successful, the government should first adjust the regulatory framework, which would increase the confidence and interest of strategic private investors. Cost-conscious and demand-oriented production in these sectors is also essential for the overall performance of the enterprise sector. The recent adjustments of utility prices, to bring them closer to cost recovery, is a first step in the right direction.

One of the outcomes of the ownership transformation process was the emergence of the so-called privatization gap. The gap resulted from the mismatch between the value of privatized assets and the value of ownership certificates given to the population (see Box 6.2). In July of 1998, the authorities decided on the list of state-owned assets that would be eligible to be exchanged for the remaining ownership certificates in PIFs, in order to remove the so-called privatization gap. Closing the privatization gap is another key element of the remaining privatization agenda that authorities must address.

Box 6.2. The Privatization Gap and the Privatization Investment Funds

Privatization Investment Funds (PIFs) were established to counterbalance insider ownership by enabling the population to (indirectly) buy shares of enterprises. PIFs collected certificates in order to buy enterprise shares, which were transferred to the Development Fund (in the value of 20 percent of social capital). The aggressive media campaign by the PIFs in mid-1994 encouraged the collection of a significant part of the ownership certificates. By the end of 1995, 14 management companies managed 81 PIFs; by the mid-1997, the number of PIFs declined to 72. The minimum required capital to establish a management company was SIT 50 million (US$375,000 at 1994 exchange rate), and SIT 100 million (or US$750,000) for establishing a PIF. About 62 percent of the start-up capital was provided by banks and insurance companies.

It is estimated that 57.7 percent of all certificates were transferred to PIFs, 34.1 percent were used for internal buyouts or public sales, whereas 8.2 percent of the certificates have not been used. The Agency for Privatization tried to estimate the excess of certificates issued beyond the value of social capital, usually referred to as the privatization gap. The problem of excess certificates would have not been as acute if the initial value of social capital appearing on the opening balance sheets had been estimated correctly. Instead, during the privatization process, the initial value of social capital decreased. It did so for different reasons, such as the transfer of agricultural land to the Agricultural Fund, restitution claims, exclusion of public utilities infrastructure and equity, bankruptcies and liquidations, and the issuance of additional certificates for the unpaid salaries.

The difference between the value on the opening balances and the adjusted value for the privatized enterprises, i.e. the privatization gap, has been calculated at SIT 148.9 billion in November of 1998, that is, just under US$1 billion or 5.5 percent of GDP. The PIFs, holding an excess supply of certificates, were guaranteed by law a replacement of their remaining certificates with shares of privatizing enterprises or with the state assets. It is expected that, by the end of 1998, the PIFs will receive the first SIT 20 billion from the government assets. Moreover, the Slovenian Development Corporation has already accumulated an additional SIT 29 billion in assets to fill the privatization gap. It is unlikely, however, that investors would agree to accept shares in firms under the SDC control.

Enterprise Sector Performance in the Transition

Improving corporate governance is a critical outcome of enterprise restructuring. In Slovenia, this is particularly important in that insiders (management and workers) have bought the majority of socially-owned enterprises. Since the management and workers of enterprises are also the owners, the incentive structure and the willingness to implement necessary reforms to improve productivity is reduced. As a result, the enterprise sector continues to under-perform. To facilitate restructuring and to improve corporate governance, the authorities have improved take-over legislation, and intend to strengthen capital markets to facilitate enterprise ownership concentration.

Theoretically, the advantage of the insider ownership was to increase the motivation of management and employees to improve the company's efficiency. Corporate governance would to improve because insiders have better access to the information needed for the efficient operation of the firm. However, in transition economies, improvements in corporate governance are likely to be reduced by insider buyouts that maintain the status quo and eliminate the division between management and ownership. By contrast, the sales to outsiders and foreign investors have improved corporate governance and performance, have provided easier access to capital and know-how, and thereby facilitated the difficult steps towards efficient restructuring (see Table 6.2).

Table 6.2. The Impact of Different Privatization Techniques

Privatization Method	Commitment for Restructuring	Access to Capital	Access to Know-how	Corporate Governance
Insiders' Distribution	-	-	-	-
Sales to Outsiders	+	+	+	+
Sales to Foreigners	+ +	+ +	+ +	+ +
State Ownership	--	+	--	--

In Slovenia, the four privatization categories illustrated in Table 2 translate into three main groups of owners:

- **Insiders** consist of management and employees, former employees, pensioners, and their family members;
- **Outsiders** consist of foreign physical and legal entities, as well as institutional investors, such as Privatization Investment Funds, banks and insurance companies;
- **State** (central authority and local communities), includes the Slovene Development Corporation; and indirectly through Restitution Fund, and Pension Fund.

These ownership groups face different working conditions. As a result, there are differences in access to financing, foreign or domestic borrowing, government contracts and guarantees, export and import markets, or labor restructuring and wages that reflect the productivity of the labor force. Because of the transition problems of the banking sector and because of the underdeveloped financial sector in general, enterprises had difficulties in financing the investments needed for restructuring. This is in part the result of high real interest rates due to prevailing operating costs and limited competition in the banking sector. Even though the privatization process allowed for the continuous ownership of banks by (now privatized) enterprises, the symbiotic relationship between banks and enterprises has not lead to widespread preferential treatment in financing to the enterprises, unlike that which occurred in other transition economies of the Central Eastern Europe.[14] On the contrary, banks limited their risk in the enterprise sector. Only in 1998 have they started to aggressively attract corporate clients in Slovenia.

The Enterprise Sector Still Generates Losses

The transition from a socialist self-management system to a market economy requires the implementation of radical enterprise reform. The privatization process was the corner stone of the enterprise sector reform, but it has not yet produced the incentive changes necessary to reverse the

---

[14] As in the Czech Republic, Slovenia has a recursive enterprise/banking/privatization fund ownership structure. Enterprises own banks, which own investment funds, which in turn own enterprises. Regional banks were implicitly privatized with their "mother" enterprises. The widespread problems generated by this relationship in other countries have not been present (thus far) to a sizable degree in Slovenia.

performance of enterprises. Instead, the enterprise sector, as a whole, has continuously reported losses during the transition. The government rehabilitation programs were designed to restructure large industrial plants and banks. These programs were executed through four different channels: (a) by direct state aid (subsidies, etc.); (b) by the Bank Rehabilitation Agency (debt restructuring and debt conversion); (c) by the Slovenian Development Corporation (enterprise sector restructuring); and (d) by nationalization of selected sectors (public utilities, ironworks and mines). In addition, the government has promoted private sector development, focusing on emergence of new small and medium-sized enterprises (SME). Currently, the SMEs constitute the large majority of enterprise sector.

In spite of all these efforts, the overall enterprise performance has not been satisfactory; further restructuring is still necessary. However, there is a large heterogeneity among different agents in the enterprise sector.   Such an outcome suggests that there is an important link between enterprise performance and ownership structure. It has been hypothesized[15] that management-employee ownership negatively affects the corporate governance. Insiders are typically unable to bring new skills to the firm and have limited capacity and incentive to raise new capital. Strategic investors, on the other hand, tend to have access to cheaper capital (especially foreign investors), to bring in new managerial techniques and technology, and to provide potential market connections abroad. Fearing that a conflict between inside and outside owners might emerge, outsiders lack the interest to invest in companies with high internal ownership.

A comprehensive research of the corporate sector in Slovenia has been launched.[16] Addressing the relationship between enterprise performance and ownership structure during the transition, the analysis was performed for the period between 1994 and 1996. It includes 2023 enterprises, broken down according to the different categories of ownership. Although the sample size seems small, accounting for only 6 percent of total number of enterprises, these comprises nonetheless 83.5 percent of equity, 77.6 percent of assets, and 78.5 percent of those employed. Moreover, these enterprises generated 76.4 percent of sales, 87.5 percent of exports and 79.7 percent of net losses of total non-financial corporate sector. Therefore, the sample is a representative group for the whole enterprise sector in the Slovenian economy. The different categories of ownership as follows:

- New Private companies   recently formed and thus have not undergone privatization;
- Foreign companies   majority foreign-owned;
- Internal companies   majority insiders-owned from insiders buyouts/ distribution;
- External companies   majority outsiders-owned by funds and small;
- Non-Privatized companies   majority owned by the Slovenian Development Corporation;
- State companies   majority state-owned and performing public services.[17]

The main characteristics of the defined groups of enterprises, at the beginning of the research period, are presented in Table 6.3. Even though the internally owned enterprises represent the largest

---

[15] See World Bank's World Development Report 1996, "From Plan to Market."

[16] See Marko Simoneti, Matija Rojec, and Marko Rems, "Enterprise Sector Restructuring and EU Accession of Slovenia," mimeo, 1998.

[17] The same analysis also assessed the presence of each of these ownership groups in different sectors. Internal enterprises are present in trade and construction, as well as in the same sectors as the external enterprises (agriculture, manufacturing, hotels and restaurants). Private enterprises are predominately in the financial and business services and trade. Foreign enterprises are concentrated in manufacturing and trade, while state enterprises are concentrated in the public services sector. Non-privatized enterprises can be found in all sectors.

category (31 percent), their equity and asset size has lagged behind the externally owned and state enterprises. As for the number of employees, internally owned enterprises are labor intensive and have employed the largest share of the workforce, while externally owned and state enterprises seem to be more capital-intensive. State and non-privatized enterprises retained an important position in the Slovenian economy, accounting for altogether 25 percent of workforce, 46 percent of total equity and 43 percent of total assets. New private and foreign enterprises, on the other hand, employed only 13 percent of the workforce; their equity and assets amounted to 8 percent and 12 percent respectively. Foreign owned firms are strongly export-oriented.

Table 6.3. Ownership Structure of Enterprises and Selected Indicators, 1995

Ownership Categories	No. of Firms	Equity	Assets	No. of Employed	Sales	Exports	Net Profit/Loss
			(percent of total)				(SIT millions)
New Private	27.4	3.4	6.4	8.3	11.1	8.4	5,109
Foreign	7.6	5.0	5.6	5.4	11.8	18.2	6,110
Internal	30.5	17.3	17.2	32.9	25.1	22.1	-5,992
External	19.2	28.9	27.0	27.9	29.3	29.7	-122
Non-Privatized	10.7	9.0	12.8	13.4	17.8	17.8	-20,802
State	4.6	36.4	31.1	12.0	3.8	3.8	3,204
Total	100.0	100.0	100.0	100.0	100.0	100.0	
Memorandum	2,023	2,639,287	4,567,212	380,315	3,502,148	981,299	-12,492

Source: Rems, M., M. Rojec and M. Simoneti (1998).

Different characteristics of ownership categories also produced different levels of sales, exports, and profits. In the first year of the analysis (1995), the enterprise sector as a whole reported a net loss. Foreign, new private and state enterprises all generated net profits. A negligible loss was generated by externally owned enterprises, while a significant loss was generated by internally owned and non-privatized enterprises. The latter were expected to generate losses since the SDC took over loss-making enterprises in the majority of cases. The external enterprises generated the largest share of sales and exports, followed by internal and non-privatized enterprises. As expected, foreign-owned and non-privatized enterprises were important exporters, since 68 percent of all assets of foreign owned, and 50 percent of all assets of non-privatized enterprises are in manufacturing. Nonetheless, some of the non-privatized enterprises can export only at a loss. Similarly, for state and private enterprises -- dominating in public services in the former case, or trade and services in the latter -- the export orientation was negligible. New private enterprises primarily serviced the domestic market.

If returns to equity are compared, the best results were achieved by the new private and foreign owned companies with 5.7 percent and 4.6 percent, respectively. By contrast, the non-privatized and internally owned enterprises reported the worst results (-8.8 percent and −1.3 percent, respectively). Similar findings were identified with regard to the value added per employee, which is measured as a sum of labor costs, provisions and net operating profit/ loss (see Table 6.4).

The findings from Table 6.4 show that enterprises with high return on equity also achieved higher profit margins (as measured by the Net Profit/Loss to Sales ratio). The best assets turnover ratio (as measured by the Net Sales to Assets ratio) was achieved by the new private and foreign owned enterprises, and the worst ratio by the non-privatized and state enterprises. The internally owned enterprises had a high index (146) since they operated with a significant loss. The next two ratios suggest that new private and foreign enterprises also achieve their profitability either due to a higher asset to equity ratio or to a relatively higher external source of financing. On the other hand, a high index for asset to equity ratio by the non-privatized companies (142) is linked to low profitability. A burden of high indebtedness is heavier for the non-privatized enterprises than for the new private and foreign owned ones, since the latter took loans to restructure and improve their activities, while the debts of non-privatized enterprises stemmed mainly from failed investment in the past or present loans for survival.

Table 6.4. Comparison of Performance Indicators by Ownership Categories, 1995

Ownership Categories	Net Profit/ Loss to Equity (in %)	Net Profit/ Loss to Sales (in %)	Value Added per Employee	Net Sales to Assets	Assets to Equity	Liabilities to Equity	Equipment in Fixed Assets	Equipment per Employee
			Index (all enterprises = 100)					
New Private	5.7	1.3	106	174	186	315	120	56
Foreign	4.6	1.5	131	210	112	133	203	168
Internal	-1.3	-0.7	92	146	99	97	96	43
External	-0.0	-0.0	107	108	94	81	99	89
Non-Privatized	-8.8	-5.1	74	91	142	208	84	72
State	0.3	0.8	118	36	85	65	93	311
Total	**-0.5**	**-0.4**	**100**	**100**	**100**	**100**	**100**	**100**

Source: Simoneti, M., M. Rojec and M. Rems (1998).

Both indicators of capital accumulation show that, besides capital-intensive state enterprises, foreign owned enterprises stand out. Internally owned, new private and non-privatized enterprises have below-average value of equipment per employee; internally owned firms are the most labor intensive of all industries. New private enterprises follow, but this result is related to their predominant concentration in services. On the other hand, new private and foreign owned enterprises have the largest indices for equipment in fixed assets, which indicates their reallocation of resources to productive capital, thereby reducing their share of non-productive assets (land and buildings) in their balance sheets.

Enterprise Restructuring is Slowly Taking Place

Following the sample of enterprises for the period 1994-96 allows us to identify a trend in enterprise restructuring, as measured by profitability. Restructuring has been faster in externally owned, internally owned and foreign owned enterprises, whereas restructuring in state firms and non-privatized enterprises has been slow. In the 1996 sample, 121 enterprises (out of the original 2,023) exited the sample group due to bankruptcy and mergers. The exit enterprises accounted for the majority of the losses in the enterprise sector and came mostly from internally and externally owned firms. This indicates that although restructuring has been taking place in Slovenia, it has been mostly through bankruptcies of loss-making enterprises. Bankruptcies have been the most intense in the non-privatized and external enterprises, particularly in the labor-intensive sector.[18] Almost none came from foreign owned enterprises, which operate with profits. The remaining sample of 1,902 enterprises shows some progress in enterprise restructuring.

As we can see Table 6.5 presents three categories of enterprise profitability. Net profit/loss from regular activity is determined by the addition of the other two categories; it represents the tradition measure of overall profitability in the enterprise sector netting out profits or losses from extraordinary operations. This is done to avoid misrepresentation due to special events such as one time sell of assets, write-offs, etc. The profitability of the enterprise sector in this category is, to a large extent, determined by the huge losses due to high financing costs. These losses have been increasing for all ownership categories and represented more than 90 percent of the total net loss from regular activity in 1995-96.

---

[18] See IMAD, Slovenian Economic Mirror, January 1998.

There are two reasons for such results. The first is the effect of the obligatory revaluation of equity, which leads to fictitious financing cost for firms whose equity exceeds the amount of those assets subject to revaluation. This is just an accounting operation, which unfortunately cannot be netted out from the data. The implication, however, is that the results are likely to be somewhat better than what the data shows. The second is the high interest rate paid by enterprises in Slovenia due to the prevailing conditions in the financial sector. The process of restructuring is thus complicated for those enterprises that depend on domestic financing.

Table 6.5. Profitability of the Enterprise Sector, 1994-96

Ownership Categories	Exit Firms (% of total)	Net Profit/Loss from Regular Activity (in SIT mil)			Net Operating Profit/Loss (in SIT mil)			Net Profit/Loss from Financing (in SIT mil)		
		1994	1995	1996	1994	1995	1996	1994	1995	1996
New Private	3.8	-2,341	2,263	-701	22	6,442	4,590	-2,363	-4,179	-5,291
Foreign	0.7	5,541	4,148	6,942	6,124	6,119	9,940	-583	-1,971	-2,998
Internal	4.9	-7,309	-13,589	-12,022	3,436	-4,613	1,178	-10,475	-8,976	-13,200
External	10.6	1,429	-4,677	-735	11,741	1,610	13,589	-10,312	-6,289	-14,324
Non-Privatized	10.1	-19,946	-26,202	-27,758	-10,897	-13,739	-10,786	-9,049	-12,463	-16,972
State	6.5	2,081	230	-28,539	937	2,977	-22,358	1,144	2,569	-6,181
Total	6.0	-20,545	-37,827	-62,813	11,363	-1,381	-3,848	-31,908	-36,446	-58,965

Source: IMAD, Slovenian Economic Mirror, February 1998.

Net operating profit/loss reveals the potential of the enterprise sector. A constant overall deterioration from 1994 to 1996 was mainly due to the poor results of state, non-privatized and internal enterprises. A significant deterioration for state enterprises in 1996 (in comparison with 1995) was the result of a massive depreciation allowance in the electricity supply sector. Excluding the state sector, the remaining categories would have generated net operating profit of SIT 18,510 million in 1996. The improvements were evident for the internally and externally owned enterprises, while the core business for non-privatized enterprises continues to report losses. The latter indicates that the government support programs, exercised by the Slovenian Development Corporation, have not adequately addressed restructuring issues. The SDC seem to have been more successful in promoting restructuring through exits (bankruptcy) of loss-making enterprises than other forms of restructuring.

Table 6.6. Profitability of the Private Enterprise Sector, 1994-96

Ownership Categories	Net Profit/Loss from Regular Activity (in SIT mil)			Net Operating Profit/Loss (in SIT mil)		
	1994	1995	1996	1994	1995	1996
New Private	-2,341	2,263	-701	22	6,442	4,590
Foreign	5,541	4,148	6,942	6,124	6,119	9,940
Internal	-7,309	-13,589	-12,022	3,436	-4,613	1,178
External	1,429	-4,677	-735	11,741	1,610	13,589
Total	-2,680	-11,855	-6,516	21,323	9,558	29,297

Source: IMAD, Slovenian Economic Mirror, February 1998.

Investment Climate Remains Weak

Enterprise restructuring requires an environment, which fosters investment. New investment is a crucial element of enterprise sector reform for bringing new technology and efficiency to the production process. In transition economies, new investments rejuvenate firms, thereby enhancing competitiveness and preparing enterprises for the strong competition that liberalization and joining the EU single market conveys. Moreover, the accumulation of capital stock, through investment, is a necessary component to generate needed high and sustainable growth rates. New investment has thus been a key ingredient of the transition to a market economy, particularly since the disintegration of the former communist blocks in the CEE -- and particularly, the former Yugoslavia -- generated enough uncertainties for most companies to postpone long-term decision, including needed investment programs.

Box 6.3. The Increasing Role of the Slovenian Development Corporation

The Law on Ownership Transformation established the Development Fund, responsible for the financial restructuring of troubled firms (transferred to the fund's portfolio on the eve of the privatization), and their subsequent privatization. It was also responsible for a transfer of 20 percent of shares of privatizing enterprises to the privatization investment funds. Its main task, restructuring of the socially-owned loss-making enterprises, was devised by the government in order to avoid politically and socially painful bankruptcy procedures. Starting in 1992, the Development Fund became the main shareholder of 98 enterprises with 56,000 workers according to the Law on Ownership Transformation and the Law on Companies in the Ownership of the Development Fund. These enterprises were adversely affected by the loss of Yugoslav markets due to the war. In the subsequent years, the Development Fund laid off 14,000 workers and started to sell the enterprises' shares. It maintained its major shareholder position only in those enterprises that investors found less attractively priced, or in which ownership status has not been resolved due to the unsolved restitution issues.

New companies were transferred to the Development Fund if they violated the Law on Ownership Transformation, or if they failed to prepare a coherent privatization program. The shares of these newly transferred companies had to be distributed to the other funds (Restitution Fund, Pension Fund, and Privatization Investment Funds), while the proceeds of the potential sales had to be allocated to the budget. Upon the completion of the privatization process in 1998, the Development Fund, the Agency for Privatization, and the Bank Rehabilitation Agency, were all merged under the new Slovene Development Corporation (SDC).

The SDC has substantially increased its size and role in the enterprise sector reform. It has recently taken firms that, by mid-1998, had not completed their privatization process. As a result, its portfolio now has around 360 enterprises, or a quarter of the firms in the original privatization pool. Moreover, the SDC role has expanded to address, not only restructuring issues for enterprises under its portfolio, but also restructuring in newly privatized enterprises. Over the years, a sizable amount of funds has been transferred to the SDC for enterprise restructuring, including SIT 10 billion in 1998. The poor performance of active non-privatized enterprises over the past indicates that the government-led restructuring policies (via SDC) have not been effective. The increasing role of the SDC, and its potential transformation into a powerful extra-budgetary agency (with no sunset clause), raises concerns about the government industrial policy.

The overall investment climate in Slovenia during the transition has been negative. This is the result of the expected uncertainties of transition, the high cost of financing and the outcome of the chosen privatization model. The latter focused on internal buyouts, thus maintaining the status quo. This has further reduced the incentives and opportunities to invest. As a result, in spite of the improvement in the business climate in recent years, investment activities remain virtually non-existent in certain ownership categories. Data indicate that externally privatized enterprises invest much more in fixed assets than internally privatized firms do. The latter lack sufficient investment to cover depreciation, thus generating negative net investment figures (see Table 6.7). Although downsizing, including disinvestment, is often the first step towards restructuring, internally owned enterprises seem to be both borrowing and disinvesting to cover losses and to maintain employment and/or wages above their long-term sustainable levels.

Table 6.7. Investment by Ownership Structure, 1995-96

	Gross Investment / Assets (in percent)		Net Investment / Assets (in percent)	
	1995	1996	1995	1996
New Private	8.41	5.98	4.61	2.10
Foreign	7.15	8.57	0.77	1.98
External	4.96	6.11	0.27	1.12
Internal	4.12	3.94	-0.32	-0.70
Non-Privatized	3.07	2.21	-0.22	-1.58
State	9.41	9.12	5.61	3.36

Source: Simoneti, M., M. Rojec and M. Rems (1998).

Overall, new investment in the enterprise sector remains low. Most of the new investment seems to be driven by the public sector – about 79 percent of the net investment in 1996 (and 43 percent of the gross investment) was initialed by the State in the public utilities sector—rather than by a developing private sector. This lack of either the capacity or the long-term strategy to invest is one of the most important incentive problems facing the enterprise sector in Slovenia today. If the enterprise sector is to compete in the EU single market, it must require improve its profitability and modernize its production processes. This in turn, will require higher private sector investment rates to modernize the production plant and to increase access to new technologies.

Low investment in Slovenia seems to be the result of a number of factors. On one hand, low investment is the result of an absence of strategic owners in the newly privatized enterprise sector with a long-term perspective. On the other hand, it is the result of the high cost and limited availability of long-term financing for all but a select group of enterprises. Moreover, investment is low in part due to lack of strategic alliances, especially with foreign investors, that could bring less expensive capital, new technologies and management practices to Slovenia. The overall performance is, however, likely to improve due to expected higher levels of foreign direct investment (FDI) in the coming years, particularly as implicit and explicit obstacles are eliminated by the EU accession process. Moreover, investment is likely to increase due to declining interest rates that will reduce the burden of high financing costs.

The Role of Foreign Investment

One of the most important differences between Slovenia and other leading accession countries has been Slovenia's reluctance to embrace foreign investment. Foreign investment in Slovenia has not reached its potential. The lower than expected levels of FDI do not result from unattractiveness of the Slovenian economy. On the contrary, given its superb location, its high level of industrial development and the quality of its labor force, Slovenia should have attracted a sizable amount of FDI. Low FDI inflows have been most likely the result of domestic impediments and government policies that have discourage FDI inflows during the transition. Government policy favored national ownership in the enterprise sector. As a result, FDI has not played the primal role in enterprise restructuring as in other transition economies, most notably Hungary. Except for Renault's investment and the more recent Goodyear Tire & Rubber joint venture with Slovenia's Sava Group, a producer of car tires, firms investing in Slovenia have been small to medium in size -- a pattern reminiscent of FDI in Poland during the initial stages of the transition, that is, before the FDI "take-off" of 1994-95.

FDI inflows to Slovenia increased from US$111 million in 1992 to around US$186 million in 1996. The average over the 1992-94 period was merely around US$117 million. The value of FDI increased by 37 percent in 1995 and remained almost flat the following year, increasing by just 5 percent. The signature of the EU agreement in mid-1996 and the favorable opinion of the EU towards Slovenia in 1997 sent a clear signal to the international community. As a result, FDI inflows increased by 73 percent in 1997, reaching US$321 million. FDI inflow in the first seven months of 1997 was US$224.8 million, whereas for the same period in 1998, the figure fell to US$141.2 million only, a 37 percent drop.

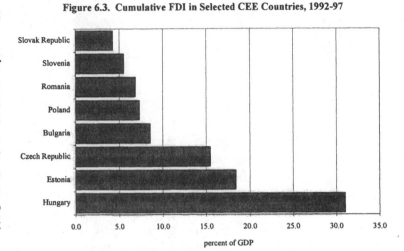

Figure 6.3. Cumulative FDI in Selected CEE Countries, 1992-97

The experience of FDI in other transition economies extends over a period long enough to draw some generalizations as to their impact on restructuring and integration into international markets. FDI has helped integrate domestic production capacities into global networks of production and distribution, by acting as a powerful vehicle for transfers of technology and the best practices in management. FDI contributes to intraindustry linkages, allowing economies of scale through greater product specialization in differentiated products – particularly important for small economies. While conventional comparative advantage brings about interindustry specialization -- as it operates on groups of products rather than within them -- the force driving two-way trade in similar differentiated products are economies of scale associated with supplying a larger market. The reason a country cannot produce a complete range of these products relates to fixed costs of production. Consequently, countries with similar factor endowments find reasons to trade with each other.

In spite of the low levels of FDI in Slovenia, its positive impact in the performance of the enterprise sector is clearly noticeable. Slovene enterprises with substantial foreign participation tend to perform better than domestic enterprises. Research by the Institute for Macroeconomic Analyses and Development (IMAD) compared enterprise data in the period from 1994 to 1996 (see Table 6.8). Firms were divided in two groups, according to the degree of foreign participation and control. During the whole period, the enterprises with foreign participation had better results than domestic enterprises in all the relevant indicators. The gap, however, has been slowly closing, as the spillover effects materialize.

The analysis reveals that operating profits are higher for enterprises with foreign participation, and that their higher profit-to-sales ratio reflects a better cost control. They use their assets more efficiently, as showed by their high total assets turnover ratio. These firms have a better, more balanced, asset structure, such as a higher proportion of productive assets in fixed assets, and most likely better quality assets, thus leading to a higher level of technology and more efficient production processes. A higher asset per equity ratio is a result of external financing resources, with better terms. Moreover, these enterprises tend to have more and better commercial links abroad, which enhances trade (exports) and makes them more competitive abroad.

While selectivity bias -from foreigners buying the best firms- could be responsible in part for the better performance of enterprises with foreign participation, the narrowing trend of the performance gap indicates that, if any, the selectivity bias was low. The gap in all performance indicators shown in Table 6.8 have been reduced, in some cases substantially, like the operating profit per equity or the value added per employee. Moreover, spillover effects may also be responsible for the closing gap.

Table 6.8. Comparative Performance of Foreign and Domestic Enterprises, 1994-96

Performance Indicators	1994		1995		1996	
	Foreign	Foreign to Domestic, Index	Foreign	Foreign to Domestic, Index	Foreign	Foreign to Domestic, Index
Operating Profit per Equity, in percent	8.5	260	7.7	226	8.3	206
Operating Profit as a Share of Net Sales, in percent	3.9	154	3.4	139	3.4	125
Net Sales per Assets, in percent	103.1	137	109.2	145	110.6	136
Assets per Equity, in percent	212.7	123	206.6	112	218.3	121
Value Added per Employee, in mil SIT	3.3	178	3.4	160	3.3	133

Source: IMAD, Slovenian Economic Mirror, September 1998.

Concluding Remarks

In the process of transferring the ownership of socially-owned enterprises, about 1,500 firms were privatized. The dominance of insider control has implied less overall restructuring and efficient enterprise governance than one might have anticipated. Companies with insiders ownership and control show the following characteristics: they (a) are inclined to under-invest; (b) prefer higher wages instead of long term growth; (c) make the firm relatively unattractive to foreign investment partnerships; (d) have inefficient management controls; (e) have low mobility of labor; and (f) are overly dependent on credit and thus likely to result in a high incidence of failures and bankruptcies in the future.

The overall picture of the enterprise sector shows that the aggregate enterprise sector continues to operate with sizable losses. However, the losses reported during 1994-96 were mostly a consequence of expensive financing (and/or the effect of accounting standards), aggravated by the poor performance of certain ownership classes, most notably non-privatized enterprises. The net operating profit has slowly improved in all private sector categories, which represent a good part of the bulk of the Slovenian enterprise sector. In non-privatized and state sectors, however, this has not been the case. The non-privatized enterprises are still generating net operating losses, which causes concern regarding the efficiency and adequacy of the restructuring efforts as well as the increasing role of the Slovenian Development Corporation. Although disaggregated data for 1997 are still not available, preliminary data, including 36,717 enterprises,.[19] show that the enterprise sector still reported aggregate losses, mostly as a consequence of high financing costs (and the effect of accounting standards). The operating activity, however, slowly but steadily improved over the last three years, which is an important sign of the gradual restructuring taking place in Slovenia.

---

[19] IMAD (1998), Spring Report.

To rejuvenate the process of enterprise reform, the government should address the unfinished privatization agenda, it should establish a legal and regulatory framework that facilitates investment, promotes private sector development, improves corporate governance and enhances efficiency. The unfinished privatization agenda includes: (a) the privatization of state-assets (public utilities, state banks, etc.); (b) the privatization of the residual stake in already privatized enterprises; (c) the resolution of the status of firms in the portfolio of the SDC; and (d) the resolution of the privatization gap problem. Moreover, advancing the stalled structural reform agenda and accelerating the transposition of the *acquis* will improve the business climate to attract needed FDI and stimulate enterprise and banking sector reforms. This, in turn, will reduce financing costs, improve performance and enhance the prospects for the enterprise sector to compete, on equal terms, in the Union's single market.

To enhance enterprise restructuring the government can implement measures that will put the right incentives in place aimed at improving corporate governance. Such measures, besides privatizing state-owned firms, should include strengthening of minority shareholders rights, improving in disclosure and quality of information by firms, establishing of international accounting standards, facilitating takeovers and mergers, enhancing banks' capacity to handle problem debtors, streamlining bankruptcy procedures and attracting FDI.

Figure 6.4. Private Sector Share in GDP

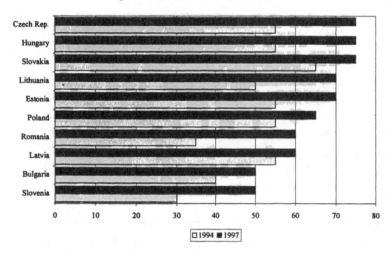

Foreign investors do not perceive Slovenia as a country with significant investment opportunities. This contrasts with other leading transition economies, where FDI has played a crucial role in restructuring. Moreover, private sector development, as measured by its share of GDP, has been pale in comparison with other candidate countries (see Figure 6.4). This puts Slovenia at the end of the enlargement group. As the process of accession to the EU advances, Slovenia has a considerable opportunity to attract foreign investment and to improve its enterprise performance; privatization with strategic foreign and domestic partners should play a critical role. Private sector development and the reduction of the public sector share in the economy, both though privatization and the rationalization of public expenditures, should be among the principal objectives of the government and a key component of Slovenia's EU accession strategy.

Labor Market and Social Policies

Introduction

Slovenia inherited the labor market conditions, laws and regulations of the Socialist Federal Republic of Yugoslavia (SFRY), but it moved faster than the other ex-Yugoslav states, after independence, to transform its economy, to reform its factor markets and to position itself as one of the leading candidates for membership in the enlarged EU. Slovenia's political and economic transformation is setting the foundation for both a modern democracy and stable market institutions. Policy and institutional reforms have produced a fast economic turnaround and fueled economic recovery.

Slovenia's dual transition -to an independent state and to a market economy- has produced serious changes in factor markets conditions. The reform agenda has advanced on many fronts, but the size of the unresolved structural problems in labor and other factor markets remains substantial. The fast turnaround of real output has not been followed by employment recovery as expected. This, however, is not a characteristic unique to Slovenia. On the contrary, this asymmetry in output-employment is becoming a stylized fact in most transition and western economies, creating what is now called structural unemployment.

Table 7.1. Annual Percentage Change in GDP and Employment, 1993-97

	Czech Republic		Hungary		Poland		Slovenia	
	Real GDP	Employment	Real GDP	Employment	Real GDP	Employment	Real GDP	Employment
1993	-0.9	-1.6	-0.6	-5.9	3.8	-2.4	2.8	-1.8
1994	2.6	0.8	2.9	-2.1	5.2	1.0	5.3	-0.4
1995	5.0	2.6	1.5	-1.9	7.0	0.3	4.1	-0.3
1996	4.8	1.7	0.2	-1.9	6.0	-0.1	3.1	-0.7
1997	1.0	-0.3	4.4	0.5	6.9	1.4	3.8	0.2
1993-1997	13.0	3.2	8.6	-10.5	32.5	0.2	20.6	-3.0

Source: The World Bank.

Structural unemployment, created in part by the mismatch between supply and demand for labor skills, remains a critical problem in Slovenia. Moreover, although the aggregated profitability of Slovenia's commercial sector is improving, it continues to be negative in 1997. Loss making firms employed about 25 percent of the working population and are concentrated in labor-intensive sectors where employees have low skills. Once unemployed, these workers are trapped outside the formal economy because the new market conditions demand higher degrees of education and skills. For this reason, social policies will have to play a crucial role during the remainder of the transition, as well as during the pre-accession period. To make those social policies fiscally sustainable and to reduce the perverse incentives they may generate in labor markets, efficient targeting and design will be crucial.

This chapter aims at contributing to the Government's effort in assessing progress and identifying areas where additional effort and policy improvements are needed to both enhance the flexibility of the labor market and to boost the Government's capacity to efficiently allocate resources. The goal is to assist Slovenia's transition to a market economy and its accession and eventual EU membership. To that end, this chapter reviews labor market conditions in Slovenia and analyzes its main characteristics and policies.

Labor Market Characteristics

The Slovenian labor market shared the same basic characteristics, and some of the same distortions, of other socialist economies. These included heavy social sector employment, full or quasi-full employment, together with some hidden unemployment; these includes sizable female participation in the labor force, a well educated labor force, heavy employment in industry, little geographic mobility, an egalitarian wage structure, overly generous fringe benefits, and government and worker involvement in the determination of wages. Consequently, during the transition Slovenia's labor market experienced the same stylized trends as did many other Central and Eastern European (CEE) transforming economies; these trends included a decline in both

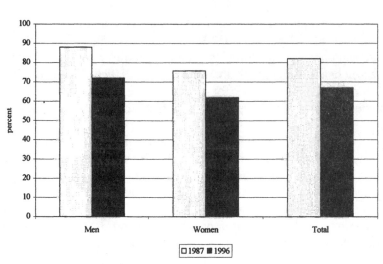

Figure 7.1. Labor Force Participation Rates

labor force participation and employment rates, an increase in unemployment rates and the appearance of structural unemployment. During the transition, the labor market also experienced, at first, a steep decline in real wages, then followed by a reversal that generated an increase in real wages well above productivity.

In Slovenia, as in other regions that have gone through a severe structural adjustment process, the return of output growth has been followed by real wage growth, but not by employment growth. In fact, unemployment pressures have not pushed wages down, thereby increasing labor demand. This outcome is partly the result of a skills mismatch between what labor markets demand and what workers can offer. The unemployed have lower education and/or skills, while labor demand is moving away from unskilled labor and toward more skilled workers. Moreover, traditional skills are no longer in demand as they once were, while new skills are sought in the market; some workers suffer because the specificity of their skills is associated with a declining sector. Hence, long term unemployment, defined as those unemployed for over 12 months, hits mostly workers with lower education or skills, and those with specific vocational training.

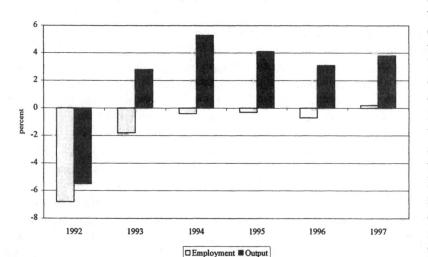

Figure 7.2. Employment and Output Growth

Skill mismatch is not the only problem. High labor costs -through taxes, social security contributions and expensive redundancy costs- a lack of flexibility in labor markets, particularly as a result of both the prevailing wage settling mechanisms and overprotective labor legislation, are further hindering labor market restructuring, thereby limiting the capacity of the market to efficiently allocate resources during the transition and to generate new job opportunities. Consequently, Slovenia urgently needs to further restructure its labor market, particularly because the highly competitive EU market will put pressure on the Slovene economy.

The Slovenian government's cautious attitude towards real sector reform is due, in large part, to the perception that unemployment is very high and could create unacceptable threats, both to social cohesion and economic performance. An examination of the relevant data, however, seems to suggest otherwise. Two sets of data exists that tell different stories: the National Employment Office (NEO) registry unemployment, which sets the unemployment rate at about 14 percent, and the Labor Force Survey (LFS) unemployment, which sets the unemployment rate at 7 percent. Because of both the lax monitoring activities of the NEO and because of the heightened incentives to register as unemployed -incentives that run beyond simple assistance in finding a job- it seems that the LFS data is the more reliable in measuring unemployment trends in Slovenia. Unquestionably, unemployment increased during the transition. Nonetheless, the level of unemployment prevailing in Slovenia today, as measured by the LFS, is among the lowest in all transforming economies, with the exception of the Czech Republic, and is substantially lower than in the EU. In particular, the unemployment rate for women is much lower in Slovenia than in the EU.

Figure 7.3. Differences in Survey and Registry Unemployment, 1996

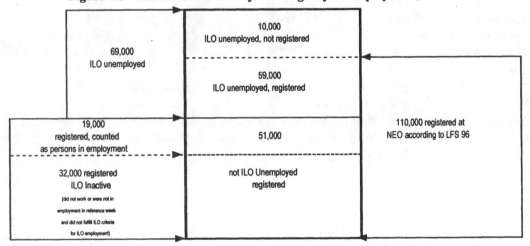

Periods of longer school attendance and early retirement programs contributed to keep the labor force participation (LFP) rates of both young and old workers at a relatively low level. This reduced the labor supply and helped buffer the unemployment pressures during transition. The fall in employment is slowly coming to an end. The reallocation of workers continues, albeit at a slow pace. As a result, labor markets are still underrepresented in the service sector and over represented in the industrial sector. This, and the potential for even higher unemployment -because the skills of workers in many industrial branches are no longer in demand- points to the need for further restructuring.

The government is concerned about unemployment, in particular about workers losing their jobs. The LFS data, however, show that the government should re-focus its concern towards making the market more flexible and facilitating job creation, rather than mainly pursuing job preservation. The lack of job opportunities for first-time job seekers, young workers, and people coming out of inactivity, rather than job loss itself, is the most important reason for unemployment. Indeed, the LFS data seems to point to a problem on the supply side of the market (the skill mix) rather than on the demand side. This result, however, may also be a signal of a labor demand adjustment being artificially repressed by policies -in the labor and other markets- which promote labor hoarding. In particular, early retirement programs, used in the early 1990s, were successful in getting workers out of the labor force but had produced a long lasting effect on public finances, increasing pension expenditures by about 50 percent to reach almost 15 percent of GDP in 1997. The demographic trends point to a deterioration of the pension situation over the coming years. Pension reform is thus a critical element of the government's reform agenda.

Not all the news about the characteristics of unemployment in Slovenia is negative. Heads of Slovenian households are not affected as severely as are similar groups in the EU; this means that the current unemployment rate affects families less in terms of income and welfare than in the EU. The area of concern regarding unemployment is the concentration among the young, especially those with less education, the high duration of unemployment (a growing trend), and the regional disparity that hints both to lack of labor mobility and a problem in the housing market. Policies that make labor markets more flexible and create the right set of incentives for the private sector to generate new job opportunities -without the use

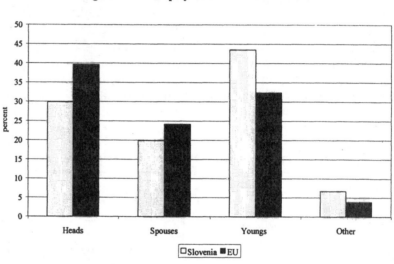

Figure 7.4. Unemployment of Households Heads

of instruments that produce labor market distortions or weakens the fiscal position of the country- should be fostered. Moreover, policies that generate sustainable growth should also be sought as the engine to promote employment and reduce unemployment.

Labor Market Adjustment

In a case like Slovenia, where the economy is being transformed to become market oriented, it was expected that fundamental changes would accelerate labor adjustment. The privatization process was expected to have produced sizable net labor flows, particularly as firms adjusted to the new competitive markets downsizing. This, however, does not seem to be happening to a significant degree. A large portion of the labor shedding seems to have taken place before privatization, that is, in the early years of the transition. It seems to have been the result of bankruptcy rather than demand adjustment to overmanning. Privatized firms ended-up primarily in the hands of insiders -workers and managers- thus weakening the privatization process as a tool for enterprise restructuring. As a result, the enterprise sector (as a whole) continues to operate with losses in 1997. These losses are concentrated in low-skill labor-intensive privatized firms (in the hands of insiders), and in those enterprises that have yet to be privatized and which are owned by the Slovene Development Fund, redefined recently as the Slovene Development Corporation.

Table 7.2. Employment Rates by Occupation and Sector, 1996

	Slovenia	EU
Legislators and Managers	5.7	8.2
Professionals	9.7	11.7
Technicians	15.0	13.7
Clerks	10.7	13.9
Service and Sales Workers	12.0	13.0
Agriculture and Fishery Workers	9.2	4.1
Crafts and Related Trades Workers	13.7	16.4
Plant and Machine Operators	18.4	8.9
Elementary Occupations	5.2	9.6
Armed Forces	0.2	0.6
Agriculture Sector	**10.2**	**5.3**
Industrial Sector	**42.2**	**30.2**
Service Sector	**47.5**	**64.5**

Source: Statistical Office of the Republic of Slovenia and OECD.

Other signs of transition coupled to weak adjustment in labor markets come from the data on labor turnover and wage heterogeneity (see Table 7.3). Labor turnover was expected to accelerate during the transition as it had in other leading transforming economies and the EU economies. This has not occurred to the degree expected. In particular, job-to-job transitions and accessions to employment have been relatively low. Wage dispersion should have intensified as certain skills (and branches) became less valuable and as other skills (and branches) became highly sought. Moreover, as the link between productivity and wages became stronger, intra- and inter- industry wage dispersion was also expected to increase. The available data shows that the effects have been significantly smaller than expected, thus hinting at labor rigidities and potential inefficiencies in the allocation of resources.

Table 7.3. Accession and Separation Rates: International Comparison

	Accession rate	Separation rate
Transition countries (average for selected years)*		
Slovenia (1990-96)**	13.2	18.2
Slovenia (1989-95)***	N.A.	13.0
Estonia (1990-94)	20.6	22.6
OECD countries (average for selected years between 1971 and 1984)		
Un-weighted average of OECD countries	25.5	26.1

Notes: *Accession rate is defined as annual number of accessions per 100 employees in a calendar year; separation rate is defined as annual number of separations per 100 employees in a calendar year. **Obtained from data on individual labor turnover. ***Obtained from group data reported by enterprises. Rate calculated from May to May. OECE average includes Finland, France, Germany, Italy, Japan, Sweden, UK and US.

Sources: For Slovenia: Abraham and Vodopivec (1993), internal material of Statistical Office of Slovenia based on Labor Force Survey and monthly employers' reports on accessions and separations. For Estonia, own computations based on 1995 Estonian Labor Force Survey. For OECD countries, OECD (1994).

Constraints to Effective Labor Market Performance

Slovenia's labor market seems to be slow in adjusting to the new economic conditions. The lack of flexibility in the labor market is limiting its capacity to allocate resources efficiently. The barriers to labor market flexibility seem to be many. The first barrier is labor skill mismatch, a natural outcome of the transition. Labor skill mismatch generates supply constraints and keeps structural unemployment from coming down. This type of unemployment is difficult to manage, since it requires a major effort to re-skill part of the workforce. The second barrier is an institutional wage negotiation and wage settling mechanism based on both social agreements and collective bargaining agreements that determine wages at almost all levels, including the minimum wage, sectoral wages and beyond. This semi-centralized mechanism is pushing lower wages up while keeping higher wages capped, with little or no link to productivity increases. As a result, the relation between wage growth and productivity growth is weak. Moreover, relatively little freedom is left to the market to generate needed adjustment in relative wages among sectors and individuals, thus further hindering labor market adjustment.

High labor costs in the form of income (personal versus corporate) and wage taxation, social security contributions, hiring and firing costs and by-law fringe benefits constitute the third barrier. As a result, these high costs are generating the wrong set of incentives for firms to promote new employment opportunities for the labor force to re-allocate. This compels some employers to offer temporary jobs, beyond their use as a screening mechanism, and in some cases pushes employers and employees to informality. Finally, overprotective employment legislation constitutes a fourth barrier, increasing both entry and exit costs, reducing labor flexibility, and hindering job creation incentives.

Table 7.4. Social Security Contribution Rates in 1997
(percent of gross wages)

	Employee	Employer	Total
Pension	15.50	8.85	24.35
Health	6.36	6.89	13.25
Unemployment	0.14	0.06	0.20
Maternity	0.10	0.10	0.20
TOTAL	22.10	15.90	38.00

Source: Ministry of Finance.

As a corrective, the newly proposed labor relations law promotes flexibility on several counts. Above all, it shortens the layoff notification period, particularly for workers with short tenure. It also proposes to eliminate the delay before the redundancy notice can become effective; it reduces severance pay for certain categories of workers; it softens the difficulty of dismissal, chiefly by dropping the current employer's requirement of retraining the redundant worker. The proposed law, however, is stricter regarding the regulation of fixed-term work. Not only does it retain the strictest definition of fixed-term work, but the proposal limits both the use of the number of successive contracts and the maximum cumulative duration of fixed-term contracts.

Social Protection and Active Labor Market Policies

The challenge for the government is to design and implement effective labor market policies in order to adequately protect individuals who have been disproportionately affected by the transition, without imposing undue fiscal and labor costs, and without creating adverse incentives to take on jobs. To that end, social protection policies -in the form of unemployment insurance, social assistance and other income support programs- must be well designed, monitored and implemented. If insufficient or poorly targeted, social protection mechanisms will not be sufficient to cope with structural issues and to avoid poverty. If excessive, they will generate perverse incentives in the labor market and possible undue fiscal costs affecting the welfare and long-term growth prospect of the country.

The Law on Employment and Unemployment Insurance was enacted in 1991 and amended in 1991-98. The law gives unemployed workers the right to: (a) unemployment compensation; (b) unemployment assistance; (c) training; (d) reimbursement for moving expenses connected with re-employment; (e) redundancy compensation; and (f) health and old-age insurance. Other indirect benefits are also available to families of the registered unemployed.

Only about a third of the unemployed registered at the NEO actually received the cash benefit (unemployment compensation and/or assistance), thus hinting that other elements of the unemployment insurance package (specifically the health and pension parts) are pushing some Slovenes to register as unemployed. Moreover, the weak monitoring of active job search and actual unemployment status of the worker biases NEO unemployment figures up. The 1998 amendment to the employment and unemployment law aimed at addressing these issues. Trends in unemployment insurance and social assistance data seems to confirm, in part, the increasing duration of unemployment. Some workers have exhausted their unemployment insurance term and moved into social assistance.

Assisting the unemployed in their effective job search is preferable to simply providing them with income support. Reliance on income support can diminish work incentives and impede the job search, making the unemployed overly dependent on social transfers as their basic income source. The goal of the NEO should be to increase the rate at which the unemployed are successfully matched to available job vacancies. This is not an easy task. It requires an adequate level of resources, and an integrated system that coordinates the administration of unemployment and related social benefits.

Since the transition started, Slovenia has relied, not only on passive, but also on active labor market programs. In addition to traditional training programs, several new programs have been introduced. These programs include public works, job preservation subsidies, and active programs to provide guidance and assistance for individuals considering self-employment. The question of whether active labor market programs have achieved their stated goal of enabling the unemployed to take a job is an important one. A matching function analysis of training and public works programs in Slovenia nonetheless indicates that targeted training programs are helping the unemployed find jobs, while public works do not seem to enhance employment prospects of participants after the program is over.

The evidence in EU and OECD countries shows that active labor market policies can potentially increase employment and/or earnings prospects of participants, vis-à-vis non-participants. Job-search assistance and counseling in the form of scheduled interviews, back-to-work plans and job clubs have showed positive outcomes with limited use of resources. These are simple measures to organize, but they do require an employment office that is sufficiently staffed and funded to support the counseling program. Slovenia can benefit from further use of these programs. Training programs for the unemployed, in contrast, have had mix results. When highly targeted to specific groups, and when having adequate resource support, they can be effective in reducing unemployment. Universal programs, however, seem to be less effective.

Direct job creation programs, in the form of subsidies for employers who create jobs or reductions in social charges for firms hiring unemployed persons, self-employment start-up grants, and public works are all used in the EU as well as Slovenia. In the EU, however these programs, have proven to produce substantial displacement and substitution effects on employment. Displacement is produced when firms taking the subsidies expand, while those not having access to the subsidy, contract. Substitution arises when firms hire workers that are eligible for a subsidy at the expense of laying-off or not hiring workers who are not subsidized. In addition, firms may receive the subsidy for workers they would have hired anyway, producing a deadweight loss. Consequently, their use as an effective tool to fight unemployment in a long lasting and efficient way is questionable.

Box 7.1. Social Protection Programs

In contrast to other former socialist economies, both unemployment insurance and social assistance benefits existed under the socialist system in Slovenia. The first regulations for protecting unemployed workers date back to 1952. The current system of unemployment insurance, modified several times after its introduction, was set up in 1974. Social assistance -means-tested financial assistance to individuals and families with insufficient means for living- was introduced in 1979.

Income Support Programs

- The Law on Employment and Unemployment Insurance was enacted in 1991 and amended in 1991-98, without reducing the generosity of the unemployment benefit. The law gives unemployed workers the right to (a) unemployment compensation; (b) unemployment assistance; (c) training; (d) reimbursement for moving expenses connected with re-employment; (e) redundancy compensation; and (f) health and old-age insurance.
- Similar to the original 1974 law, the current law resembles unemployment insurance legislation in Germany and Austria. Nonetheless, the law deviates from that of other European countries in two respects. First, in addition to a non-means tested benefit, namely unemployment compensation, it also offers a means-tested benefit -- unemployment assistance. Second, the duration of potential entitlement to unemployment compensation is not uniform but rather contingent on the individual's years of service.

Social Assistance Programs

- Means-tested financial assistance to needy individuals -available also to those capable of work- was introduced in 1979. For able-bodied individuals, several types of assistance were offered: financial assistance as a supplementary source of income, financed from the budget of the Republic of Slovenia on the one hand, and temporary and one-time assistance, financed by the local governments (communes) on the other.
- In 1992, a new law was enacted, preserving the principles but shifting the bulk of the financing to the central budget. The 1992 law distinguishes two types of social assistance: (i) social assistance as a supplementary source of income ("denarni dodatek"). It is offered to those individuals and their families who are without sufficient means due to causes beyond their control; and (ii) social assistance as the sole source of income, which is restricted to persons permanently unable to work and to those above 60 without other income sources.
- Eligibility for social assistance is income-tested, with property being considered on an ad-hoc basis. The level of the benefit equals the difference between the prescribed threshold income for the individual or family and the actual incomes of the individual or family. Additional benefits include a housing subsidy, if the recipient rents an apartment. The threshold income is expressed in terms of a guaranteed wage, with no apparent relationship to a poverty line. For the unemployed, the receipt is conditional upon registration at employment offices, and may also be further made conditional upon signing a contract specifying the actions to be taken by the recipient (such as health treatment, participation in public works). The maximum duration of the benefit is 6 months (the average duration for 37,000 cases awarded in the first half of 1995 was 4 months, with 40 percent of cases awarded the maximum duration of six months). The benefit is renewable, depending on circumstances. Conditions for keeping the benefit after being awarded are only implicit: recipients must report changes of relevant circumstances, but the law does not specify actions to be taken if this happens. There is no active job search requirement stated as a condition for keeping the benefit. The social assistance is administered through 62 local centers for social work, and financed primarily through the central budget.

Trends in Unemployment Benefit. Reflecting increasing unemployment during the transition, unemployment benefit recipients and expenditures dramatically increased. The number of recipients increased from 7,000 in 1988 to 65,000 in 1993, with strong increase in the recipients of both unemployment compensation and unemployment assistance. Since 1993, however, there has been a reduction in the number of recipients, and about 39,000 of these received these benefits at the end of 1996. Because the potential duration of unemployment assistance was shortened by the amendment of the law at the end of 1993, the number of recipients of unemployment assistance declined considerably.

Not only did the number of recipients increase during the transition, so did the average duration of the recipients, from 4.6 months in 1988 to 13 months in 1996. The average duration of the receipt of unemployment assistance increased until 1993 when it peaked at 19 months, but was dramatically reduced by the change of the law in 1993, to 5.9 months in 1996.

Table 7.5. Unemployment Benefits, 1988-96

	1988	1989	1990	1991	1992	1993	1994	1995	1996
A. Number of recipients (as of the end of the year)									
Total	6813	11649	30388	49396	51905	64817	43696	35417	38708
Unemployment compensation	4256	6114	18451	31818	32533	42582	31452	28305	33715
Unemployment assistance	2361	3710	8784	14110	18229	20052	11036	5936	4112
Lump-sum grants (total in the year)	196	1825	3153	3468	1143	2183	1208	1176	881
B. Average duration of the benefit (in months)									
Unemployment compensation	4.6	4.0	4.8	4.2	8.5	14.3	14.4	12.7	13.1
Unemployment assistance	8.8	5.4	7.5	7.6	10.4	19.0	8.0	7.3	5.9
C. Average monthly real benefit, in 1000 of 1995 SIT									
Unemployment compensation	36.3	51.5	27.8	29.8	29.8	44.9	50.2	48.5	51.0
Unemployment assistance	29.6	35.0	26.1	14.3	21.9	20.3	18.0	19.9	20.6
Lump-sum self-employment grants	973.3	N/A.	1339.6	647.4	519.4	N/A.	616.6	632.4	644.0
D. Expenditures on unemployment benefits									
Total expenditures, in percent of GDP	0.47	0.73	0.43	0.67	0.85	1.22	1.15	0.78	0.73
Unemployment compensation (a)	0.47	0.73	0.17	0.46	0.59	0.97	0.91	0.66	0.66
Unemployment assistance	N/A.	N/A.	0.08	0.10	0.23	0.25	0.20	0.08	0.04
Lump-sum self-employment grants	N/A.	N/A.	0.18	0.11	0.03	N/A.	0.04	0.03	0.03
Memorandum items									
Registered unemployed (in thousands, yearly average)	21.3	28.2	44.6	75.1	102.6	129.1	127.1	121.5	119.8
Labor force (in thousands, yearly average)	953.9	943.5	909.4	841.3	791.0	766.5	752.3	750.2	744.9
Unemployment rate based on registered unemployment	2.2	2.9	4.7	8.2	11.5	14.4	14.4	13.9	13.9
Unemployment rate based on labor force survey	N/A.	N/A.	N/A.	7.3	8.3	9.1	9.0	7.4	7.3
Expenditure on labor market programs, in percent of GDP	0.74	2.59	0.82	1.62	2.10	2.02	1.83	1.51	1.40
Number of monthly recipients of social assistance in cash	10240	11303	9413	10321	8466	17544	22623	26466	32822
Expenditures for social assistance, in percent of GDP	0.04	0.04	0.07	0.09	0.08	0.17	0.20	0.24	0.28

Notes: (a) Data for 1988 and 1989 includes unemployment assistance and self-employment grants, and data for 1993 includes self-employment grants.

Source: National Employment Office of Slovenia, Work Report 1988-1995; Statistical Yearbook of Slovenia, 1994; Bulletin of the Bank of Slovenia, August 1996.

Unemployment compensation became more generous during the later phase of the transition, while unemployment assistance became less generous. In the 1988-92 period -excluding the unreliable year of 1989- average real monthly unemployment compensation ranged from 30,000 to 36,000 SIT (in real 1995 prices); after 1992, it ranged from 45,000 to 51,000 SIT. This can be explained by the combination of two factors: the 1991 increase of the replacement rate in the first three months of the receipt, and the increase in real wages after 1992. In contrast, the reduction of real value of unemployment assistance from 1988 to 1996 by one third shows the erosion of the guaranteed wage to which the benefit has been tied. Ad-hoc adjustments of the guaranteed wage obviously did not match price increases.

Unemployment insurance expenditures, expressed as a share of GDP, increased during 1991-93, reaching a peak of 1.22 percent of GDP in 1993. It declined both in 1994 but particularly in 1995 -so much so that by the end of 1996 it amounted to 0.73 percent of GDP. Expenditures in both unemployment compensation and assistance declined as a percent of GDP since 1993 -the latter much more dramatically. Lump-sum payments of unemployment benefit played an important role until 1991 (when they were mostly paid to employers as a type of a subsidy for giving a job to the unemployed). Since 1992, they have been kept at about 0.03 percent of GDP.

Table 7.6. Social Assistance, 1988-96

	1988	1989	1990	1991	1992 (a)	1993	1994	1995	1996
A. Number of recipients (monthly average)									
Total	10240	11303	9413	10321	8466	17544	22623	26466	32822
Recipients of SA as the only source of income	2226	2040	1893	1830	1785	1770	1709	1558	1494
Recipients of SA as a supplementary source	5985	6700	5100	4639	6681	15774	20914	24908	29988
One-time assistance	702	854	1572	2006	N/A.	----	----	----	1340
Temporary assistance	1327	1709	848	1846	N/A.	----	----	----	----
B. Average monthly real benefit, in 1000 of 1995 SIT									
Average for all types of social assistance in cash	9937	8774	15403	13506	8702	16285	15483	16951	16951
C. Expenditures on social assistance, in percent of GDP									
Total for all types of social assistance in cash	0.04	0.04	0.07	0.09	0.08	0.17	0.20	0.24	0.28
Memorandum items									
Institutional and foster care in percent of GDP	0.18	0.25	0.27	0.27	0.21	0.26	0.24	0.25	N/A.
Recipients of unemployment benefit, end of the year	6813	11649	30388	49396	51905	64817	43696	35417	38708
Expenditures on unemployment benefits, in percent of GDP	0.47	0.73	0.43	0.67	0.85	1.22	1.15	0.78	0.73

Notes: (a) Data in 1992 is underreported. Part of social assistance and other social care expenses was covered from local sources, and the reported data do not account for them completely (due to merging of administrative control under the new law of 1992).

Source: Ministry of Labor, Family, and Social Affairs, internal material; Statistical Yearbook of Slovenia, 1994; Bulletin of the Bank of Slovenia, August 1996.

In the pre-transition period, as well as in the early 1990s, there were about 10,000 social assistance recipients per month. This number strongly increased in the post-1992 period, reaching 17,000 in 1993 and 33,000 by 1996.[1] It is interesting to note that after 1989, average real monthly benefits almost doubled. They have remained relatively stable since, amounting in 1996 to about 17,000 SIT (in 1995 prices), or about US$135. The share of social assistance expenditures as a percent of GDP has been consistently increasing, from 0.04 percent in 1988 to 0.28 percent in 1996, reflecting increasing trends of recipients and the increased post 1989 level of average benefits. While the increase of social expenditures in the last two years could not compensate for the much larger reduction in the total amount of unemployment benefits paid out, undoubtedly many unemployment benefit claimants, after exhausting those benefits, shifted to social assistance.

Trends in Early Retirement. To protect workers from increased hardship brought about by transition reforms -and possibly to "make room" for the employment of young workers- the Slovenian government encouraged and subsidized early retirement. Before the change of the pension law in March of 1992, women qualified for early retirement at the age of 50 and men at the age of 55, five years before the regular retirement age. Qualifying individuals had to have sufficient years of service and had to buy the missing pension credits -at a price, which had no bearing with the actuarially fair price. As a rule,

---

[1] Data for 1992, both for number of recipients and for expenditures, are unreliable -- most likely underreported.

employers paid the missing pension credits for the early retirees, and the government compensated the employers for about 50 percent of the costs.

Early retirement was certainly a good deal: pension levels for early retirees were only slightly reduced in comparison to their normal retirement levels (there was a penalty of one percentage point of a full pension for each missing year of pension credits) -and even then the reduction was effective only until they reached normal retirement age. In addition, given the pension benefit formula and changes in the wage structure during the transitional period, pension levels for newly retiring workers, tended to be better protected from inflation than wages were. For some groups of workers, pension levels at retirement even exceeded the wages received immediately before retirement (this applied mostly to low skilled workers).

It thus comes as no surprise that the early retirement policy was very effective in getting some workers out of the labor force and into retirement. From 1987 to 1991, there were sizable reductions of employment for workers in the highest experience groups (measured by the length of total employment); this was accompanied by wage increases for those in these groups that remained working. The outcome of these policies -however effective in coping with transitional unemployment- was to substantially increase the share of expenditures devoted to pensions, as well as the number of pensioners. Although active programs of early retirement were terminated and although conditions for early retirement were made stringent, the impact on the government's fiscal accounts will prove lasting. In 1996, pension expenditures represented 14 percent of GDP, almost twice as much than before the transition. This level of pension expenditure implies a 3.5 percent of GDP deficit in the pension system. The need for a comprehensive reform of the current pay-as-you-go pension system is thus critical. The government has been working on designing a new multi-pillar pension system that aims to solve the problems of the current pension system.

EU Accession and the Labor Market

As the process of accession to the EU advances, the Slovene authorities are making a considerable effort to adjust the regulatory framework of the labor market to EU requirements. New legislation affecting labor relationships addresses key issues to make labor markets more flexible, thereby reducing rigidities and implicit costs, and approximating the norms to those of the EU. These laws pave the way towards satisfying the requirements for accession. Provisions concerning health and safety in the workplace, as well as equal employment opportunity and working time are contained in the new draft legislation, which the authorities hope to have approved by Parliament in 1999.

The Copenhagen criteria require Slovenia (and any other signatories to Europe Agreements) to: have a "functioning market economy," have the capacity to cope with competitive pressures and market forces within the EU, and adhere to the aims of political, economic and monetary union in the EU. This requires an efficient labor market capable of both absorbing shocks and reallocating resources during the pre-accession period and beyond. The Copenhagen criteria also require that members have established stable institutions guaranteeing democracy, the rule of law, human rights and the respect for, and protection of, minorities. As all EU members, Slovenia will be required to eventually adopt the entire *acquis*. There is, however, no presumption that all aspects of the *acquis* must be implemented before admission. Even today, for instance, many EU members have not complied with all aspects of the Single Market Program laid out in the 1986 Single European Act. Nonetheless, the number of derogations and transition periods granted to new member states, will most likely be kept very limited, and will certainly be lower than in previous enlargements. To guarantee the proper functioning of the single market, the room for negotiations is expected to be narrow.

Slovenia's accession to the EU is driving both the pace and direction of policy and institutional reform. In the area of the labor market, Slovenia's compliance with the *acquis communautaire* implies recognizing both a set of minimum rights for workers and standardized labor conditions resembling those prevailing in the EU. The White Paper prepared by the EU identified four areas of social legislation (linked with labor markets) where legal harmonization and convergence is needed, namely: (a) equal opportunity for men and women; (b) health and safety at work; (c) labor law and working conditions; and (d) coordination of social security schemes.

The gap between Slovenia and the EU is not substantial; considerable effort is being made to adjust the regulatory framework of the labor market to the EU accession requirements laid down in the White Paper. The process of legal harmonization is underway, and a new labor relations code and other pieces of legislation are being prepared with the assistance of PHARE. Nonetheless, as the authorities work to meet the White Paper requirements, they should not lose sight of the implications of the EU accession process for the labor market. They should consequently prepare the ground for admission beyond mere legal adjustments. Indeed, the economy is likely to experience increasing competitive pressures as the process of economic approximation to EU markets advances. This points to the need for further restructuring, for a flexible environment that promotes both labor mobility and allows a greater diversification of wages across sectors and individuals.

Accession to the EU will encourage/compel Slovenia to remove existing inconsistencies in the regulation of foreign employment. The free movement of workers envisioned under the EU single market legislation would require changes in the national laws prior to Slovenia's gaining full EU membership. Access of foreign workers, from EU countries, to employment will have to be free from discrimination on the ground of nationality. Residency requirement for enterprise managers will have to be eliminated. Access to the EU will also open further opportunity for Slovenian workers abroad. The employment of foreign workers will remain dependent on labor market conditions, but will encourage cooperation between Slovene and foreign firms.

In the area of labor legislation, the government needs to focus on policies that will encourage a more flexible labor market. There is a wide range of choice in these standards, which vary greatly across countries. Strict employment protection standards are two-fold: countries with high standards of protection appear to have higher rates of long-term unemployment as well as higher rates of unemployment among young persons (age 14-24) relative to adults. Slovenia should also avoid introducing measures that are not really required for accession but that could prove detrimental to a successful adjustment in the labor market. As small and medium-sized firms represent the engine of employment growth, it would be highly undesirable to hinder their expansion. The need for a decentralized wage policy to encourage enterprise-level bargaining should be increased. Indeed, most EU countries are currently expanding the scope of their decentralized wage bargaining and linking wage setting to firm performance.

As the authorities work assiduously to meet the White Paper requirements, they should not lose sight of the implications of the EU accession process for the labor market, and should consequently prepare the ground for admission beyond mere legal adjustments. In fact, the economy is likely to experience increasing competitive pressures, with the increasing economic approximation to EU markets, particularly in the case of sectors that have been lagging behind. This points to the need for further restructuring, and for a flexible environment that promotes labor mobility and allows a greater diversification of wages across sectors.

Box 7.2. Slovenia's Labor Market and the *Acquis Communautaire*

I. Equal Opportunities for Men and Women. Stage I key measures require that the country comply with the contents of Directives 75/117/EEC and 76/202/EEC, which contain provisions on (i) equal pay and (ii) equal treatment for men and women in access to jobs, promotion, training and working conditions. Stage II key measures require the country to comply with Directives 79/7/EEC and 86/378/EEC, which apply the principle of equal treatment for men and women to statutory and occupational social security schemes.

- *The Constitution of the Republic of Slovenia has a provision that guarantees equality of men and women. Thus, all subordinate legislation (such as labor laws) conveys equal fundamental rights.*

II. Co-ordination of Social Security Schemes. Although no harmonization in the social security schemes needs to be carried out, certain rules that prevent workers who are moving from one Member State to another from losing their social security rights have to be in place. There are no Stage I measures, but it is advised that adaptation begin at an early stage. The Community provisions on the legislation are based on four principles: (i) only one legislation can be applicable (to avoid double social security contribution); (ii) equality of treatment (same obligations and same benefits as nationals); (iii) retention of rights acquired; (iv) aggregation of periods of insurance or residence.

- *Slovenian laws that regulate social security schemes treat foreigners and nationals equally. Compulsory pension and invalidity insurance schemes also include foreign citizens. Social assistance is allowed only for Slovenian permanent residents and, in the Law of Family Benefits, certain rights are provided only for Slovenian citizens. In terms of international coordination, social security in Slovenia is regulated by bilateral agreements (18 countries, of which the majority are members of EU or have applied for membership).*

III. Health and Safety at Work. Measures at Stage I require compliance with Directive 89/391/EEC, which stipulates that the employer has to assess the risks to safety and health at work, to make sure that workers receive appropriate safety and health information and to provide workers with adequate safety and health training. Legislation should also include provisions regarding protective and preventive services, health surveillance and the participation of workers on health and safety issues at work. At Stage II, countries are required to examine and comply with a set of 13 Directives which contain regulations on the achievement of satisfactory level of health and safety of workers in the most critical areas (workplace equipment, safety signs, chemical exposure).

- *The Law on Safety at Work in Slovenia covers regulations required at Stage I and most of the areas comprised in the 13 directives. Nonetheless, some of the regulations are 40 years old. Parliament is in the process of adopting a new law, which would cover the necessary changes, related to individual fields of safety at work. Enforcement in this field is regulated by the Law on Labor Inspection.*

IV. Labor Law and Working Conditions. At Stage I, countries are required to comply with the contents of four Directives which provide protection of worker rights on the issues of: (i) collective redundancies; (ii) undertakings, businesses, or part of businesses; (iii) insolvency of employers; (iv) young people at work. At Stage II, they are required to comply with the contents of three additional Directives, which regulate terms and working conditions, working time, and information and consultation.

- *The Labor Relations Act regulates the procedures of dismissal for operational reasons (technological, organizational, economic or measures imposed by the State). The Law contains provisions for collective dismissals in the event of a large number of redundancies. On the other hand, the law does not explicitly provide a provision for the continuation of the contract of employment in the event of change of ownership, nor does it include change of ownership as a reason for termination of employment. The takeover of workers in case of activity transfer is defined in the general collective agreement for the commercial sector. Future legislation will stipulate that employment contracts will not terminate in cases of legal and, organizational changes, mergers, affiliation or division of the employer, and transfers of part of businesses. The Labor Relations Act regulates issues concerning persons in employment -- defined as persons over 15 years of age. The Law has provisions that protect young people, such as students and pupils, who can work only if they are 15 years of age or older and can then work only under temporary contracts. It also has provisions for workers under 18 years of age, who may not work more than full-time (defined as 42 hours a week). Finally, labor legislation contains the basic limitations and arrangements concerning working time, which are in accordance with the fifth Directive.*

Compliance with some EU regulations could increase labor costs and adversely affect labor demand and enterprise competitiveness. Implementing such regulations means also setting up ways to monitor compliance by firms (labor inspection, for instance) and allowing workers to exercise their rights (through administrative and judiciary bodies). Budgetary resources will need to be devoted to these activities. Once the broader impact of reforms is factored in, however, the net impact on economic efficiency and welfare is likely to be positive. For one, health costs may come down and (after accession) the coordination of social security systems could enhance labor mobility, thus reducing unemployment pressures. In some areas, adoption of EU legislation could help increase labor market flexibility, thus bringing down the cost of labor and increasing potential labor demand. The pre-accession strategy should thus focus on: a) the early adoption of those EU norms that would make labor market institutions more flexible; b) the gradual adoption of those reforms/or enforcing the compliance with existing laws in cases where benefits exist but also entail transitional costs (health and safety at work); and c) delaying adoption of EU norms which will restrict flexibility (the case of firing costs).

In the run-up to accession, there is an opportunity to make Slovenia's labor markets more efficient. In a time of rapid economic change, labor market flexibility would ease the reallocation of factors of production from non-competitive to competitive firms, thus feeding economic growth while reducing unemployment. Moving quickly towards mutual recognition of educational and training systems and professional qualifications with the EU will help Slovenia strengthen its human capital. Investments in education are likely to have the highest returns. The rapid professionalization of its civil service needs to be part of this process. Preparing for, negotiating, legislating, and implementing EU norms requires intensifying the training of civil servants, including intermediate and technical staff.

Another impediment to a successful labor market lies in the resistance of employers to high social insurance contributions and to other types of payroll taxation. One reason for weak employment growth appears to be the perverse incentives of the tax system. At a time when the government is concerned about employment, Slovenia has a tax system that is pro-capital when it comes to the selection of production technique. This may be an outcome of the need to promote modernization of the industrial sector through generous capital depreciation schedules. Nonetheless, the privatization process, biased in favor of insider ownership, couple to the still high cost of capital, may have, in part, actually neutralized the pro-capital tax effort. The tax system labor bias -as large as those observed in many LDCs- is due to the high social security contributions, payroll and wage taxes, high personal income tax rates (relative to corporate income tax rates), and the generous depreciation schedule for capital. All add up to a substantial bias against labor, thus limiting the creation of new job opportunities.

Table 7.7. Statutory Social Contributions Rates in Slovenia, Europe, and the OECD
(percent of gross wage bill)

Country	Employers	Employees	Total	o/w Pensions	Share of Pensions
Slovenia	**15.9**	**22.1**	**38.0**	**24.4**	**64**
European Union [1]	23.6	12.9	36.5	20.6	56
Western Europe [2]	22.1	11.7	33.8	19.3	57
OECD [3]	16.2	8.6	24.8	13.2	53

Notes: 1/ Un-weighted average of the EU-15 excluding Denmark.
2/ The above plus un-weighted average of Iceland, Norway, and Switzerland.
3/ The above plus un-weighted average of Australia, Japan, Mexico, New Zealand, and the US.
Source: Ministry of Finance and OECD, *The Tax and Benefit Position of Production Workers,* Paris.

Surveys of small employers[2] suggest that excessive labor taxation, including social security contributions, represent an important impediment to the development of small enterprises (in addition to a lack of credit and to severe procedural obstacles to the start-up of new businesses). Total social security contributions in Slovenia amount to 38 percent of gross wages, whereas the average contribution rate for the EU countries is 36 percent. However, social security is not the only tax (contribution) affecting the wage bill. For workers under temporary contracts, a 25 percent *payroll tax* is levied. There is also a *tax on wages*, with progressive rates assessed according to a monthly gross wage paid by employers. This

---

[2] OECD (1996), *Small Business in Transition Economies*, Working Papers, Vol. IV, Paris.

tax-based income policy taxes wages that deviate upward from the average wage. In sum, with a 17-50 percent marginal income tax rate, a 16 percent social security contribution rate paid by employers and up to a 15 percent wage tax, labor related taxes for the firm seem to be disproportionally high compared to capital taxes.

As the fiscal situation permits, there should be efforts to reduce taxes on labor, in particular the wage tax and contributions for pensions, sickness and employment insurance. High taxes on labor are not only harmful to job creation but may also encourage tax evasion. While it is likely that this is currently less a problem in Slovenia than in other transition economies, small firms typically cannot afford the same compensation costs as larger enterprises; they are more difficult to target for audit and enforcement. Thus, if taxes are too high, fewer small firms will be established, wages will tend to be under-reported, and the size of the informal sector will tend to increase. The experience of other transitional economies suggests that, in an economy undergoing rapid structural change, a vicious circle of increasingly high tax rates and a shrinking tax base could be set in motion.

Perhaps reflecting a more favorable starting position, Slovenia took the lead among CEE countries in stabilizing and transforming its economy. Tight macroeconomic policies and early structural reforms positioned Slovenia well ahead of the others for early EU membership. This leadership, however, has been endangered by the recent stalling of the reform agenda, which threatens strong and sustainable economic growth. While GDP has increased since 1993, growth has been modest in comparison with other leading CEE transition economies. Structural reforms have advanced but remain largely incomplete. Most pressing, employment has not recovered in spite of the return of output growth.

Slovenia's bid to join the EU provides an opportunity for a new "push" of profound structural reforms that will accelerate adjustment and modernization of policies and institutions. Membership will require Slovenia to adjust its policies and laws to the norms set out in the EU's treaties, directives and regulations, known collectively as the *acquis communautaire*. This will also require the development of human and institutional capacity to implement and enforce the *acquis* in a sustained and systematic way. For some EU directives, compliance will mean sizable investments. The *acquis* will act both as a benchmark and a powerful lever for advancing structural reform. Slovenia's membership in the EU will not only require massive restructuring and modernization of most sectors, but will encourage a crucial reallocation of resources in the economy. Labor markets will thus play a crucial role, not only in the process of adjustment, but for Slovenia to compete in the EU internal market.

Agricultural Sector in Transition

Introduction

The Slovenian agriculture sector is economically small but environmentally and socially important. More than half of Slovenia is covered with forests and more than 70 percent of the total land is made of high mountains or areas with very difficult agricultural production conditions. With the exception of the eastern part of the country, meadows and pastures dominate the agricultural land, leaving little land for production. The agricultural sector is characterized by a differentiated system i) of part-time agricultural labor activities serving as a social buffer; ii) full-time intensive private family farming often with non-farm incomes; and iii) a few large state agricultural enterprises (the so-called "social" sector), mostly developed in the post-war period in the flat land.

Over the past years, the Slovenian agricultural sector has remained relatively unreformed. Considering much higher level of competition that Slovenia will face as part of the single European market, the process of strengthening the agricultural economy appears slow. In particular, the agricultural and food sector has not undergone a significant process of adjustment since Slovenia achieved independence in 1991. Candidacy to the EU is becoming a major factor in the shaping of agriculture and agro-industry policies in Slovenia. While in most sectors, Slovenia's bid to join the EU provides an opportunity for more radical reforms, in agriculture an early adoption of some specific and potentially costly regulations -e.g., the price structure of the Common Agricultural Policy (CAP)- could become a significant impediment, both economically and ecologically.

The transition toward the CAP and, in particular, the speed of the transition is a crucial factor that needs to be carefully assessed in view of the anticipated reforms of the CAP. In this respect, support to rural development should progressively become de-coupled from agricultural production. The government could consider developing a rural development policy, de-coupled from the traditional and largely distortive policy of protection, price support and market intervention. In addition, tourism represents a major strength for the Slovenian economy, and the image of Slovenia - an ecologically protected garden of Europe - is already being promoted. Along these two lines, a medium-term strategy for Slovenia can be built around a well-designed de-coupled policy (i.e., de-coupled from market intervention) and promote an economically sustainable protection of the environment.

Slovenia remains a predominately rural country, and thus the economic welfare of rural Slovenia cannot be overlooked. Simply put, Slovenia depends on the ability of its agriculture sector to develop. It appears that the economic welfare of Slovenia will be submitted to various new incentives resulting in: (i) the transition policy that will be developed by the Government; (ii) emerging opportunities resulting from the new economic environment; and (iii) a more competitive environment and new market incentives and constraints to farmers and entrepreneurs. These challenges affect, not only the agriculture and food sectors, but also the fragile Slovenia eco-systems (mountains; karst). Sustainable development in Slovenia is, therefore, not so much an agricultural development issue, but an issue of sustainability in rural development that simultaneously encompasses social, economic and ecological aspects. The Government of Slovenia (GOS) now faces the difficult challenge of simultaneously addressing the increasingly pressing need for harmonization to prepare the country to be in line with the *acquis communautaire,* and the equally pressing need to protect its fragile eco-systems. These two objectives, with the recent attention paid to rural development, remain compatible although still difficult to balance.

This chapter reviews the Slovenian agricultural and food sector. It describes the main policies affecting the sector, their impact on both the competitiveness of the sector and its compatibility with the *acquis communautaire*. Finally, the chapter suggests priorities and lines for a medium-term adjustment policy.

Overview of the Agriculture Sector

The Agriculture sector's contribution to the economy is small and has remained stable over the past few years, at about 4.4 percent of GDP. The share of the agricultural sector in total employment is about 10 percent. Although Slovenia is a net importer of food products, farms supply the country with much of its needs for food consumption in dairy products, eggs, pig meat, potatoes, fruit and vegetables.

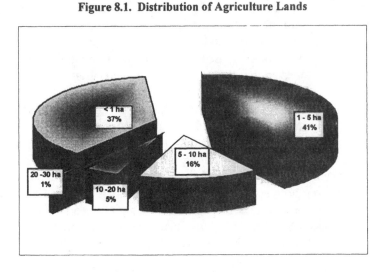

Figure 8.1. Distribution of Agriculture Lands

Slovenia's agriculture displays a strong dualism in the farming sector, with a large number of small, often labor intensive, family farms, and some large farms from the "social sector". Small farms characterize the first part of Slovenia's dual farm sector. Less than 5 percent of all farms are larger than the average European Union (EU) farm -- about 14 hectare. They cultivate about 11 percent of the agricultural land, while, in the EU, the same class of farms, cultivate about 75 percent of the agricultural land. In Slovenia, very small lots are cultivated in the absence of land consolidation. Large farms, from the so-called social sector, for which ownership is not fully clarified comprise the second category of the dual sector. Most of the family farms have developed labor intensive production - however, because of the large grasslands, dairy and cattle low intensity production prevails. Because of the high protection of the sector and the resulting high agricultural prices, only about 20 percent of private farmers secure their income exclusively from their farming. About 58 percent of the agricultural labor force thus has other economic activities; part-time farming is pervasive.

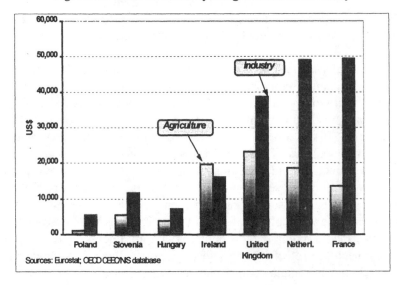

Figure 8.2. Labor Productivity in Agriculture and Industry

Sources: Eurostat; OECD CEEC/NS database

Labor productivity in Slovenian agriculture fares relatively poorly when compared to EU countries. These statistics, however, largely reflect the high level of protection and support Slovenian farmers receive from the state. Moreover, the farming sector has a highly contrasted, dual nature with mostly small family farms and the "social" sector farms. In the absence of clear statistics on the actual support the two types of farms – that is, small or "social" sector farms -- receive quantitative evidence about who benefits the most from the various price support mechanisms does not exist. It appears that while the administration of milk prices appears to benefit both types of farms, the Ministry of Economic Relations and Development (MOERD) and State Reserves interventions on wheat, rye, sugar tend to benefit the large farms from the social sector. Given relatively high support prices in numerous agricultural subsectors, statistics also show that labor productivity in agriculture is about half what it is in the Slovenian industry.

Changes observed in agricultural production since 1991 are, in part, the consequence of the sharp reduction in the exchange of products between Slovenia and the other parts of the former Yugoslavia. Nonetheless, because of the specific position as a net importer, and because of the moderate change in farm structure and ownership, Slovenia experienced a rather short fall of its agricultural production. It appears that the transition shock was not as dramatic as in most other Central and Eastern European countries (CEECs). The real issue that Slovenia now faces is preparation for the next shock that will result from further trade liberalization and, specifically, from its role within the EU single market.

Slovenia is a net importer of agricultural and food products. The agriculture and food trade deficit has stabilized over the past two years (US$475 million). Agriculture represents about 4 percent of total exports and 8.5 percent of total imports. The structure of foreign trade has remained relatively stable over the years: Slovenia's main exports, in value terms, are milk and milk products, meat and meat products (mainly poultry), beverages (alcoholic and non-alcoholic); fresh fruits (apples and pears); potatoes; hops; its main imports are wheat and coarse grains (maize), fruits, cheese, vegetables, meat.

Figure 8.3. Agriculture Trade Balance

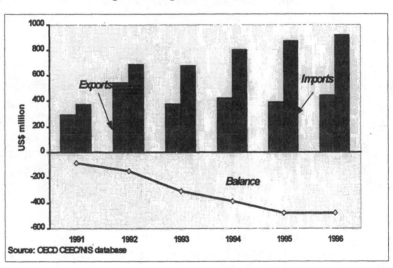

Source: OECD CEEC/NIS database

Trade with the EU fell in 1996 to 32 percent of total agri-food exports (38 percent in 1995) and represents 46 percent of agri-food imports (48 percent in 1995). Slovenia's main trading partners are the countries of the former Yugoslavia: 55.5 percent of total agri-food exports in 1996 (48 percent in 1995) and a stable 13 percent on the import side.

Slovenian agriculture is currently protected at about the same level as the EU, but the instruments of protection differ. Those instruments are not based on competitive private markets but, in sub-sectors such as wheat, rye and sugar, they remain rooted to the former centrally-planned system. Prices are supported by various mechanisms ranging from market intervention and export subsidies to trade protection (tariffs and quantitative restrictions through State trading under the direction of the MOERD). In addition, prices are still influenced by monopolistic pressures exercised by the large farms encouraged by the administrative pricing system for several crop and animal products (wheat, rye, sugar, milk, pork meat). Such monopolistic pressures are significant in the poultry sector, but are loosing significance in milk production. One can also mention the formal harmonization of prices paid for grapes and wine by the professionals in the marketing chain: the benefits from the protection against imports of wine could be subject to review from the perspective of monopolistic behavior. The Producer Subsidy Equivalent (PSE) in Slovenia was, in 1995, about 42 percent (EU: 49 percent).

Government intervention in agricultural markets has several negative long-term consequences - a policy largely inherited from the former Yugoslavia. The main consequences of the current policies are:

- The economic incentives created by the Government's interventions favor the production of low-value added agri-food products. Most measures taken either by MOERD, or by the Ministry of Agriculture, Forestry and Food (MOAFF), are still largely aimed at self-sufficiency. Neither economic incentives from actual market demand nor comparative advantage can, under such conditions, develop. Current policies create strong disincentives against high value agri-food products. This is most evident when looking at the support given to wheat or sugar producers at the expense of other products. Similarly, the export subsidies given for fresh milk - transported in tanks to Croatia - do not favor the further processing of milk into fresh dairy products or differentiated cheeses. Yet another example can be found in the wine industry, which does not feel the pressure from imports; the resulting relatively high domestic prices fail to create the incentives necessary to export. Market intervention also slows down the process of farm restructuring and largely prevents the land market from actively functioning. State-controlled farms do not feel the real need to adjust to market incentives, and family farms receive less incentives towards restructuring. A majority of these policies basically favor intensification at the expense of higher-value productions;

- Agro-industries and agricultural marketing services display a significant potential for development that remains largely untapped. The relative lack of access to competitive raw material (domestic and foreign) and the lack of incentives to adjust agricultural production toward markets, form as a major constraint to agro-industrial development. Similarly the relatively under-developed wholesale marketing enterprises in charge of assembling agricultural products and delivering them to wholesale markets or agro-processing firms, is another major constraint to the efficient supply of processing firms; and

- The State Reserves Administration remains a significant economic burden on Slovenia's budget as well as its economic development. The principles under which it operates, at present, do not concur with the EU principles as listed by the Treaty of Rome, nor do they concern with the *acquis communautaire* and the institutions of the Common Agricultural Policy (CAP).

The opening of Slovenia to foreign markets, and, in the case of accession to the EU, to competition from other EU countries, will undoubtedly come as a shock to Slovenia's largely unprepared agricultural sector. Although PSEs for both Slovenia and the EU appear of the same order of magnitude, the instruments of the respective policies are different. In Slovenia, these differences result in the relative absence of efficient marketing channels at the wholesale level. Moreover, they are constrained by i) direct intervention by the State Reserves Administration; ii) a weak marketing cooperative industry; iii) the lack of incentives to add value to agricultural products and, iv) as the domestic market is artificially very attractive, the lack of incentives to export. In the coming years, Slovenia faces a difficult challenge. On one hand, Slovenia must strengthen its agriculture and food sector, preparing it for this new and increased competition in the single EU market. On the other hand, Slovenia must protect its fragile eco-system against potentially negative consequences of an intensification of its agriculture and a poorly managed land consolidation process. With the objective of harmonizing the Slovenian legislation with the EU regulations in agriculture and food, it would be appropriate to progressively open the domestic markets to foreign competition and, take into consideration the on-going discussions on the reform of the CAP.

Foreign investment would not only contribute to the necessary restructuring of the food sector but would add higher-value to agricultural products. Foreign investment in the sector, thus far constrained for various reasons, would facilitate the restructuring process, both in agriculture and in agroindustry. Slovenia's good transport infrastructure will be a major asset for the country, particularly, its well-equipped and well-organized port of Koper, good railway infrastructure and improving roads.

The strengthening of the MOAFF in relation to the up-coming negotiations with the EU and the harmonization process should be urgently addressed. A handful of hard working civil servants will no longer be able to respond to the new tasks in terms of policy adjustment and implementing capability. In this process, outsourcing of selected services could be developed. Contracting specific tasks to private sector or Universities for example could help alleviate the current burden the MOAFF faces. Significant budget savings would also result from the modification of the role of the MOERD in the areas of price administration, foreign trading activities and State Reserves. Similarly, the restructuring and partial privatization of selected state agencies in charge of consumer protection, food quality inspection - particularly improving food and live animal inspection at the borders of the country - could be prepared and launched. (The example of New Zealand could be used in this field.) This new approach, frequently used in market economies, would transform the role of Government and Universities in the direction of a proactive support to a new food quality management and control system.

The government policy toward self-sufficiency is unsustainable. The current policies directly support agriculture through price controls and direct subsidies; these policies would benefit from a open review of their real objective. One might well question why central authorities still expect a high degree of difficulty in supplying food to a population of only 2 million. Most families, farmers and non-farmers, have a garden, usually well cultivated; transportation by train and port infrastructure is largely adequate; neighboring countries are mostly net exporters of basic food staples such as cereals and sugar. It is thus not clear why the country still believes it is important to centrally administer the supply of these products.

The current incentive framework does not adequately prepare the country for future competition. Market demand is poorly transmitted to farmers by often-inefficient marketing channels and by a centrally-planned system largely inherited from the former Yugoslavia. In most sectors of the economy, Slovenia's bid to join the EU will provide an opportunity for more radical reform. In agriculture, however, the continuation of a highly protective policy and the early adoption of the instruments of the CAP would slow down the restructuring process that the sector urgently needs. The early adoption of some specific and potentially costly regulations, such as the price structure, could become not only a significant economic impediment but could also have negative ecological implications -- pushing further intensification of production in areas where soils should be protected. Admittedly the country faces a dilemma for products for which production and marketing quotas are enforced in the EU. How, for instance, will Slovenia develop a good starting position in the dairy industry without affecting the quantities the country will be allowed to produce. In any event, it still appears that an early restructuring of the dairy industry based on market forces and less protection would only strengthen the sector and prepare it for future competition.

Addressing the relative absence of budget resources targeting rural development would provide the best opportunity given to the government to re-think its policies regarding rural regions and agriculture. In doing so, Slovenia would participate in the recent trend, observed in the EU and other countries, toward the de-coupling of income support from market intervention and protection of eco-systems (soils erosion, clean water, etc.). In the long run, a clean and attractive environment is, the best comparative advantage that Slovenia could develop for both its own population and for the image of its food products.

Measures pertaining to social policy toward agriculture as well as the protection of the environment would need to be de-coupled from price support and market interference by the state institutions. It appears that the economic welfare of Slovenia will be submitted to various new incentives resulting from: i) the transition policy toward the EU; ii) emerging opportunities resulting from the new economic environment, and iii) a more competitive environment under the new mostly market-based incentives to farmers and entrepreneurs. These new challenges could affect not only the agriculture and food sectors, but also the fragile Slovenian eco-systems (mountains; karst). Sustainable development in Slovenia is, therefore, not so much an agricultural development issue as much as an issue of sustainability in rural development that would encompass simultaneously social, economic, and ecological aspects. The government is now facing the difficult challenge of simultaneously addressing the increasingly pressing needs for harmonization to prepare the country to be in line with the *acquis communautaire*, and the equally pressing needs to protect its fragile eco-systems.

Agro-industrial Sector Policies

Slovenia's input processing industry is relatively undeveloped. In the past, most of its agricultural inputs were produced in other republics of the former Yugoslavia, and therefore, a large share of Slovenia's farm input supply is imported. The fertilizers industry is composed of four enterprises -- the largest one representing, in 1994, about 83 percent of the total output of the industry.

Confusion over the definition of agro-industry,[1] and difficulties in accessing data[2] make it difficult to present a global picture of the structure of the industry. The Slovene food industry is composed of 271 enterprises (1996) with a total of 14,150 employees. The largest processing enterprises, in terms of employees are in the dairy, non-alcoholic beverages and milling industry; in terms of output, the largest processing firms are in the dairy, brewing and tobacco sector. A 1993 survey gives a global picture of the food industry showing, in first place, the meat processing industry with less than 30 percent of the total food industry; it is followed by five subsectors representing each about 13 percent of the total gross output: dairy, grain, sugar and confectionery, fruit and vegetables and alcoholic beverages. Although exact figures on the overall profitability of agroindustry is not known but is likely to benefit from the high protection against imports.

The dairy industry started its restructuring in only one enterprise, the Ljubljana factory which processes about 150,000 tons per year -- accounting for about 37 percent of the total milk processed in the country. Six other factories process only between 22,000 and 50,000 tons of raw milk. One third of the dairy enterprises are private. Out of the 388 million of liters processed in 1995, about 35 percent were sold as fresh pasteurized and sterilized UHT milk. Although the range of product is wide, from fresh dairy products to various types of cheeses, domestic and export marketing strategies - in particular product differentiation and new products - are weak.

The structure of the industry in terms of the number of agroindustrial factories does not correctly reflect the situation in terms of ownership. As a matter of fact, one privatized company, Mercator, prominent in the retail industry, also has majority stakes in eight enterprises (oilseed crushing and refinery; dairy processing; meat processing; bakery; pasta processing; etc.) and minority stakes in a large

---

[1] Particularly in the type of ownership and in the classification of food industries.

[2] Particularly in the cereal processing sector.

number of so-called cooperative enterprises (see below). This prominent participant in the food industry[3] has developed a strategy to devolve processing activities to specialize in retailing activities.

Table 8.1. Structure of Food Industry (Private and Public Sector)

	Number of enterprises	Share in total output of the sub-sector (percent)-		Average value added per capita
		Largest enterprise	Three largest ent..	US$
Non alcoholic beverages.	20	46	82	30,000
Malting and brewing	8	51	99	95,000
Alcoholic beverages.	22	31	71	23,000
Sugar confectionery and chocolate	4	63	99	18,000
Biscuit, bakery and pastry	88	21	41	23,000
Pasta	12	79	89	8,000
Ice cream	1	100	100	34,000
Other food products	134	10	24	26,000
Tobacco	1	100	100	45,000

Source: Ministry of Economic Affairs, European Union Questionnaire update (1997).

There are four main areas through which Slovenian agro-industrial enterprises could improve their profitability and competitiveness. Strengthening these four areas would help them better compete in the new single market environment. The four areas are:

- The sub-optimal allocation of raw agricultural products. With a large number of small farms, processing enterprises are obliged to organize for very small deliveries of agricultural products. This is particularly true for milk, cereals, or fruits (to be processed). In the dairy sector, cooperatives around the world provide good intermediation services between processing firms and individual farmers; in Slovenia, private wholesale merchants and marketing cooperatives acting as real enterprises (as opposed to facilitators to intermediation only) need to be developed. The current situation results in relatively high costs (logistics, quality control, administration). This is, in part, the consequence of the relatively under-developed market intermediation services for allocating agricultural products over: (i) time (mostly within one crop year); (ii) space (between surplus and deficit areas, domestically and abroad); and (iii) quality (adjusting the various qualities to the various users). As seen above, centrally-administered prices and margins in several sub-sectors prevent markets from playing their allocative role. In the context of the single EU market, and in the absence of substantial improvement of the wholesale marketing system, food processing enterprises are likely to turn to other EU countries to supply their agricultural inputs (e.g., in large shipments of standardized raw agricultural products). The main impediments to the development of trading enterprises are, in particular, the interference by the MOERD and the State Reserves Administration, and the imperfect level of competition observed in several sub-sectors largely protected from foreign competitors;

- The respective roles of individual enterprises and State agencies in the management of food quality. The responsibility of the participants in the food marketing chain is to determine the quality of the products delivered to their clients, particularly in relation to potential health hazards and environmental impact. This responsibility applies, not only to domestic markets, but also to imports and exports. The GOS is aware of the pending problems of harmonization

---

[3] The eight majority Mercator food processing factories constitute about 13 percent of the total turnover of the company (81 percent being retail), i.e., about US$120 million. The management of the company indicates that the share of Mercator in the total food industry output of Slovenia is about 20 percent.

with the EU system (legislation, implementation and enforcement). Accordingly, the GOS will have to make a number of decisions including: a transfer to the private sector of a rather large reduction in the number, and a substantial reassignment of the roles, of state agencies regarding standards, quality control and health safety. During negotiations for EU membership, Slovenia will soon have to demonstrate that its food legislation as well as the ability of its enforcement agencies are fully compatible with the EU directives on food hygiene, inspection and certification, and legal responsibilities of producers. Not only is such ability crucial for Slovenian products, but also to control products imported into the EU from third countries through Slovenian borders;

- Marketing strategies (differentiation of consumer products). There is a significant scope for a larger contribution of agro-industry to the economic growth of Slovenia. At present, most of the marketing strategies in the food and wine sector target the domestic market. Although adapted to the specificities of the domestic market, technological choices will be re-shaped in the case of accession to the EU single market by three main elements:

  - the new market environment, particularly by the new competition for market share by a highly concentrated retail industry (in Slovenia, large retailing enterprises with super- or hyper-markets in the suburbs of the largest cities, mostly owned by foreign investors, have started to emerge);
  - the new set of incentives resulting from the harmonization of legislation regarding food quality; and
  - the new opportunities that could result from a second set of reforms of the CAP for agricultural commodities.

- Industrial strategies (consolidation through mergers and acquisitions). Market pressure for economies of scale and for new industrial and commercial strategies will lead to consolidation through mergers and acquisitions. Some factories might have to close and others to develop new activities. For undifferentiated products, the reduction of processing costs will lead to mergers and acquisitions in sub-sectors such as dairy processing, for which the size of the individual units are sub-optimal. This restructuring process has already started (e.g., dis-investment by Mercator, and consolidation of several dairy processing plants). Finally, direct transfers from budget to selected enterprises such as in the milling, sugar or poultry sector are not viable in the long-run, and new strategies should be sought to adjust the concerned enterprises.

Rural Finance and the Cooperative Sector

Slovenia is characterized by a weak cooperative sector largely oriented toward intermediation, with minimal value added in this process. It is characterized by a network of credit cooperatives dependent on a few founding enterprises, and on its role in the distribution of credit subsidies. A majority of marketing cooperatives are multi-purpose enterprises; within their various activities and accounts, they tend to balance loss-making sub-sectors through direct transfers from their profit-making activities. In an environment with stronger market pressures, such practices are often dangerous. They can create unhealthy conflicts of interest within the membership of the coop. In addition, marketing cooperatives are very often, at most, the accounting agent for food processing enterprises (e.g., in the dairy sector). Similarly, credit cooperatives display significant weaknesses; they do not add significant value in terms of financial intermediation to the agricultural and food sector. Their weaknesses come, in part, as a result of their legal statute. They mix, in their membership, individual members - mostly farmers and employees of cooperatives - and, generally, two to four founding cooperatives. Their existence remains largely based on a captive "*clientele*" of members using their services for the transfer of payments, including salaries, and the transfer of credit subsidies to farmers.

The weak credit cooperative sector does not bring efficient financial services to the agricultural sector. With its close political links to the MOAFF, cooperatives remain in part an informal arm of the Government to implement agricultural policy. The weakness of the credit cooperatives thus seems to come from: (i) the confusion in their role regarding the development of the agricultural and agro-industrial sector (as opposed to their limited number of marketing and processing enterprises in their membership); (ii) their dependence on direct State support to farmers; and (iii) their inability to develop self-guided and self-financed business strategies for their members (e.g., independent from Government). The implementation of the new Bank Law, with its more stringent financial requirements from savings banks, might accelerate the restructuring of credit cooperatives.

Figure 8.4. Structure of the Cooperative Sector

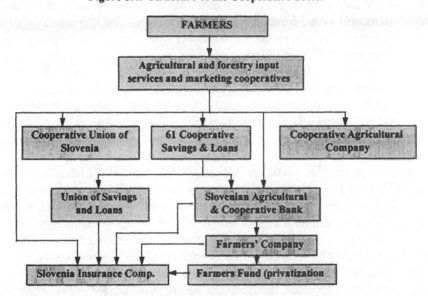

The co-existence of two categories of members in the same legal entity is inappropriate because it can create conflict between the two kinds of members in the management of the enterprise. In the case of financial problems, it can create conflict over the sharing of financial losses and liabilities among members. This prevents small farmers from taking real interest in both the management of their cooperative and in the design of its commercial and industrial strategy. As a result, a large number of Slovenian cooperatives have not been able to play a major role in adding value to agricultural products. In this context, their ambition to take over the majority of the newly privatized food processing enterprises can be questioned from the viewpoint of the overall economic development of the country. This same weakness is also reflected in the membership of the Cooperative Savings and Loans (CSL), which further constrains their development. As a matter of fact, the founding members of the CSL are liable for the totality of the losses without any limitation, while the individual members do not face the same risk. It appears that the CSL act as a pump of relatively cheap financing to: (i) the founding enterprises (usually 2 to 4 founding members per CSL) by channeling individual members' deposits to finance investments and working capital for the founding enterprises[4]; and (ii) to selected individual farmers for some of their inputs and investments at subsidized rates.

---

[4] Indicative figures show that, while deposits in the CSL come 70 percent from individual members and 30 percent from founding enterprises, the majority of credit (possibly up to 70 percent) would go to the founding enterprises.

Preferential credit programs to agriculture and agro-industry will need to be revised; they should remain at rates at least higher than the interest paid on term-deposit accounts. In the context of the EU, it is likely that credit subsidies will not be allowed at the national level as they would distort competition among member countries.

Private Sector Development in the Service Industries to Agriculture

Under market pressures, job transfers between agriculture and the agri-service industry (inputs and output), or to other sectors should be anticipated. Appropriate planning and accompanying measures, such as training programs or streamlined procedures for enterprise creation, need to be developed. The land market remains too small/narrow to facilitate the consolidation of land in larger farms easier to cultivate. The relative increase in labor productivity expected in agriculture will release a number of individuals from farming activities. In rural areas, parallel with the natural reduction in employment at the farm level, a significant shift from farm to agricultural and other services in rural areas, is expected. Part of the adjustment will come from natural attrition. With the recommended reforms toward more market and less protection, improvement in the access to modern agricultural inputs and to efficient marketing and processing services will facilitate the transfer of jobs from agriculture *stricto sensu* to agri-services and to other emerging sectors. The percentage of agricultural production actually commercialized remains very low.[5] With higher incomes, stricter quality control procedures, and the need to improve post-harvest technologies, there is scope for a substantial increase in these figures, and accordingly, in employment in relation with marketing services. The question over the next five to ten years is whether such increase can counterbalance the reduction expected in farm employment.

The education system, in particular secondary agricultural schools, have already moved toward the training in skills related to service industries and non-agricultural part-time activities such as tourism. At the graduate and post-graduate levels, the current effort (education and research) by specialized universities in the area of agricultural economics, agribusiness, food technology, and quality management should be actively supported, particularly through joint programs with foreign Universities. While part-time farming is likely to remain a significant characteristic of Slovenian agriculture, with an appropriate effort in training (technical skills as well as managerial skills), in the development of rural infrastructure and in the financing of rural services, the expected significant transfer of the labor force from agriculture to the agricultural service sector could be facilitated.

Adjustment of the Central Administration

To prepare and strengthen Slovenia's various state agencies for changes in the role of State versus private sector and for harmonization with the EU's *acquis communautaire*, a thorough review of the strengths and weaknesses of these institutions is necessary. Two areas appear of particular urgency: the State Reserves Administration has been already discussed; in addition, the growing administrative burden to be expected in the context of the negotiations with the EU, and the actual changes in the role of the State. With the expected harmonization of regulations with the EU, Slovenia needs to be a credible partner for the enforcement of policies regarding agriculture and food, rural development, environment and consumer protection. The relatively small civil service must be strengthened to address the dialogue with the foreign partners of Slovenia; procedures in the dialogue with the EU must be streamlined.

---

[5] The Statistical Office of Slovenia indicates the following figures for 1995 (given as a percentage actually commercialized out of total production): wheat = 51; maize = 8; potatoes = 3; apples = 34; pears = 24; peaches = 23; grape = 31; vegetables 5; eggs = 42; beef and veal = 68; pig meat = 49; poultry meat = 89; and milk = 67.

Control of the implementation of the various policies should be transferred, as much as possible, to the private sector. In this context, the MOAFF's actions in both negotiations and collaboration with the European Commission (EC), might be facilitated by increasingly contracting (outsourcing) with outside institutions (private sector, University, professional associations).

Strengthen Private Sector Links

Representation of private interest for each profession in the various agricultural and food subsectors remains a weak element. In the EU, such representation is a crucial element of the CAP. It helps foster a better cross-understanding of private interests by the EC and the governments, and symmetrically, a better understanding and implementation of government policies by the private sector. In addition, many decisions related to trade, research and technology, market information, and training could be collectively by operators belonging to the same profession or those belonging to the same marketing chain (the so-called interprofessional associations). In Slovenia, these private professional associations and interprofessional associations, independent from the government, do not cover the full spectrum of the concerned marketing chains from farmers to retailers and traders.[6] The strengthening of such organizations should be promoted; technical cooperation with similar foreign organizations should be developed. They should also be scrutinized from the view point of the risk of cartelization. Among the services that agriculture and agro-industries lacks, one can list the following:

- Consultation with state agencies intervening in the subsector;
- Analysis and information on markets and regulations (domestic and foreign);
- Organization of technical or commercial training programs;
- Contracting for research on issues of common interest with domestic or foreign institutions;
- Organization of first instance arbitration of trade conflicts; and
- Development of facilitating procedures and instruments for the exchange of products.

Agriculture and the EU Accession Process

The original principles of the CAP were aimed at achieving food security through high prices in the original six country members of what was, at the time, the European Economic Community (EEC). The Treaty of Rome of 1957 and the conference of Stresa in 1958 assigned a series of objectives to the CAP that were chiefly aimed at achieving food security through a pricing system at levels higher than world prices. In 1962, after the establishment of the CAP, national market price support systems were consolidated at the Community level. These systems were exclusive of other national price and trade policy instruments, which they replaced for all the main EEC's agricultural products. Specific regulatory instruments for individual agricultural subsectors were progressively introduced and adjusted over the years. Until 1992, the CAP was based mostly on a combination of: (a) market management instruments through price support mechanisms (intervention), protection against imports (minimum threshold price and variable import levies), and exports refunds; (b) supply management instruments (production quotas); and (c) direct income support to producers when the GATT did not permit high variable tariffs.

The administration of the CAP is implemented through national intervention agencies. The set of administrative prices to be introduced for the following crop year is decided by the Council of Ministers of the member countries, based on proposals made by the European Commission. The budget for these

---

[6] The most important association covering several elements of the agricultural and food marketing chain is the Business Association of Food Industry of Slovenia, with 85 members covering most food branches with the exception of wheat (bakeries, millers), sugar and confectionery, and wine.

activities is voted by the European Parliament. It must be noted that the budget discussions are the principle means by which the European Parliament can influence the CAP. The administration of the instruments of the CAP constitutes a rather complex system based on: (a) market-management committees where the European Commission, together with the representatives of each member country, decide upon adjustment of the implementation of the CAP (e.g., export refunds or export taxes); and (b) intervention agencies. Such agencies are charged with the gathering and dissemination of market information, the administration of the purchase of commodities at the support price from wholesale agents, and their storage and release on domestic or third countries markets. As a result, for the two leading prices -- the import price[7] and the support price[8] -- the private sector operates freely and at market prices in the internal EU common market. In addition, intervention boards in each individual member country implement the CAP through the private sector. Such principles and instruments require significant adjustment of the Slovenian price and trade policy. Although favorable in the short-term for farm incomes, the CAP -with the limitation of production the EU system implies for milk[9]- would create a significant constraint to the restructuring of the Slovenian dairy industry and to its long-term competitive ability.

---

[7] Until 1993, for most agricultural products, an administrative price was fixed for the entire crop year, with a system of variable import levies to reach that price. With the GATT/WTO agreement, this was transformed into an *ad-valorem* tariff.

[8] The intervention price is guaranteed to licensed wholesalers (private traders, cooperatives or processing firms). As such, the resulting level of farmers' support is below the official intervention price-i.e., after a marketing margin is taken by the private intermediaries. The fact that intervention does not interfere with the free allocation of products over regions in the EU is illustrated by the fact that only intervention centers located in surplus regions of the EU are activated by the private sector.

[9] Particularly if the production quotas are based on the current low yields and low intensity of production of Slovenia.

Public Services and Municipal Infrastructure

Introduction

In order to improve the quality of life of its people, increase environmental protection standards and facilitate the country's accession to the European Union (EU), Slovenia will have to design and put into operation a consistent set of policy measures aimed at improving and expanding the provision of public services in the country. Efficient, reliable and user-oriented public utilities are an important component of a well-functioning market economy. The quantity and quality of infrastructure services is therefore an important determinant of a country's overall productivity, regional development and growth prospects. Given that the municipal infrastructure in Slovenia has been strongly under-financed during the transition,[1] the sector is becoming a growing obstacle for the country's economic development and its expeditious accession to the EU. Meeting EU directives in number of areas, like environment, transport, water supply, waste water collection and treatment and solid waste management, requires from the country large investments, in particular at the municipal level.

This chapter analyses the current status of municipal infrastructure development in Slovenia in view of its accession to the EU. Within this general framework, the chapter has the following three specific objectives: (i) to review municipal infrastructure as an integral part of the country's economic infrastructure development, (ii) to identify the main issues, strengths and weaknesses, of municipal infrastructure in Slovenia, and (iii) to suggest policy measures aimed at market-oriented municipal sector development that is consistent with the EU requirements. The second section discusses the municipal sector in the context of overall economic infrastructure development in Slovenia, analyzing the main characteristics of each of the three economic infrastructure sectors (energy, transport and telecommunications and municipal services). The section there quantifies both medium-term investment needs of these sectors, contrasting them with the availability of public funds. The third section addresses key issues in municipal infrastructure development: it presents the existing institutional, legal and regulatory environment for municipal infrastructure development. The section focuses on the analysis of the financial performance of municipal infrastructure service providers and on municipal infrastructure investment trends and prospects. Finally, in the last concludes with section policy measures.

Infrastructure Development at the Municipal Level

Current Status of Economic Infrastructure Development

Energy, transport and telecommunications, and the provision of municipal services by public utilities, such as water supply, waste water collection and treatment, and solid waste management, are the corner stone of the economic infrastructure. This economic infrastructure links all elements of the economy and facilitates or hinders adequate flows of production factors, goods and services. The economic infrastructure contributes to about 15 percent of Slovenia's GDP and accounts for some 20 percent of the country's total investment (equivalent to 5 percent of GDP). Although combined budgetary

---

[1] See Mojmir Mrak, *Infrastructure Investment Needs in Slovenia.* IB Revija (Ljubljana), Vol. 31, No. 12, 1997 and *Communal Infrastructure in Slovenia: Survey of Investment Needs and Policies Aimed at Stimulating Private Sector Participation.* Ljubljana, 1998.

allocations -- state budget and local community budgets -- for economic infrastructure investment increased from 1.6 to around 2 percent of GDP during 1992-96, the relative importance of state budget financing, as a principal funding source, almost halved in this period (from 69 percent in 1992 to 39 percent in 1996). This trend has been caused, not only by a growing volume of infrastructure financing need, but also by an improved access of service providers to various forms of debt financing and the tight fiscal policy of the government during the transition.

Slovenia's physical stock of infrastructure and its infrastructure policies are not adequately suited to its needs as an emerging market economy. In the energy sector, for example, the main legacies of the past are high-energy intensity, insufficient capacity,[2] maintenance and renewal, as well as inadequate environmental performance. The transportation sector is also confronted with several problems. Traffic flows are strongly concentrated on road transportation, exposing the country to significant environmental risks; these flows have also been associated with a low level of road safety. There are several factors behind the relatively small share of the railway sector in total transportation in Slovenia. These factors are partly related to geographical characteristics of the country (short distances among major destinations in the country) and partly to the railway's technical and technological patterns, especially to its poor accessibility. As far as telecommunications are concerned, its penetration rate is relatively high relative to other transition economies, although further modernization is necessary. In the municipal infrastructure sector, some services, such as water, were abundantly supplied with limited regard to economic or environmental costs while others, such as wastewater treatment, were largely under-supplied.

The strategic objective for infrastructure development in Slovenia is to move towards reliable and cost efficient energy, transportation, telecommunication and public utility services, which will take due account of security of supply, the safety of the population, rational use of energy and protection of the environment. In order to achieve this, a whole range of co-ordinated policy measures must be designed and put into operation. Their common denominator is a more commercial approach to infrastructure sectors development.

One of the key elements of the market-oriented transformation of public utilities in Slovenia is the introduction of cost-conscious and demand-oriented production, as well as more careful pricing of services. The price reform and effective collection of tariffs are crucial in balancing the supply and demand for infrastructure services as well as achieving the financial viability, and accountability, of infrastructure service providers. In the past, the overall level of prices and tariffs for services provided by public utilities has tended to be below that level which allows cost recovery. As a result of the government's general policy of containing inflation, this is still the case -with end-user prices of many services provided by utilities, including gas, transport fuels, electricity, municipal services, fixed telephony services and public transport. The gap between actual and cost recovery prices and tariffs has been narrowed over the years. Prices for domestic coal are, however, higher than import prices; it is part of the strategy for the gradual closing-down of non-profitable coal mines.

In spite of numerous sector specific patterns, the economic infrastructure sectors in Slovenia also have many things in common: (i) provision of services continues to be the rear exclusive domain of the public sector; (ii) the sectors are currently involved in some type of reform aimed at harmonizing the legislation and adjusting the institutional framework in line with the EU standards and requirements as set out by the *acquis*; (iii) tariff structures continue to be distorted, especially in the municipal sector, where the tariffs still do not cover all the costs and where households are still subsidized from the business sector; (iv) financial viability of infrastructure service providers in many economic infrastructure sub-sectors, such as railways and municipal infrastructure, continues to be depressed; and (v) all the sectors,

---

[2] Capacity is limited due to the planned decommissioning of the nuclear power plant Krško.

and especially municipal services, have experienced significant infrastructure investment delays over the transition years.

The main characteristics of each economic infrastructure sectors -- including ownership patterns, price setting mechanisms, financial status of service providers and the investment trends of recent years -- are presented in some detail below:

Energy Sector

- *Import dependence.* Slovenia produces lignite and coal, but is highly dependent on oil and gas imports. In the early 1990s, imports of oil and gas were at a level of around 60 percent of the country's total primary energy supply. By the year 2010, this dependence is expected to increase to 70 percent. To lessen the country's import dependence, there are plans to broaden the supply base, to maintain an economically justifiable level of domestic coal production, to enhance efficiency and to promote renewable energy sources.

- *Ownership structure.* The energy industry, including the production and distribution of electricity, is still almost entirely publicly owned. The only exceptions are petroleum and gas industries where ownership is distributed predominantly among the state, other publicly owned companies, state funds and employees.

- *Prices.* As part of the government's general policy of containing inflation and protecting household consumers, some of the end-user prices, such as prices for gas, transport fuels and electricity, are still below the level of Western European countries. Prices for domestic coal are, however, higher than import prices, as part of the strategy for the gradual closing-down of non-profitable coal mines.

- *Policy orientation.* The long-term energy policy objectives and main priorities for the development of the energy sector are defined in the Strategy for Energy Use and Supply of Slovenia, adopted by the Parliament in January of 1996. Its main goals are: (i) to increase energy efficiency in all sectors of consumption, and thus to decrease overall energy intensity in the country; (ii) to minimize the growth of energy dependence, which includes building oil and gas storage capacities; (iii) to maintain a sustainable level of electric power production in the newly constructed thermal power plants; (iv) to disengage from nuclear power production in the long run; (v) to increase the share of natural gas consumed by commercial sector and households; (vi) to maintain the present rate of exploitation of domestic coal while shifting the sector away from its consumption; and (vii) to substantially increase the share of renewable energy sources, especially of hydro power.

- *Investments in the recent years.* Over the period 1992-96, investment in the energy sector had the following characteristics: (i) around 1 percent of GDP was allocated for investments in this sector; (ii) state budget resources contributed with less than 20 percent in the total energy investment financing bill; (iii) less than 10 percent of total infrastructure budget financing was channeled for energy financing, although the sector participated with over 20 percent in total infrastructure investment.

Transport and Telecommunications

- *Strong forward and backward linkages.* The sector accounts for between 6 and 7 percent of GDP. It is of strategic importance not only because it establishes conditions for mobility of goods, services, capital and persons, but also because it has strong upstream and downstream linkages with other sectors of the economy. The impact of transport and telecommunications in Slovenia extends beyond enhancing productivity and output growth, determining the way in which markets and market institutions develop.

- *Ownership structure.* A large part of the infrastructure in this sector, such as roads, railways and post services, is still entirely publicly owned. In ports, airports and telecommunications, on the other hand, ownership is typically distributed, in various proportions, among the state, employees and other owners. Foreigners do not participate as owners in any segment of Slovenia's transport and telecommunication infrastructure, except for a recent mobile telephony concession, SiMobil, that is still non-operational.[3]

- *Prices.* Many transport and telecommunication charges, such as highway tolls, prices for the transport of passengers, or post service tariffs and telecommunication tariffs, are under more or less strict government control. Prices are set on a case-by-case basis. There are, however, some segments of the transportation sector, like air traffic and maritime transport, where companies set their prices freely.

- *Policy orientation.* The strategic orientation for transport and telecommunication development has been developed in the 1995 government strategy paper, *Strategy for Economic Development of Slovenia by the Year 2000.* For both sectors, objectives can be classified in two groups. The first group is of intensified infrastructure development to strengthen transport and telecommunication links between different parts of the country, as well as with neighboring countries, and to increase competitiveness through lower-prices and improved access to infrastructure services. The second group of transportation and telecommunication objectives is differentiated. As far as transportation policy is concerned, it includes safety for all traffic participants, rational use of energy, regional development, protection of the environment and other economic objectives. Among those objectives, the most important are internalization of the transport's external costs and the creation of a regulatory environment aimed at increased commercialization and competition. A commercial approach, including gradual liberalization of prices and credible reform of tariff structures, is to be followed in the area of telecommunications. As far as postal service development is concerned, the government considers its network as satisfactory; the government's main development orientation is to improve the quality of services as well as the system's efficiency.

- *Investments in the recent period.* Over the 1992-96 period, the transport and telecommunications sectors increased the annual level of investment by more than 7 times, primarily due to investment in highway construction. As a consequence, the share of these investments increased from 1.2 percent of GDP in 1992 to 3.6 percent of GDP in 1996. Given that investments in other infrastructure sectors grew much more slowly in this period, the share of transportation and telecommunications in total infrastructure investments rose 19

---

[3] SiMobil, a company owned by an international consortium that includes Telia of Sweden, was awarded the country's second GSM in mid-1998. SiMobil is currently awaiting the issuance of the final concession agreement. SiMobil has expressed concern about the apparent slow pace of the concession granting process. Until it has entered into the concession agreement, SiMobil will be unable to obtain financing or hire employees. Under the terms of its concession, SiMobil is permitted to build its own microwave links if Telekom Slovenije cannot provide the required leased lines within three months. An open question is whether SiMobil can lease lines from alternative providers such as the railways, power companies or highway companies, which would likely be priced substantially lower than Telekom Slovenije's facilities.

percentage points, from 51 to 70 percent in the same period. The sector also attracted around three-quarters of all budgetary resources channeled for infrastructure investment. This figure includes resources earmarked and raised through the so-called gasoline tolar (a 16 percent levy on the price of gasoline) and channeled for the highway construction through the budget.

Municipal Services

- *Sector organization and ownership structure.* In contrast to energy, transport and telecommunication sectors, municipal services are managed at the local community level. Municipalities are owners of assets and have responsibility for providing the services. This has typically been done by municipality-owned public utilities.

- *Financial situation and price setting.* By and large, municipal public utilities are financially weak. The reasons for this are numerous, and many of them are rooted in the pre-transition period. At that time, municipal infrastructure relied on a centralized system for a significant share of its funding, particularly for capital investments. Tariffs were kept low, subsidizing both households and enterprises. Over the transition period, responsibility for the provision of services has been turned over to municipalities, while the flow of funds from the center has been sharply reduced. As price-setting for most services has remained under government control, tariffs have not been raised sufficiently to cover operating and capital costs. The weak financial position of municipal public utilities is one of the main reasons for investment lags in this sector.

- *Investments over the last few years.* In contrast to transport and telecommunications, where investments in nominal terms have increased by 3.5 times during 1993-96, and in contrast to the energy sector, where investments more than doubled in the same period, municipal public utilities investment stagnated in nominal and real terms over this period. As a consequence, the sector deteriorated vis-a-vis other economic infrastructure areas. Its investments, as a proportion of GDP, declined from 0.7 to 0.4 percent between 1993-96; as a proportion of total infrastructure investments, the decline was even sharper, from 20 to 8 percent. Another contrasting feature of the municipal public utilities sector is its investment financing structure, with budget transfers by far the most prominent source. In 1996, for example, budgetary funding accounted for 93 per cent of total municipal infrastructure investment. Due to their weak financial situation, service providers were practically without internal financial resources and without good access to credit financing.

Investment Needs and Funding Gap

The recent study on infrastructure investment requirements[4] has developed a rough quantification of the volume of economic infrastructure investment needs and of the funding gap between needed investments and available public funds. The study was based on two scenarios for infrastructure investment. The first one, *Investment Needs Scenario*, reflects infrastructure investment needs, as articulated by line-ministries and providers of infrastructure services. This scenario is likely to overestimate the true investment requirements. In order to obtain a meaningful assessment of the gap between Slovenia's infrastructure investment needs and its capacity for funding these investments, another scenario, *Macroeconomic Scenario* was designed. It is based on macroeconomic investment projections for Slovenia as defined in the government's official projections based on the 1997 Spring Report of the Institute for Macroeconomic Analysis and Development (IMAD).

---

[4] See Mrak, M. (1997) op. cit.

Two main conclusions can be drawn from the study with respect to infrastructure investment needs and the funding gap in Slovenia by the turn of the century. First, the line ministries and providers set infrastructure investments needs at a much higher level than corresponding sustainable investments projected by IMAD. The infrastructure investment needs for 1997 to 2000 are estimated at 8.7 percent of GDP. On the other hand, IMAD's projection estimates that the sustainable level of infrastructure investment cannot exceed 5.1 percent of GDP. According to the two scenarios, the infrastructure-funding gap amounts to almost SIT 400 billion[5] in the period 1997-2000. This is equivalent to 3.6 percent of Slovenia's GDP.

Second, the funding gap is not proportionally distributed among the different infrastructure sectors - the largest gap is estimated to be in the municipal sector. Table 9.1 shows that the funding gap in this sector is about SIT 154.1 billion. This implies that municipal sector claims are 3.5 times more than those foreseen in the government's macroeconomic projections. This gap could indicate substantial under-investments in the sector or a high overshooting in investment demands. Past under-investment is also claimed as the main reason for a significant funding gap is in the energy sector. Here, the funding gap is estimated at SIT 108.5 billion. For the 1997-2000 period, real investment needs, expressed as a percentage of GDP, are almost twice as high as estimated sustainable investments for this sub-sector. In contrast to these two sectors, investments in transport and telecommunications are considered to be much closer to the desired level of investment. The financing gap of SIT 136.9 billion amounts to 34 percent of total investment needs. The result, however, masks significant differences between individual transport branches. While the highway program seems to be relatively well off, some other segments, such as railways share the history of delayed investments characteristic of most of activities.

Table 9.1. Infrastructure Investment Needs and Funding Gap, 1997 - 2000
(in SIT million at 1996 prices)

	Investment Needs Scenario		Macroeconomic Scenario		Funding Gap	
	Volume	% of GDP	Volume	% of GDP	Volume	% of GDP
Total Planned Investment	969.5	8.7	570.0	5.1	399.5	3.6
Energy	242.6	2.2	134.1	1.2	108.5	1.0
Transport and Telecommunications	528.1	4.7	391.2	3.5	136.9	1.2
Municipal Infrastructure	198.8	1.8	44.7	0.4	154.1	1.4

Source: Mrak, M., *Infrastructure Investment Needs in Slovenia.*

Key Issues in Municipal Infrastructure Development

Legal and Institutional Framework

Before 1991, socially-owned enterprises providing public utilities were responsible for providing municipal services as well as for investing in municipal infrastructure. In many respects, these enterprises had patterns similar to enterprises in any other segment of the Slovenian economy. Although prices of municipal services were controlled by the State at the time, the sector had two stable sources for funding municipal infrastructure investment - depreciation charges and transfers from a state fund established especially for this purpose.[6]

---

[5] The amounts are estimated at 1996 prices.

[6] See Kelvišar, Marjan, *Public Sector and its Role in Financing New Infrastructure Projects*, Svetovalni Center, Ljubljana, 1998 (in Slovenian language).

In the post-independence period, the legal environment and institutional framework in which Slovenian local communities and their respective public utilities operate has dramatically changed. Under these changes, ownership of municipal infrastructure has been transferred into the hands of local communities. They have become responsible for the provision of municipal services as well as for municipal infrastructure investment. Both have been negatively affected by the fragmentation of local communities. Public utilities that have previously operated on the "one local community, one local service provider" principle have now been faced with a situation where they have to operate with more than one local community, and therefore often with more than one legal regime and tariff system.

The legal, regulatory and institutional framework addressing the municipal services and service providers consists of five laws. They are: (i) the Environmental Protection Act (adopted in 1993); (ii) the Law on Public Commercial Services (adopted in 1993); (iii) the Law on Local Self-Government (adopted in 1993); (iv) the Law on Financing Municipalities (adopted in 1994); and (v) the Law on Prices (adopted in 1991). Some of the key provisions contained in this package of legislation are addressed in the ensuing paragraphs.

Determination of "public commercial services". Although the Law on Public Commercial Services does not give a specific definition, it nevertheless provides guidance in this respect by describing them as services that are intended to guarantee products and services that are in the public interest. These services are to be provided by entities that are directly or indirectly controlled by the state or by local communities. They can be either obligatory or optional services. The former must be defined by a sectoral law, in this case by the Environmental Protection Act. They include: (i) supply of drinking water; (ii) disposal and purification of municipal waste and precipitation water; (iii) handling of municipal waste; (iv) dumping of the remains of municipal waste; (v) public hygiene and cleaning of public areas; and (vi) maintenance of public ways and green areas as well as regular control and cleaning of heating places. Local communities have the discretion to define certain other municipal services as obligatory.

Ownership transformation of municipal sector enterprises. The Law on Public Commercial Services has guided the process in conjunction with a decree that established the criteria for determining the share of socially-owned capital in the overall capital of public utilities. Based on these legal provisions (affecting 76 municipal public utilities), ownership of both municipal infrastructure and socially-owned capital (all those assets used for carrying out services that are in the "special public interest") was transferred into the hands of local communities. Once the process was completed, local communities became exclusive owners in 43 percent of all public utilities. They also acquired majority ownership shares in another 32 percent of enterprises and became minority equity holders in the remaining 25 percent of enterprises.

Legal forms of carrying out municipal services. According to the Law on Public Commercial Services and the Law on Local Self-Government, commercial public services (including local), can be provided by one of the five following legal forms: (i) administrative enterprise, (ii) public economic institution, (iii) public enterprise, (iv) concession, and (v) joint venture with public capital. In practice, public enterprises form, by far, the most frequent legal form of providing municipal services. At a time when there were 65 local communities in Slovenia, in around 80 percent of them services were provided through public enterprises, in another 13 percent through concessions, and in the remaining 7 percent of local communities through joint ventures with public capital.

Financing of Local Communities

There are three main sources of financing for local communities:

- *Local community's original revenues.* Local communities are entitled to raise their own revenues to finance public expenditure. These revenues are of two types: (i) tax.revenues; these include corporate tax, personal income tax, other personal taxes, tax on payroll, sales taxes on services and taxes on the use of goods. Some of these taxes are the exclusive revenue of local communities, while others are distributed among the State and local communities. (ii) non-tax revenues; these include duties on the use of agricultural land, administrative and other fees, fees on gambling machines, fines and some others. As shown in Table 9.2, original revenues account for around 70 to 80 percent of total local communities' budgets.

- *Transfers from the State budget.* At present, local communities can obtain resources from the state budget from two sources. The first source is the so-called financial equalization. According to the legislation, all local communities in Slovenia must provide their populations with a similar level and quality of public services. When a local community does not have sufficient resources of its own to cover expenditure for these services (so-called guaranteed expenditures), the State provides the difference. The other forms include transfers for demographically endangered regions, a water pollution tax (it can be retained in a local community if used for precisely determined investment purposes) and other special purpose transfers. In volume terms, this channel of local community funding is much less important than financial equalization (see Table 9.2).

- *Borrowing.* The State is not only the legislator but it also determines the framework for raising debt financing and continues to control the prices of many communal services. Local communities are allowed to borrow short-term to cover current expenditure, while long-term debt can be raised only for infrastructure financing. It must be underscored, however, that debt levels have to be kept within limits strictly determined by the central government.

Table 9.2 Financing of Local Communities, 1992–98
(in SIT billion)

	1992	1993	1994	1995	1996	1997*	1998**
A. Revenues	51.1	75.6	100.7	108.9	131.0	143.1	158.3
1. Original Revenues	40.4	62.0	80.5	81.2	103.3	112.1	126.3
- Tax Revenues	28.6	41.7	53.7	50.3	59.8	62.2	73.1
- Nontax Revenues	11.8	20.2	26.8	30.9	43.5	49.8	53.2
2. Transfers from the State Budget	10.7	13.6	20.3	27.7	27.6	31.1	32.0
- Financial Equalisation	10.7	13.6	19.0	24.4	23.0	28.0	29.0
- Other Transfers	--	--	1.2	3.2	4.6	3.1	3.0
B. Expenditures	51.0	75.1	99.2	103.8	125.6	142.9	157.1
1. Transfers to Social Services	21.7	30.3	39.4	46.9	51.7	57.8	62.7
2. Subsidies and Other Transfers	15.8	24.7	33.8	36.7	50.8	58.0	64.9
3. Wages	10.4	14.8	20.1	13.3	15.4	18.0	19.5
Surplus/Deficit (A - B)	0.1	0.5	1.6	5.1	5.3	0.2	1.2
C. Borrowing	1.4	1.3	1.2	0.5	1.3	1.1	0.6
1. Domestic Borrowing	0.7	1.1	1.2	0.5	1.3	1.1	0.6
2. Sales of Securities	0.8	0.2	0.1	-	-	-	-
D. Amortization	0.6	1.1	1.0	1.7	1.6	1.8	1.7
E. Net Borrowing (C – D)	0.7	0.2	0.3	-1.2	-0.3	-0.8	-1.1

Note: * Estimates.
        ** Proposed 1998 Buget Projections.
Source: Ministry of Finance.

Price Setting for Public Services and Tariff Structures

Until 1989, each municipality had a consumer-supplier council under which negotiations concerning the conditions of providing local public services took place. In principle, the consumer-supplier council set the prices for services. In practice, however, the state had a great deal of formal and informal influence on price setting, to keep public-service prices down.

One of the first steps taken by the newly independent Slovenia in 1991 was to pass the Law on Prices. As a result, prices of municipal services have continuously been under the control of the government. Although various price adjustment procedures have been applied in recent years, their common feature has been to allow prices of public utility services to rise by 80 percent of the inflation rate (as determined by the retail price index or industrial producer prices). This price-setting policy has not allowed municipal service providers to cover all their operating and capital costs. In most cases, tariffs have only been sufficient to cover current expenditures, but not to finance regular maintenance, rehabilitation or new investments.

In addition, there is another distinguishing feature of prices of municipal services in Slovenia. As in many other transition economies, there are significant differences in the price levels for water supply, wastewater and waste disposal for different groups of customers. Different prices are usually set for the four following groups of customers: (i) households, (ii) business entities, (iii) non-business entities, and (iv) other users. Table 9.3 shows that in recent years prices for municipal services have been lowest for households and highest for business entities (only in the case of waste disposal, the highest prices have been paid by the category called other users). The table also shows that the range of prices paid by different categories of users has narrowed over time.

Table 9.3. Average Prices of Municipal Services, 1991-96

	June 1991	End 1991	End 1992	End 1993	End 1994	End 1995	Aug. 1996
Water Supply*							
-Households	10.22	15.51	28.05	35.28	45.43	51.80	56.80
-Business Entities	20.91	31.37	55.63	69.20	85.81	98.58	106.38
-Non-Business Entities	15.94	24.28	40.15	49.89	64.94	84.31	92.32
-Other Users	15.97	22.54	42.30	55.39	75.64	88.12	98.96
Waste Water*							
-Households	3.07	4.44	7.77	9.84	12.97	16.87	18.03
-Business Entities	6.22	9.17	15.17	19.47	25.92	31.91	33.56
-Non-Business Entities	4.95	7.62	11.71	14.55	17.59	26.85	28.01
-Other Users	4.99	7.06	14.10	15.98	23.24	36.45	40.96
Waste Disposal**							
-Households	1.18	1.78	3.13	4.09	4.94	6.08	7.08
-Business Entities	2.89	4.31	7.28	9.58	11.92	13.81	15.23
-Non-Business Entities	1.82	2.97	5.08	6.84	7.71	10.09	11.03
-Other Users	3.30	4.50	7.18	8.67	13. 76	16.57	17.61

Notes: *   SIT/m³
            ** SIT/m²

Source: Strategy of Communal Sector Development in the Republic of Slovenia, Svetovalni Center, Ljubljana, 1997.

The existing tariff structures accompanied by changes in the structure of municipal services' consumption have strongly influenced the financial performance of service providers. In the water supply segment, for example, total water consumption remained at the same level between 1980 and 1994. In the structure of consumption, however, the share of the enterprise sector was almost halved, from 63 percent to 36 percent. This can be explained by the high increase in household sector consumption (increasing by more than 50 percent) and by the economic decline of the late 1980s and early transition years.

Financial Performance of Municipal Public Utilities

Based on the Agency for Payments database, we analysed the 1995-97 financial performance of all 78 municipal sector enterprises in Slovenia. These public utilities employed 6,224 employees in 1997. The analysis below compares the financial performance of (municipal) public utilities with that of the entire enterprise sector in the country (36,717 enterprises with 460,376 employees in 1997).

Although many different indicators can be used to assess the financial performance of enterprises, the single most important is whether the enterprise generates profits. For analytical reasons,[7] it is sensible to distinguish between different categories of financial results and consequently net profit/losses accounts. Table 9.4 shows net profit/loss position of the municipal sector enterprises in Slovenia in 1997.

Table 9.4. Municipal Sector Enterprise Performance, 1997
(in SIT million)

	Enterprise Sector	Municipal Sector
1. Net Overall Profit (+) / Loss (-)	17,859	-314
2. Net Profit (+) / Loss (-) from Regular Activity	-51,584	-1,215
3. Net Operating Profit (+) / Loss (-)	50,516	-1,378
4. Net Profit (+) / Loss (-) from Financing	-102,100	163
5. Net Profit (+) / Loss (-) from Extraordinary Revenues and Expenditures	69,443	901

Source: Calculated from Agency of Payments Database.

Net overall profit/loss balance incorporates net profit/loss from regular activity (point 2 in Table 9.4) and net profit/loss from extraordinary revenues and expenditures (point 5 in Table 9.4). The analytical value of this category is limited due to high amounts of net profit/loss from extraordinary revenues and expenses. These are a consequence of two types of accounting operations: (i) high valuation of assets and gradual spending of accumulated provisions via extraordinary revenues, and (ii) extraordinary expenses from write-offs.[8] However, in contrast to the enterprises sector that had net overall profit of SIT 17.9 billion in 1997, the municipal sector enterprises registered net overall loss of SIT 314 million.

Net profit/loss from regular activity includes net operating profit/loss (point 3 in Table 9.4) and net profit/loss from financing (point 4 in Table 9.4). In this net profit/loss category, there is a striking difference between the municipal sector enterprises and the Slovenian enterprises. Although both categories of enterprises registered net losses from regular activity in 1997, its source was very different. In the regular enterprise sector, the net loss was a combination of net operating profit (it reveals a real potential of a company for growth and development) and net loss from financing (it indicates that a company is burdened by the costs of financing). By contrast, the net losses from regular activity of municipal sector enterprises were of a completely different origin. They were the result of a net operating loss (this confirms the poor potential of these companies for growth and development) combined with a net profit from financing.

---

[7] Slovenia's accounting standards bias profit/loss accounts due to the requirement to revalue some assets.
[8] For an extended explanation of these categories see Simoneti, M., M. Rojec and M. Rems, Enterprise Sector Restructuring and EU Accession in Slovenia, Mimeo, 1998.

Net operating profit/loss is the single most important net profit/loss category for measuring a company's potential for growth and development. In contrast to the economy as a whole, which improved its financial performance over recent years, specifically, from a net loss of up to SIT 2.5 billion a year in 1995 and 1996 to a net profit of SIT 50.5 billion in 1997, municipal sector enterprises are taking just the opposite trend. In 1995 and 1996, they still had an annual net operating loss of around SIT 1 billion; in 1997, however, the net loss increased to as much as SIT 13.7 billion. This clearly confirms that the financial performance of municipal sector enterprises (public utilities) has deteriorated.

Major performance indicators for municipal sector enterprises shed some additional light on the financial performance of these enterprises and confirm the above findings. Measured by return (net operating profit/loss) on equity and sales, the municipal sector enterprises performed much more poorly in 1997 than the enterprise sector in general. A similar negative result was registered with respect to total asset turnover ratio. In municipal public utilities, the sales to assets ratio was several times higher than in the rest of the economy. High assets to equity and debt to equity ratios confirm that municipal sector enterprises are undercapitalized and that they are highly indebted. For 1997, both indicators were several times higher than the corresponding indicators for the whole enterprise sector in Slovenia.

Table 9.5. Selected Performance Indicators for Enterprises, 1997

	All Enterprises	Municipal Sector Enterprises
	(in percent)	
Return on Equity*	1.3	-1.7
Profit Margin**	0.8	-0.3
Total Asset Turnover***	81	21
Asset to Equity Ratio	194	250
Long and Short -Term Debt to Equity Ratio	85	134

Notes: *Net operating profit/loss per equity.
       ** Net operating profit/loss to net sales.
       *** Net sales to assets ratio.
Source: Calculated from Agency of Payments Database.

Recent Trends in Municipal Infrastructure Investment

In order to understand the investment trends in municipal infrastructure, in mid-1998, a survey on municipal infrastructure investment was taken for a sample of local communities in Slovenia. The analysis is based on replies to the questionnaire received from a sample of 26 local communities in Slovenia (1/6 of the total number of local communities), with a total population of 307,000 inhabitants (again roughly 1/6 of the total population). The sample included an equal distribution of small, medium-sized and large local communities and of all geographical regions of Slovenia.[9]

The survey allow us to identify trends and financing patterns in municipal infrastructure investment for the period of 1995 to 1997. They include the following:

- municipal infrastructure was, together with investment in roads, at the top of local communities' investment priorities;
- more than half of total municipal infrastructure investment was allocated for water supply and sewage;

---

[9] For further details see Mojmir Mrak, *Communal Infrastructure in Slovenia: Survey of Investment Needs and Policies Aimed at Stimulating Private Sector Participation*, Mimeo, Ljubljana, 1998.

- over two thirds of municipal infrastructure investment was financed from state and local budgets, the latter being significantly more important of the two;
- actual implementation of 1995–97 municipal infrastructure investment plans varied widely across individual local communities; and
- in the cases where municipal infrastructure investment implementation was poor, local authorities identified financial problems as the main culprit.

The survey also allows us to identify municipal infrastructure investment plans related to the 1998-2002 period. In this case, the following conclusions can be stated:

- municipal infrastructure investments are planned to be, on average, 3 times higher than achieved in recent years;
- investment priorities shift away from water supply to sewage, wastewater treatment and solid waste management;
- the growing demand for municipal services and the need to adjust to the EU norms are the main driving force behind ambitious municipal infrastructure investment plans; and
- the lack of financial resources is considered the single most important reason for possible delays in investment plan implementation.

Finally, the survey identifies issues related to projected funding for the 1998-2002 municipal investment programs. The structure of municipal infrastructure financing for the 1998–2002 period, as envisaged by the respondents, is dramatically different from the one prevailing during 1995–97. The main differences are the following:

- overall budget financing of municipal infrastructure investments, i.e., from both local and state budgets, is expected to become relatively less important than it was in the past (its share is expected to fall from 68 percent in the 1995-97 period to 53 percent in the 1998-2002 period);
- in contrast to recent years, when local budgets had a dominant share of total budget financing of municipal infrastructure investment, for the next medium-term period the state budget is expected to assume the leading position of total budget financing;
- the suggested shift in the sources of budget financing clearly indicates local communities' expectation that the State budget will be one of the main funding sources available for meeting ambitious municipal infrastructure investment plans; taking into account the existing fiscal position of the country, this view seems to be far removed from the current reality;
- municipal sector enterprises (public utilities) and the EcoFund are expected to retain their share (around 15 and 5 percent respectively) in the overall funding structure of municipal infrastructure investment;
- in contrast to the past, bank credits are expected to become an important source of municipal infrastructure funding in the years to come; their participation in the overall funding structure is expected to reach 13 percent in the 1998–2002 period. In the 1995–97 period, this source of financing was practically not used at all; and
- only one local community in the sample has explicitly put BOT project financing as a funding source for its municipal infrastructure investments.

There are at least two important conclusions that can be drawn from the survey. First, following the traditional path of public sector financing of municipal infrastructure projects will not allow the undertaking of all investments required. In fact, estimates regarding municipal investment needs and public funds available reveal a gap in financing of SIT 134.4 billion for the period 1998-2002, which is equivalent to 0.8 percent of Slovenia's projected GDP. This funding gap actually means that municipal investment needs are estimated at a level three times higher than the level foreseen in the country's macroeconomic projections (1.2 percent of GDP against 0.4 percent of GDP). Although the survey provides data on municipal investment needs, as perceived by local authorities, these data are broadly consistent with the infrastructure investment needs data gathered at the national level and presented in Table 9.1.

Second, under existing funding patterns, characterized by a low level of internal financing and no access to borrowing, ambitious municipal infrastructure investment plans can be financed only through strong reliance on traditional budget finance. As this is not consistent with the country's macro economic and budgetary limits, the overall structure of investment funding has to be revised. Without an increase in access to non-budgetary sources of finance, investment in the municipal infrastructure will continue to be depressed. The primary source for these sources of funding is private investment.

Compliance with the EU Legislation

As mentioned above, the strategic objective of municipal infrastructure development in Slovenia is to move towards a reliable and cost efficient provision of municipal services, which takes due account of security of supply and to the use of economic instruments. Policy priorities aimed at achieving this objective also include systematic actions to reduce pressure on the environment and to protect air, water, soils and natural systems, with precise goals for further improved sanitation coverage, improved quality of water supplies and safe storage and disposal of waste. These policy priorities are expected to bring Slovenia gradually in line with the environmental policies of the EU *acquis*, and to meet the country's obligations under international environmental agreements.

Despite significant progress achieved thus far, compliance with the requirements of the EU environmental directives remains an important challenge. There are several reasons that validate this assumption. First and foremost, the EU *acquis* includes a large body of environmental and other legislation, much more than the one faced by the 1980s enlargement candidates. Some of these directives implied highly specific requirements concerning environmental management and local communities' development. Second, the local capacity to transpose and implement the EU directives is weak and needs to be further developed. Third, there seems to be a low correlation between Slovenia's perception of its immediate national priorities and the requirements of the EU directives in this sector. Fourth, progress towards meeting the EU requirements will require substantial investment in municipal infrastructure. This, in turn, has several implications towards macroeconomic management.

There is no doubt that Slovenia will derive substantial environmental benefits from meeting EU standards as quickly as possible. The process should, however, be designed and implemented by taking into account that necessary investments required to attain EU environmental norms are of such a magnitude that early compliance, i.e., by the period 2002-05, is likely to be financially and technically difficult. A much longer period will be needed. Moreover, while in some segments, such as local air pollution, direct environmental benefits are quicker and relatively easy to measure, in other areas, such as water quality and wastewater treatment, these benefits are less immediate and more difficult to measure.

From the municipal sector development point of view, by far the largest potential costs of complying with EU environmental legislation are associated with the implementation of: (i) the urban wastewater treatment directive; (ii) the drinking water directive; and (iii) some aspects of the waste management legislation. According to the urban wastewater directive (91/271/EEC), all urban areas with a total wastewater discharge between 2,000 and 15,000 population equivalent, are required to have a sewage system for collecting wastewater by the end of 2005. Those with a discharge of over 15,000 population equivalent are required to do so by the year 2000. In addition, by the same time, discharges of sewage that is to be collected must be subject to at least secondary treatment and, in so-called sensitive areas, tertiary treatment.

The requirements presented above have implications on municipal expenditure needs.[10] It is estimated that the investments required to meet the urban wastewater directive would be of the order of ECU 889 million over the period 1998-2020. Another ECU 235 million is expected to be required over the same period to meet the requirements of the drinking water directive (80/778/EEC). This directive relates to the quality of water for human consumption. It will soon be replaced with a new framework directive that would establish much more stringent standards for lead and some other quality parameters. Moreover, for Slovenia, pre-treatment of surface and ground waters that are used for drinking is one of the most relevant, and potentially costly, aspects of the drinking water directive.

As far as waste management is concerned, compliance with the two pieces of EU legislation will require large investments at the municipal level. The first piece of EU legislation is linked with meeting the directive on landfill of waste. There are currently over 50 landfills in Slovenia, where it is mostly municipal waste that is deposited and where most of the landfills will be filled in less than 5 years. The closure of the existing landfills requires full compliance with the directive, including leakage control, groundwater monitoring and gas extraction. Compliance with this directive is expected to cost Slovenia about ECU 321 million over the 1998-2020 period. Investments in municipal waste incineration for both existing installations and new installations will require close to ECU 311 million over 1998–2020 – a sum that takes into account incineration of both industrial and municipal waste. Costs to comply with hazardous waste incineration are not included in this estimate.

Complying with EU environmental legislation will depend on building institutional capacity and structures capable of transposing and implementing the *acquis*. The government, however, needs to elaborate credible strategies to meet EU requirements over a realistic time horizon, and to generate public support that is required to implement the agreed strategies and policy priorities successfully.

Strategy for Municipal Infrastructure Development

In order to achieve the strategic objectives of municipal infrastructure development, a whole range of coordinated policy measures must be designed and put into operation. Their common denominator is a more commercial approach to municipal infrastructure operation and development. Market-based policies and practices for infrastructure services are the cornerstone of the reform. This means the introduction of pricing policies that reflect real costs of production, the introduction of further competition and private sector involvement in provision and development, and the proper regulatory framework to operate public utilities.

Introduction of Cost-Reflecting Prices of Municipal Infrastructure Services

One of the core elements of the market-oriented transformation of public utilities in Slovenia is the introduction of cost-conscious and demand-oriented production practices as well as closer cost-recovering pricing policies. The price reform and effective collection of tariffs are crucial in both balancing the supply and demand for municipal infrastructure services and in achieving the financial viability and accountability of infrastructure service providers. In the past, the overall level of prices and tariffs for services provided by public utilities has tended to be below that which allows the cost recovery.

---

[10] All the estimated costs come from PHARE (1998).

As a result of the government's general policy of containing inflation, this is still the case with end-user prices of many services provided by utilities, including municipal services.

Tariff reform involves, not only a general increase of prices and tariffs, but also their rebalancing. At present, the structure of tariffs in some municipal infrastructure segments, such as water supply, wastewater collection and treatment and solid waste management, weighs more heavily on enterprises than on households. This reflects the social role of municipal infrastructure services in the pre-transition period and the public resistance to rebalancing tariff structures due to their potential negative social implications.

There is no doubt that the alignment of public service prices and tariffs could aggravate the inflation level in Slovenia, at least on the short-term. This should, however, be judged against the trade-off of low prices of public services and their implication in distorting economic decision of the firms and households as a whole. Not only to customers get misleading signals as to the real value of infrastructure services and not only are the incentives for municipal service efficiency reduced, but the perpetuation of low pricing policies has also resulted in the deferment of urgent investments in municipal infrastructure. As EU accession approaches, the process of compliance with the *acquis* will increase investment requirements, thus altering pricing policies.

A price increase for municipal infrastructure services will have to be accompanied by policy measures that will address the negative implication of price and tariff increases on vulnerable segments of the population. The traditional system of indirect subsidy support through low tariffs must be replaced with an income targeting strategy in which support will come directly from the social safety net policy, rather than from the entire population.

Competition and Private Sector Involvement

Tariff reform will not be successful if it is not accompanied with an increased scope for competition. An extremely important policy for cost-effective provision of municipal infrastructure services is the introduction of competition wherever possible. This private entry into various municipal infrastructure sectors and sub-sectors will take two forms, the application of each depending on the specific characteristics of individual modes of infrastructure. The two forms are:

- Competition within the market, where firms compete to provide the same service, such as transportation service between two points. This form of competition is typically more feasible and desirable for the supply of infrastructure services than that of infrastructure per se. This form of competition, however, has rather limited prospects in the area of public utilities due to regional monopoly characteristics.

- Competition for the market, where firms compete for the right to provide service for a given period of time under concession or lease contract. This form of competition can bring efficiency gains in many areas of infrastructure provision of management, particularly in small countries like Slovenia. Concessions and leases should become an important instrument of competition in all segments of municipal service provision.

The introduction of competition in infrastructure sectors has typically been accompanied with continuous and more or less drastic restructuring of infrastructure service providers. These providers will have to adapt to new circumstances, including the requirements of the EU single market in these areas. Closely associated with restructuring of municipal infrastructure service providers are issues related to the involvement of the private sector in the financing, construction and operation of new infrastructure projects. Within this context, there is a need for the government to design and put into operation a policy framework for borrowing by local communities. This framework should find a feasible balance between potentially conflicting objectives: on the one hand, to allow local communities to undertake investments required to upgrade and develop municipal infrastructure and services and, on the other hand, to maintain tight central government control over fiscal policy in order to secure macroeconomic stability in the country. The danger of over-borrowing by local authorities is always a constant threat to public finances.

Legal Framework and Institutional Support

Another important condition for improving the financial viability of municipal infrastructure service providers is appropriate legislation. Although the transformation of enterprises in the municipal infrastructure sector to join-stock status has been formally completed in Slovenia, the process of actual separation of ownership and management functions is still not complete. Therefore, further adjustments of the legal framework are needed to clarify operational responsibilities as well systems for accountability for managers and those within the government who perform an ownership role. It is also necessary that the same rules of the game apply to all participants: state-owned enterprises must be subject to the same market discipline as private sector enterprise.

In order to provide a clear legislative framework for private sector involvement in municipal infrastructure investment as well as in provision of municipal services, a new concession law should be designed and adopted. The law should contain general rules under which a concession may be allocated and negotiated, and under which a project may be designed, constructed, operated, maintained and then transferred or terminated at the end of the concession period.[11] Such a law would provide the needed guidance to private investors and government authorities. It would also serve as an important vehicle for the government to make its concession policy explicit and transparent.

An appropriate legal framework is a necessary, but in itself not a sufficient, condition for an efficient implementation of the concession law. Adoption of the law should thus be accompanied by the creation of an adequate institutional arrangement. Within this context, it would be useful to establish a concession unit staffed with a small number of project finance specialists that would assist local communities (and also line ministries) in the preparation and even negotiation of individual municipal infrastructure projects. Based on a review of the project proposal and its documentation, the unit could be, among other things, responsible for giving consent on the draft concession agreement. Taking into account potentially large obligations taken over by a local community when it enters into a concession agreement, there is an absolute need for an institutional mechanism at the State level that will keep these potential obligations within agreed limits and will therefore also reduce government risk in case the project fails, and the concession agreement interrupted, regardless of the reason.

Regulatory Framework

Infrastructure service providers must be properly supervised, particularly in situations of natural monopoly or exclusive rights. Rules for evaluating their performance, and for setting their tariffs structures, must be transparent and balanced for both, investors and public interests alike. At present, Slovenia pursues a policy of informal supervision by the line ministries, with authority stemming from the state's part ownership in most service providers. This will not be sufficient where private companies enter the market.

---

[11] See *Slovenia: Private Investment in the Infrastructure of the Republic of Slovenia*. Foreign Investment Advisory Service (FIAS), Washington, D.C., 1997. The FIAS report also recommends the creation of an institutional support unit designed to assist municipalities with BOT-type investments.

Independent, yet accountable institutions in practically all infrastructure sectors are needed to oversee competition. The nature of necessary regulation depends largely on the nature of the prevailing and potential competition. In the case of so-called competition in the market, regulators should be less concerned with the price control and more concerned with issues related to safety, environmental and technical standards. If conditions for granting licenses to operators are reasonably clear and non-discriminatory, and if an appropriate safety regime is enforced, than the regulation of these services can be left to the proper agencies. When there is competition for the market, some amount of regulation is necessary to monitor compliance with the concession agreements signed between public authorities and private concessionaires. However, regulation should not be so excessive as to eliminate the prospects of private sector participation.

Concluding Remark

Slovenia's accession to the EU poses unique challenges and opportunities for the government to overcome institutional and policy inertia and to build consensus for a substantial program of structural reform. To the extent that legal harmonization is a prerequisite for accession, the government could use the prospect of membership as a means to overcome vested interests in implementing economically painful and somehow costly reforms. Moreover, the EU accession process and its regulatory procedures and directives have provided a policy model, thereby setting the path for speeding the design and passage of relevant legislation and the implementation of policies to accelerate Slovenia's transition and its development prospects.

Solutions to the large investment requirements and regulatory problems that arise in municipal industries undergoing a transition from public monopoly to competition and deregulation, generally involve sophisticated economic instruments and techniques. Difficulties are likely to arise from the inexperience with economic regulation, its pitfalls, and the safeguards that tend to keep its social costs within reasonable bounds. The development and implementation of a strategy for the municipal infrastructure sector is a pre-requisite for a smooth accession process. Its implementation will help Slovenia's capacity to benefit the most form EU membership.

While private sector involvement in the area of municipal infrastructure and the delivery of municipal services will have to be the primary strategy of Slovenian municipalities in the coming years, central government institutional support and assistance to co-ordinate municipal investment activities is necessary. Many municipalities do not have the resources to make informed decisions on this respect, thus the need for co-operation with the central authorities. The central authorities, on the one hand, should not wash their hands pointing out at local governments' autonomy when these important decisions are taken. Municipalities, on the other, would not have to compromise their autonomy by asking for assistance from the center. The interaction will be beneficial for Slovenia.

Statistical Appendix

Section I	**Social Indicators, Population and Employment**
Table 1.1	Social Indicators
Table 1.2	Total Population
Table 1.3	Employment by Sectors
Table 1.4	Registered Unemployment
Section II	**National Accounts**
Table 2.1	Gross Domestic Product, 1992-98
Table 2.2	Gross Domestic Product by Sector, 1992-98
Table 2.3	Money Income and Expenditure of Households, 1992-96
Table 2.4	Investment in Economic Infrastructure, 1992-99
Table 2.5	Gross Domestic Product - Annual Growth Rates, 1992-98
Table 2.6	Agricultural Production, 1992-97
Section III	**Balance of Payments**
Table 3.1	Balance of Payments, 1993-98
Table 3.2	Services Balance, 1993-98
Table 3.3	Geographical Composition of Trade, Exports, 1993-98
Table 3.4	Geographical Composition of Trade, Imports, 1993-98
Table 3.5	Merchandise Trade by SITC and by End Use - Exports, F.O.B., 1993-98
Table 3.6	Merchandise Trade by SITC and by End Use - Imports, C.I.F., 1993-98
Table 3.7	Decomposition of U.S. Dollar Export Values, 1993-98
Table 3.8	Decomposition of U.S. Dollar Import Values, 1993-98
Table 3.9	International Reserves, 1993-98
Table 3.10	International Investment Position, 1994-97
Section IV	**External Debt**
Table 4.1	External Debt, 1993-98
Table 4.2	Debt Service, 1993-97
Section V	**Public Finance**
Table 5.1	Consolidated General Government Operations, 1993-98
Table 5.2	General Government Revenue, 1993-98
Table 5.3	General Government Expenditure, 1993-98
Table 5.4	Central Government Expenditure on Restructuring Programs, 1993-97
Table 5.5	Social Security Contribution Rates, 1992-98
Section VI	**Monetary Statistics**
Table 6.1	Monetary Survey, 1993-98
Table 6.2	Balance Sheet of the Bank of Slovenia, 1993-98
Table 6.3	Balance Sheet of Deposit Money Banks, 1993-98
Section VII	**Prices and Wages**
Table 7.1	Price Developments, 1993-97
Table 7.2	Average Monthly Net Wages
Table 7.3	Selected Interest Rates, 1993-98
Table 7.4	Average Monthly Net Wage By Sector of Activities, 1992-97
Section VIII	**Economic Organization**
Table 8.1	Number of Enterprises by Ownership and Activity, 1995-97
Table 8.2	Distribution of Enterprises by Size in 1997
Table 8.3	Distribution of Enterprises by Ownership in 1997
Table 8.4	Ownership Structure, 1992-97
Section IX	**International Comparisons**
Table 9.1	GDP Growth in Central Europe and Asia
Table 9.2	Annual Inflation in Central Europe and Asia
Table 9.3	Fiscal Balances in Central Europe and Asia
Table 9.4	Current Account Balances in Central Europe and Asia
Table 9.5	Tax Rates in Selected Countries

Table 1.1. Social Indicators

	1992	1993	1994	1995	1996	1997
Population and Vital Statistics						
Total Population (in thousands)	1,995.8	1,990.6	1,988.9	1,987.5	1,991.2	1,986.8
Total Population growth (%)	-0.3	-0.3	-0.1	-0.1	0.2	-0.2
Life expectancy at birth (in years)	73.3	73.3	73.5	74.0	74.6	74.9
Male	69.4	69.4	69.4	70.3	70.8	71.0
Female	77.2	77.3	77.4	77.8	78.2	78.6
Population age structure (in %)						
0-14	19.8	19.3	18.8	18.4	17.8	17.3
15-64	69.0	69.1	69.3	69.3	69.5	69.7
65 and above	11.2	11.6	11.9	12.3	12.7	13.0
Crude birth rate (per thousand)	10.0	9.9	9.8	9.5	9.5	9.1
Crude death rate (per thousand)	9.7	10.0	9.7	9.5	9.4	9.4
Infant mortality rate (per thousand)	8.9	6.8	6.5	5.5	4.7	5.2
Food, health, and nutrition						
Physicians (per 1,000 people)	2.1	2.1	2.2	2.1	2.1	2.2
Hospital beds (per 1,000 people)	5.9	5.9	5.8	5.7	6.0	5.6
Adult Illiteracy Rate (%)						
Primary School Enrollment						
Male	97	98	98	99	99	99
Female	97	98	98	99	99	99
Pupil-teacher ratio						
Elementary	14.5	14.2	13.8	13.5	12.9	..
Secondary	13.7	13.2	12.8	12.5	15.2	..
Other						
Telephone Subscribers	494,268	527,827	577,173	614,796	661,902	710,044
Private cars (per thousand)	304	318	330	352	365	386

Source: Statistical Yearbook, Statistical Office of the Republic of Slovenia.

Table 1.2. Total Population [1]

	Total Population	Growth Rate in percent
1980	1,901,200	1.0
1981	1,917,500	0.9
1982	1,924,900	0.4
1983	1,933,100	0.4
1984	1,942,800	0.5
1985	1,973,200	1.6
1986	1,980,700	0.4
1987	1,989,500	0.4
1988	2,000,000	0.5
1989	1,999,400	0.0
1990	1,998,100	-0.1
1991	2,001,800	0.2
1992	1,995,800	-0.3
1993	1,990,600	-0.3
1994	1,988,900	-0.1
1995	1,987,500	-0.1
1996	1,991,200	0.2
1997	1,986,800	-0.2

Note: 1/ mid-year
Source: Statistical Office of the Republic of Slovenia.

Table 1.3. Employment by Sectors

	1992	1993	1994	1995	1996	1997
	(in thousands)					
Total Employment [1/] [2/]	656,966	626,806	605,326	593,848	581,651	593,086
Agriculture, Hunting and Forestry	15,181	13,643	12,244	8,945	8,377	8,228
Fishing	190	177	155	205	171	175
Mining and Quarrying	9,989	9,427	8,993	8,344	7,632	7,256
Manufacturing	282,105	256,959	244,786	233,694	219,557	212,802
Electricity, Gas and Water Supply	11,792	11,762	11,515	11,807	11,995	11,816
Construction	36,463	32,180	32,499	31,067	31,975	33,171
Wholesale, Reatil: Certain Repair	71,985	68,162	64,671	67,593	65,979	74,615
Hotels and Restaurants	17,082	15,445	14,891	14,340	14,043	13,980
Transport, Storage and Communications	44,766	42,038	37,547	34,768	32,418	32,513
Financial Intermediation	13,200	13,097	13,266	14,106	15,082	15,536
Real Estate, Renting & Business Activities	27,389	26,443	22,793	26,833	27,965	32,101
Public Administration & Defence: comp. Soc. Sec.	26,485	35,122	37,024	38,479	40,403	42,333
Education	34,232	35,999	37,063	48,012	49,425	50,600
Health and Social Work	51,608	51,555	52,336	42,972	43,717	44,287
Other Social and Personal Services	14,499	14,797	15,543	12,683	12,912	13,673
Registered Unemployed Persons	102,593	129,087	127,056	121,483	119,799	125,188
Self-employed Persons and Farmers [3/]	-	102,224	105,164	107,709	109,639	92,204
Total Active Population	892,223	893,949	879,295	871,706	864,689	868,619

Notes: 1/ The data include only persons in paid employment in enterprises, companies and organizations.

2/ Source: Monthly survey on employment and Employment register.

3/ Source: Employment register and Labour Force Survey.

Source: Statistical Office of the Republic of Slovenia.

Table 1.4. Registered Unemployment

	1992	1993	1994	1995	1996	1997
Registered unemployment (in thousands)[1]	102.6	129.1	127.1	121.5	119.8	125.2
Of which (in percent):						
Women	43.9	43.8	44.9	46.7	48.1	48.8
Under 26	40.7	37.4	33.5	32.2	31.4	29.1
Semi skilled and Unskilled	46.5	45.3	45.8	46.6	47.0	47.1
Over 40[2]	25.0	28.2	32.4	34.0	37.7	43.0
Unemployed more than one year[2]	50.9	54.8	62.1	59.0	53.8	59.6
Those receiving unemployment benefit	45.0	43.1	42.1	30.3	30.3	32.6
Rate of Registered Unemployment (in percent)	11.5	14.4	14.4	13.9	13.9	14.4
Job vacancies (monthly average) (in thousands)	6.9	9.1	12.6	12.9	13.1	11.2
Average number of unemployed per job vacancy	15.0	14.2	10.1	9.4	9.1	11.2

Note: 1/ Average annual.
         2/ December 31.
Source: National Employment Office of the Republic of Slovenia.

Table 2.1. Gross Domestic Product, 1992–98

	1992	1993	1994	1995	1996	1997
	(In millions of tolars, current prices)					
By Activities						
Agriculture, forestry and fishing	52,880	64,716	73,389	87,458	98,699	107,473
Industry	365,100	479,730	637,094	725,017	835,952	977,568
Services	490,748	716,134	907,425	1,115,784	1,290,276	1,481,512
Taxes on production and on imports	150,962	229,385	298,936	368,834	418,577	444,236
Subsidies	25,139	29,630	30,892	31,686	35,709	41,894
By Expenditure						
Total Consumption	768,124	1,141,855	1,424,453	1,738,562	1,980,982	2,252,739
Private Consumption	561,120	839,249	1,050,165	1,290,411	1,463,249	1,660,326
Government Final Consumption	207,004	302,606	374,288	448,151	517,733	592,413
Gross Capital Formation	179,022	277,632	388,000	519,366	596,825	687,846
Gross Fixed Capital Formation	189,608	270,237	372,663	475,605	573,355	682,672
Change in Inventories	-10,586	7,395	15,337	43,761	23,470	5,174
Resource balance	70,819	15,608	40,544	-36,468	-25,139	-33,898
Exports of Goods and Nonfactor-Services	642,772	843,148	1,111,321	1,225,660	1,419,884	1,660,733
Imports of Goods and Services	571,953	827,540	1,070,777	1,262,128	1,445,023	1,694,631
Gross Domestic Product	1,017,965	1,435,095	1,852,997	2,221,459	2,552,668	2,906,687
Net income from abroad	-1,899	4,064	13,886	24,698	20,716	20,766
Gross National Income	1,016,066	1,439,159	1,866,883	2,246,157	2,573,384	2,927,453
Net Current Transfers	5,630	11,313	17,125	10,937	8,878	16,034
Gross National Disposable Income	1,021,696	1,450,472	1,884,008	2,257,094	2,582,262	2,943,487

Source: Statistical Office of the Republic of Slovenia for 1992-96, IMAD for 1997.

Table 2.2. Gross Domestic Product by Sector, 1992–98

	1992	1993	1994	1995	1996	1997	1998
	(In millions of tolars, current prices)						
Agriculture, hunting, forestry, and fishing	52,880	64,716	73,389	87,458	98,699	107,473	117,397
Mining and quarrying	17,618	14,681	23,702	26,006	30,683	33,661	36,598
Manufacturing	288,613	371,638	486,015	545,730	616,410	720,445	806,661
Electricity, gas, and water supply	20,171	34,553	50,954	56,693	65,032	76,310	83,379
Construction	38,698	58,858	76,423	96,588	123,827	147,152	165,557
Wholesale and retail trade	95,791	139,346	190,893	232,286	257,273	293,360	330,053
Hotels and restaurants	22,671	36,509	48,410	57,164	68,467	80,050	90,495
Transport and communications	66,489	97,909	121,401	148,746	169,275	196,278	221,995
Financial intermediation	32,043	49,839	53,460	77,067	93,181	106,129	121,068
Real estate and other business services	95,260	133,606	181,983	226,191	263,568	301,440	338,283
Public administration and defense	40,405	61,768	82,328	102,937	118,746	138,381	155,614
Education	45,017	67,905	87,103	108,178	123,881	141,013	156,973
Health and social work	48,148	63,914	83,398	99,385	118,454	134,198	148,731
Other community and personal services	44,924	65,338	58,449	63,829	77,431	90,663	103,404
FISIM	-16,586	-25,240	-32,955	-43,947	-55,127	-62,207	-68,266
Total value added	892,142	1,235,340	1,584,953	1,884,311	2,169,800	2,504,346	2,807,942
Plus: Taxes on production and on imports	150,962	229,385	298,936	368,834	418,577	444,236	506,052
Minus: Subsidies	25,139	29,630	30,892	31,686	35,709	41,895	46,194
Gross Domestic Product	1,017,965	1,435,095	1,852,997	2,221,459	2,552,668	2,906,687	3,267,800
	(In percent of GDP)						
Agriculture, hunting, forestry, and fishing	5.2	4.5	4.0	3.9	3.9	3.7	3.6
Industry and construction	35.9	33.4	34.4	32.6	32.7	33.6	33.4
Industry	32.1	29.3	30.3	28.3	27.9	28.6	28.4
Construction	3.8	4.1	4.1	4.3	4.9	5.1	5.1
Services	48.2	49.9	49.0	50.2	50.5	51.0	51.0

Sources: Statistical Office, Statistical Yearbook for 1992-96 and Institute of Macroeconomic Analysis and Development's Autumn Report - estimations for 1997 and 1998.

Table 2.3. Money Income and Expenditure of Households, 1992–96[1]

	1992	1993	1994	1995	1996
	(In millions of tolars, current prices)				
Total income	1,048,736	1,443,355	1,857,470	2,188,710	2,440,594
Compensation of employees	652,814	861,937	1,074,494	1,271,699	1,400,005
Wages and allowances (net)	369,355	485,062	622,566	739,556	852,477
Taxes on employees' income	67,304	87,888	110,340	132,830	156,109
Employees' social contributions	108,526	145,737	169,466	199,470	227,183
Employers' social contributions	107,629	143,250	172,454	201,689	186,180
Operating surplus of self-employed	156,544	230,808	303,276	361,978	397,090
Social benefits	194,582	285,642	374,205	437,439	494,079
Imputed social benefits	581	772	925	1,041	1,142
Actual interest received	22,341	17,847	26,268	27,024	28,200
Income from intangible assets	5,646	8,383	10,511	12,427	14,314
Accident insurance claims	8,090	22,540	27,946	34,422	37,761
Private international transfers	3,138	6,531	10,100	11,486	10,551
Miscellaneous transfers	5,000	8,895	29,745	30,924	35,176
Deductions	374,196	512,284	634,955	741,489	817,780
Actual social contributions	216,155	288,987	341,588	399,583	413,695
Imputed social contributions	41,637	55,441	71,626	86,393	97,617
Net accident insurance premiums	14,006	32,269	37,000	46,053	50,521
Current taxes on income and wealth	75,572	102,695	137,226	157,611	184,653
Actual interest paid	12,555	14,373	25,170	27,383	43,800
Private international transfers	5,950	6,676	8,547	9,991	9,531
Compensation of employees to ROW		1,778	1,662	1,505	3,113
Miscellaneous current transfers	8,321	10,065	12,136	12,970	14,850
Disposable income	674,540	931,071	1,222,515	1,447,221	1,622,814
Gross saving	125,872	107,612	190,096	184,597	212,094
Private consumption	548,668	823,459	1,033,094	1,266,058	1,437,756

Note: 1/ Since 1994 entire turnover of duty-free shops has been considered in private consumption.
Sources: Statistical Office of the Republic of Slovenia.

Table 2.4. Investment in Economic Infrastructure, 1992–99

	1992	1993	1994	1995	1996 Estimate	1997 Estimate	1998 Estimate	1999 Estimate
					(In millions of tolars, current prices)			
1. ABSOLUTE FIGURES, SIT MILLON, CURRENT PRICES								
ECONOMIC INFRASTRUCTURE	24,387	48,737	75,115	91,459	122,488	148,475	167,000	193,480
Energy sector	7,697	12,324	22,389	22,747	29,800	32,881	39,000	43,230
Electricity supply	6,709	11,048	21,240	21,151	23,161	25,130	30,500	33,300
Other	988	1,276	1,149	1,596	6,639	7,751	8,500	9,930
Transport infrastructure	12,414	26,549	40,402	57,012	82,256	102,540	113,900	135,550
Railways	1,315	2,578	6,195	8,307	10,355	13,454	26,000	29,200
Air traffic	316	767	847	717	183	600	2,000	1,550
Roads, motor-ways	1,857	8,036	14,925	29,333	39,768	55,990	53,000	70,000
PTT services	7,024	12,491	16,430					
Post				3,500	6,200	6,400	6,000	6,300
Telecommunications				12,183	21,212	21,440	22,000	23,400
Other	1,902	2,677	2,005	2,972	4,538	4,656	4,900	5,100
Water supply	233	299	213	200	1,332	864	1,000	1,100
Public utilities	4,043	9,565	12,111	11,500	9,100	12,190	13,100	13,600
					(In percent of gross fixed investment)			
2. STRUCTURE IN %, (TOTAL = 100)								
ECONOMIC INFRASTRUCTURE	12.9	18.0	20.2	19.2	21.4	21.7	21.3	21.7
Energy sector	4.1	4.6	6.0	4.8	5.2	4.8	5.0	4.9
Electricity supply	3.5	4.1	5.7	4.4	4.0	3.7	3.9	3.7
Other	0.5	0.5	0.3	0.3	1.2	1.1	1.1	1.1
Transport infrastructure	6.5	9.8	10.8	12.0	14.3	15.0	14.5	15.2
Railways	0.7	1.0	1.7	1.7	1.8	2.0	3.3	3.3
Air traffic	0.2	0.3	0.2	0.2	0.0	0.1	0.3	0.2
Roads, motorways	1.0	3.0	4.0	6.2	6.9	8.2	6.8	7.9
PTT services	3.7	4.6	4.4					
Post				0.7	1.1	0.9	0.8	0.7
Telecommunications				2.6	3.7	3.1	2.8	2.6
Other	1.0	1.0	0.5	0.6	0.8	0.7	0.6	0.6
Water supply	0.1	0.1	0.1	0.0	0.2	0.1	0.1	0.1
Public utilities	2.1	3.5	3.2	2.4	1.6	1.8	1.7	1.5
					(In percent of GDP)			
3. INVESTMENT AS A % OF GROSS DOMESTIC PRODUCT								
ECONOMIC INFRASTRUCTURE	2.4	3.4	4.1	4.1	4.8	5.1	5.1	5.3
Energy sector	0.8	0.9	1.2	1.0	1.2	1.1	1.2	1.2
Electricity supply	0.7	0.8	1.1	1.0	0.9	0.9	0.9	0.9
Other	0.1	0.1	0.1	0.1	0.3	0.3	0.3	0.3
Transport infrastructure	1.2	1.8	2.2	2.6	3.2	3.5	3.5	3.7
Railways	0.1	0.2	0.3	0.4	0.4	0.5	0.8	0.8
Air traffic	0.0	0.1	0.0	0.0	0.0	0.0	0.1	0.0
Roads, motorways	0.2	0.6	0.8	1.3	1.6	1.9	1.6	1.9
PTT services	0.7	0.9	0.9					
Post				0.2	0.2	0.2	0.2	0.2
Telecommunications				0.5	0.8	0.7	0.7	0.6
Other	0.2	0.2	0.1	0.1	0.2	0.2	0.1	0.1
Water supply	0.0	0.0	0.0	0.0	0.1	0.0	0.0	0.0
Public utilities	0.4	0.7	0.7	0.5	0.4	0.4	0.4	0.4

Sources: Statistical Office of the Republic of Slovenia 1992-1995; Rapid Reports; and Institute of Macroeconomic
Analysis and Development estimate for 1996 and 1997.

Table 2.5. Gross Domestic Product - Annual Growth Rates, 1992–98

	1992	1993	1994	1995	1996	1997	1998
	(Percentage changes, in real terms)						
Total aggregate demand	-9.5	4.3	6.6	5.0	3.4	5.8	4.3
Exports of goods and nonfactor services	-23.5	0.6	12.3	1.1	3.3	11.3	5.6
Total domestic demand	-5.1	5.3	5.3	6.0	3.4	4.4	4.0
Private consumption	-3.6	13.9	4.0	9.1	2.4	3.6	3.4
Government final consumption expendit.	-1.8	5.3	2.0	2.4	3.2	3.2	4.6
Gross fixed capital formation	-12.9	10.7	14.1	16.8	8.4	11.2	6.7
Imports of goods and services	-22.9	17.6	13.1	11.3	2.4	12.2	6.4
Gross Domestic Product	-5.5	2.8	5.3	4.1	3.3	3.8	4.0
Agriculture, forestry and fishing	-6.7	-4.2	4.2	1.6	2.2	-2.1	1.0
Industry	-11.9	-3.1	6.0	2.9	2.8	5.1	3.3
Services	0.8	4.8	4.3	4.0	3.4	3.2	4.0
Real average net wages per employee	-0.9	14.8	7.1	5.3	4.7	2.9	2.0
	(In percent of GDP)						
Gross fixed capital formation	18.6	18.8	20.1	21.4	22.5	23.5	24.0
Gross national savings	24.9	21.5	24.8	23.3	23.6	23.8	24.3

Source: Statistical Office of the Republic of Slovenia Yearbook for 1992-97. Institute of Macroeconomic
Analysis and Development's Autumn Report - estimations for 1998.

Table 2.6. Agricultural Production, 1992–97

	1992	1993	1994	1995	1996	1997
	(Thousands of tons)					
Production of selected commodities						
Wheat	153	143	155	155	137	139
Corn	172	238	312	296	297	355
Sugar beets	97	133	222	265	308	289
Sunflower seeds	0	0	0	0	0	0
Meat	142	163	158	161	170	167
Of which:						
Beef	38	54	49	46	52	54
Pork	41	60	61	59	60	53
Poultry	58	49	48	56	58	60
Milk (millions of liters)	563	533	559	590	576	551
	(Volume indices: 1969-1971=100)					
Production of selected commodities						
Wheat	104	98	106	106	94	95
Corn	123	169	222	211	211	253
Sugar beets 1/	...	...	...	...	...	...
Sunflower seeds	21	43	32	21	11	11
Meat	143	164	169	162	171	
Of which:						
Beef	104	148	134	126	142	148
Pork	137	201	204	197	201	177
Poultry	212	179	175	204	212	219
Milk	147	139	146	154	150	144
	(Percentage share of agricultural production)					
Crop production	33.2	41.4	39.4	36.0	30.4	32.2
Fruit growing	5.4	4.7	4.4	3.6	4.6	3.3
Viticulture	7.0	6.4	5.7	3.8	6.2	9.0
Totals	100.0	100.0	100.0	100.0	100.0	100
Socialized sector	29.7	...	...	...	...	...
Private sector	70.3	...	...	...	...	...

Note: 1/ There was not yet any production of sugar beets in the years 1969–71.
Source: Statistical Office of the Republic of Slovenia.

Table 3.1. Balance of Payments, 1993-98

	1993	1994	1995	1996	1997	1998 Jan.-Nov.
	(In millions of U.S. dollars)					
Current account	191.9	600.1	-22.8	39.0	36.6	49.4
Trade balance	-154.2	-337.5	-954.3	-881.7	-771.6	-654.8
Exports f.o.b.	6,082.9	6,830.3	8,350.2	8,370.0	8,407.1	8,376.3
Imports f.o.b.	-6,237.1	-7,167.8	-9,304.5	-9,251.7	-9,178.7	9,031.1
Services	375.3	675.8	631.1	704.2	590.0	469.7
Exports	1,392.7	1,804.3	2,022.9	2,126.9	2,042.6	1,855.2
Of which:						
Transportation	446.2	486.3	504.8	480.4	465.4	482.9
Travel	734.1	911.3	1,082.4	1,229.9	1,187.6	1,032.3
Construction	0.0	125.1	135.5	93.6	76.3	66.5
Imports	-1,017.3	-1,128.5	-1,391.8	-1,422.6	-1,452.6	1,385.4
Income	-51.4	169.6	209.5	154.9	130.6	137.3
Receipts	114.7	334.3	439.0	419.5	416.8	419.5
Expenditures	-166.0	-164.7	-229.4	-264.6	-286.2	282.2
Current transfers	22.2	92.2	90.8	61.6	87.6	97.1
Capital and financial account [1]	-202.0	-523.6	168.2	-46.8	-102.8	-190.9
Capital account	4.1	-4.4	-17.9	-4.9	-4.2	-5.3
Capital transfers	4.7	-2.8	-15.6	-2.4	-3.0	-4.3
Nonproduced nonfinancial assets	-0.6	-1.6	-2.3	-2.5	-1.2	-1.0
Financial account [1]	-206.1	-519.2	186.0	-47.3	-98.7	-185.6
Direct investment	111.3	131.0	170.5	177.7	295.3	138.2
Portfolio investment	3.1	-32.5	-13.5	636.9	235.5	92.2
Other investment	-209.2	27.3	264.5	-269.7	657.6	-117.6
Assets	-313.5	-306.3	-357.0	-425.6	288.2	-455.9
Commercial credits	93.3	-0.1	0.0	-161.6	-264.2	-467.3
Loans	11.5	-10.8	-14.4	-7.2	-67.2	-30.1
Currency and deposits	-383.7	-185.1	-181.9	-474.3	678.9	32.7
Other assets	-34.6	-110.3	-754.6	157.5	-59.3	8.8
Liabilities	104.3	333.5	615.4	155.3	369.4	338.3
Commercial credits	-13.0	-11.1	-3.7	19.2	14.1	24.3
Loans	161.2	325.9	572.2	-11.6	334.2	320.1
Deposits	-40.3	32.3	39.2	154.9	20.4	-11.4
Other liabilities	-3.7	-13.5	7.7	-4.6	0.7	5.3
Official reserves (increase -)	-111.7	-644.3	-235.4	-586.8	-1,287.1	-298.3
Net errors and omissions	9.8	-76.5	-145.4	7.7	66.2	141.6
	(Percentage change)					
Memorandum items:						
Merchandise exports [2]	-9.0	12.3	22.3	0.2	0.4	6.8
Merchandise imports [2]	5.9	14.9	29.8	-0.6	-0.8	3.9
Tourism receipts	9.4	24.1	18.8	13.6	-3.4	-9.2
Trade balance	-1.2	-2.3	-5.1	-4.8	-4.2	...
Current account	1.5	4.2	-0.1	0.2	0.2	...
Capital and financial account [1] [3]	-1.6	3.6	0.9	-0.2	-0.6	...
Change in official reserves	0.9	4.5	1.3	3.2	7.1	...
GDP (in billions of US$)	12.7	14.4	18.7	18.8	18.2	...

Notes: 1/ Excludes Slovenia's share of debt associated with the 1988 New Financing Agreement as settled in June 1996.

2/ Data for 1998 are compared to January average 1997.

3/ Includes net errors and omissions.

Source: Bank of Slovenia.

Table 3.2. Services Balance, 1993–98

(In millions of U.S. dollars)

	1993	1994	1995	1996	1997	1998 Jan.-Nov.
Services, net	375	676	631	704	590	470
Credit	1,393	1,804	2,023	2,127	2,043	1,855
Transport	446	486	505	480	465	483
Travel	734	911	1,082	1,230	1,188	1,032
Tourism	734	911	1,082	1,230	1,188	1,032
Communications services	5	13	12	14	23	22
Construction services	0	125	136	94	76	67
Insurance services	1	1	1	1	1	1
Financial services	7	7	8	11	11	8
Computer and information services	5	5	12	29	32	41
Royalties and license fees	4	3	4	6	5	7
Other business services	185	244	247	242	221	183
Operational leasing services	30	11	13	11	11	10
Merchanting	46	81	109	123	102	75
Miscellaneous business, professions, and technical services	109	153	125	108	108	98
Personal, cultural, and recreational services	6	6	5	9	10	11
Government services	1	3	11	11	10	2
Other services	0	0	0	0	0	0
Debit	-1,017	-1,129	-1,392	1,423	-1,453	-1,385
Transport	-389	-418	-435	-405	-365	-359
Travel	-305	-374	-524	-542	-544	-537
Tourism	-245	-314	-461	-479	-486	-481
Communications services	-2	-6	-10	-15	-26	-27
Construction services	0	-3	-24	-36	-51	-35
Insurance services	-2	-1	-2	-2	-2	-1
Financial services	-14	-12	-15	-20	-22	-20
Computer and information services	-18	-19	-27	-31	-50	-41
Royalties and license fees	-13	-16	-23	-27	-52	-35
Other business services	-257	-249	-297	-309	-300	-291
Operational leasing services	-78	-60	-56	-37	-30	-24
Merchanting	-69	-69	-78	-79	-84	76
Miscellaneous business, professions, and technical services	-110	-120	-163	-192	-185	-190
Personal, cultural, and recreational services	-10	-13	-19	-22	-27	-28
Government services	-7	-16	-16	-14	-13	-12
Other services	0	0	0	0	0	0

Source: Bank of Slovenia.

Table 3.3. Geographical Composition of Trade, Exports, 1993–98

	1993	1994	1995	1996	1997	1998 Jan.-Nov.
	(In millions of U.S. dollars)					
EU [1]	3,847	4,480	5,575	5,367	5,320	5,474
Of which:						
Austria	303	373	535	551	565	575
France	528	586	681	598	463	706
Germany	1,798	2,068	2,508	2,545	2,459	2,369
Italy	756	923	1,212	1,103	1,248	1,147
United Kingdom	148	208	229	162	150	149
EFTA [1]	65	75	87	83	87	88
Of which:						
Switzerland	52	58	71	68	70	64
CEFTA	261	308	403	451	504	537
Czech and Slovak Republics	86	113	184	204	204	201
Hungary	88	99	115	105	120	132
Poland	87	96	105	142	155	165
Romania					24	39
Others	1,910	1,965	2,251	2,410	2,458	2,233
Of which:						
U.S.A.	216	250	261	246	243	230
Former U.S.S.R.	298	316	375	390	432	310
Countries of former SFRY	964	1,040	1,209	1,385	1,387	1,287
Total	6,083	6,828	8,316	8,310	8,369	8,332
	(In percent)					
EU [1]	63.2	65.6	67.0	64.6	63.6	65.7
Of which:						
Austria	5.0	5.5	6.4	6.6	6.8	6.9
France	8.7	8.6	8.2	7.2	5.5	8.5
Germany	29.6	30.3	30.2	30.6	29.4	28.4
Italy	12.4	13.5	14.6	13.3	14.9	13.8
United Kingdom	2.4	3.0	2.8	1.9	1.8	1.8
EFTA [1]	1.1	1.1	1.0	1.0	1.0	1.1
Of which:						
Switzerland	0.9	0.8	0.9	0.8	0.8	0.8
CEFTA	4.3	4.5	4.8	5.4	6.0	6.4
Czech and Slovak Republics	1.4	1.7	2.2	2.5	2.4	2.4
Hungary	1.4	1.4	1.4	1.3	1.4	1.6
Poland	1.4	1.4	1.3	1.7	1.9	2.0
Romania					0.3	0.5
Others	31.4	28.8	27.1	29.0	29.4	26.8
Of which:						
U.S.A.	3.6	3.7	3.1	3.0	2.9	2.8
Former U.S.S.R.	4.9	4.6	4.5	4.7	5.2	3.7
Countries of former SFRY	15.8	15.2	14.5	16.7	16.6	15.4
Total	100.0	100.0	100.0	100.0	100.0	100.0

Note: 1/ Former EFTA countries Austria, Finland, Sweden) are included in EU data since 1993.
2/ Romania is included in CEFTA data since 1997.

Sources: Statistical Office and Bank of Slovenia.

Table 3.4. Geographical Composition of Trade, Imports, 1993–98

	1993	1994	1995	1996	1997	1998 Jan.-Nov.
	(In millions of U.S. dollars)					
EU [1]	4,266	5,052	6,532	6,360	6,312	6,409
Of which:						
Austria	553	756	919	835	789	730
France	522	613	798	925	980	1,147
Germany	1,626	1,734	2,206	2,044	1,936	1,908
Italy	1,051	1,258	1,611	1,593	1,558	1,565
United Kingdom	103	130	190	208	241	211
EFTA [1]	135	188	237	249	194	190
Of which:						
Switzerland	127	154	199	178	162	156
CEFTA [2]	331	451	634	616	705	662
Czech and Slovak Republics	152	236	329	329	337	329
Hungary	165	193	267	239	293	222
Poland	14	22	38	48	58	69
Romania					17	42
Others	1,769	1,613	2,089	2,197	2,155	1,979
Of which:						
Japan	125	126	157	163	161	
U.S.A.	188	197	291	325	287	269
Former U.S.S.R.	217	169	275	236	284	200
Countries of former SFRY	696	584	671	709	594	544
Total imports	6,501	7,304	9,492	9,421	9,366	9,240
	(In percent)					
EU [1]	65.6	69.2	68.8	67.5	67.4	69.4
Of which:						
Austria	8.5	10.4	9.7	8.9	8.4	7.9
France	8.0	8.4	8.4	9.8	10.5	12.4
Germany	25.0	23.7	23.2	21.7	20.7	20.6
Italy	16.2	17.2	17.0	16.9	16.6	16.9
United Kingdom	1.6	1.8	2.0	2.2	2.6	2.3
EFTA [1]	2.1	2.6	2.5	2.6	2.1	2.1
Of which:						
Switzerland	2.0	2.1	2.1	1.9	1.7	1.7
CEFTA	5.1	6.2	6.7	6.5	7.5	7.2
Czech and Slovak Republics	2.3	3.2	3.5	3.5	3.6	3.6
Hungary	2.5	2.6	2.8	2.5	3.1	2.4
Poland	0.2	0.3	0.4	0.5	0.6	0.7
Romania					0.2	0.5
Others	27.2	22.1	22.0	23.3	23.0	21.4
Of which:						
Japan	1.9	1.7	1.7	1.7	1.7	0.0
U.S.A.	2.9	2.7	3.1	3.4	3.1	2.9
Former U.S.S.R.	3.3	2.3	2.9	2.5	3.0	2.2
Countries of former SFRY	10.7	8.0	7.1	7.5	6.3	5.9
Total imports	100.0	100.0	100.0	100.0	100.0	100.0

Note: 1/ Former EFTA countries Austria, Finland, Sweden) are included in EU data since 1993.
          2/ Romania is included in CEFTA data since 1997.

Sources: Statistical Office and Bank of Slovenia.

Table 3.5. Merchandise Trade by SITC and by End Use - Exports, F.O.B., 1993–98

	1993	1994	1995	1996	1997	1998 Jan.-Oct.
	(In millions of U.S. dollars)					
Food and live animals	239	274	263	264	240	197
Beverages and tobacco	45	50	51	72	71	75
Crude materials, edible, except fuels	108	131	171	139	166	145
Mineral fuels, lubricants, and related materials	313	76	99	77	101	73
Animal and vegetable oils and fats	7	7	7	9	16	14
Chemicals	552	706	871	881	941	795
Manufactured goods classified by material	1,586	1,866	2,373	2,277	2,265	1,965
Machinery and transport equipment	1,664	2,067	2,614	2,773	2,813	2,681
Miscellaneous manufactured goods	1,557	1,636	1,848	1,815	1,753	1,521
Others	11	14	18	1	1	1
Total [1]	6,083	6,828	8,316	8,310	8,369	7,465
	(In percent)					
Food and live animals	3.9	4.0	3.2	3.2	2.9	2.6
Beverages and tobacco	0.7	0.7	0.6	0.9	0.8	1.0
Crude materials, edible, except fuels	1.8	1.9	2.1	1.7	2.0	1.9
Mineral fuels, lubricants, and related materials	5.2	1.1	1.2	0.9	1.2	1.0
Animal and vegetable oils and fats	0.1	0.1	0.1	0.1	0.2	0.2
Chemicals	9.1	10.3	10.5	10.6	11.2	10.6
Manufactured goods classified by material	26.1	27.3	28.5	27.4	27.1	26.3
Machinery and transport equipment	27.4	30.3	31.4	33.4	33.6	35.9
Miscellaneous manufactured goods	25.6	24.0	22.2	21.8	21.0	20.4
Others	0.2	0.2	0.2	0.0	0.0	0.0
Total	100.0	100.0	100.0	100.0	100.0	100.0

Note: 1/ These totals may differ from those compiled by the Bank of Slovenia for balance of payments.
Source: Statistical Office of the Republic of Slovenia.

Table 3.6. Merchandise Trade by SITC and by End Use - Imports, C.I.F., 1993–98

	1993	1994	1995	1996	1997	1998 Jan.-Oct.
	(In millions of U.S. dollars)					
Food and live animals	478	555	637	637	596	474
Beverages and tobacco	44	47	61	60	58	48
Crude materials, edible, except fuels	345	473	620	476	488	418
Mineral fuels, lubricants, and related materials	700	521	624	755	782	476
Animal and vegetable oils and fats	23	30	38	39	41	47
Chemicals	750	891	1,145	1,125	1,133	1,012
Manufactured goods classified by materials	1,147	1,419	1,876	1,856	1,921	1,821
Machinery and transport equipments	1,969	2,324	3,205	3,175	3,096	2,948
Miscellaneous manufactured goods	783	800	1,009	1,289	1,242	1,038
Others	262	245	277	10	10	11
Total [1]	6,501	7,304	9,492	9,421	9,366	8,292
	(In percent)					
Food and live animals	7.4	7.6	6.7	6.8	6.4	5.7
Beverages and tobacco	0.7	0.6	0.6	0.6	0.6	0.6
Crude materials, edible, except fuels	5.3	6.5	6.5	5.1	5.2	5.0
Mineral fuels, lubricants, and related materials	10.8	7.1	6.6	8.0	8.4	5.7
Animal and vegetable oils and fats	0.4	0.4	0.4	0.4	0.4	0.6
Chemicals	11.5	12.2	12.1	11.9	12.1	12.2
Manufactured goods classified by materials	17.6	19.4	19.8	19.7	20.5	22.0
Machinery and transport equipments	30.3	31.8	33.8	33.7	33.1	35.6
Miscellaneous manufactured goods	12.0	11.0	10.6	13.7	13.3	12.5
Others	4.0	3.4	2.9	0.1	0.1	0.1
Total	100.0	100.0	100.0	100.0	100.0	100.0

Note: 1/ These totals may differ from those compiled by the Bank of Slovenia for balance of payments.
Source: Statistical Office of the Republic of Slovenia.

Table 3.7. Decomposition of U.S. Dollar Export Values, 1993–98

	1993	1994	1995	1996	1997	1998 Jan.–Nov. [1]
			(Index: 1995=100)			
Total export value	73.1	82.1	100.0	99.9	100.6	109.3
Price	76.8	82.9	100.0	100.8	90.9	90.4
Of which:						
Inter-currency valuation	90.8	91.6	100.0	97.0	86.5	84.7
Partner country prices	84.6	90.5	100.0	103.9	105.0	106.7
Volume	95.2	98.8	100.0	99.2	110.9	120.9
			(Percent change)			
Total export value	-9.0	12.2	21.8	-0.1	0.7	8.6
Price	-4.4	7.9	20.6	0.8	-9.9	-0.5
Of which:						
Inter-currency valuation	-6.6	0.8	9.2	-3.0	-10.9	-2.2
Partner country prices	2.4	7.0	10.4	3.9	1.1	1.7
Volume	-4.9	3.8	1.2	-0.8	11.8	9.1

Note: 1/ In 1998, percentage change with respect to the same period in the previous year.
Source: Bank of Slovenia and Statistical Office.

Table 3.8. Decomposition of U.S. Dollar Import Values, 1993–98

	1993	1994	1995	1996	1997	1998 Jan.-Nov. [1]
			(Index: 1995=100)			
Total import value	68.5	77.0	100.0	99.3	98.7	106.2
Price	84.3	85.8	100.0	98.9	89.4	86.9
Of which:						
Inter-currency valuation	91.3	92.3	100.0	97.7	87.7	85.8
Partner country prices	92.3	93.0	100.0	101.2	101.9	101.3
Volume	81.3	89.7	100.0	100.4	110.7	122.2
			(Percent change)			
Total import value	5.9	12.4	30.0	-0.7	-0.6	7.3
Price	-10.0	1.8	16.5	-1.1	-9.6	-2.8
Of which:						
Inter-currency valuation	-5.8	1.0	8.4	-2.3	-10.3	-2.3
Partner country prices	-4.4	0.8	7.5	1.2	0.8	-0.5
Volume	17.3	10.3	11.5	0.4	10.2	10.4

Note: 1/ In 1998, percentage change with respect to the same period in the previous year.
Sources: Bank of Slovenia and Statistical Office .

Table 3.9. International Reserves, 1993–98

	1993	1994	1995	1996	1997	1998 Aug.
	(In millions of U.S. dollars, end of period)					
Bank of Slovenia						
Total reserves minus gold	788	1,499	1,821	2,298	3,315	3,570
SDRs	0	0	0	0	0	0
Reserve position in IMF	18	19	19	19	17	40
Foreign exchange	770	1,480	1,802	2,279	3,297	3,530
Other foreign assets [1/]	1	103	170	34	41	47
Use of IMF credit	-12	-7	-4	-1	...	...
Commercial banks						
Foreign exchange	797	1,284	1,624	1,851	1,059	971
Short-term liabilities to financial institutions	-45	-75	-52	-88	-78	-14
Gross foreign exchange reserves [2/]	1,567	2,764	3,426	4,130	4,357	4,502
Memorandum item:						
Gold [3/]	0.13	0.12	0.13	0.12	0.1	...

Notes: 1/ 1996 reflects the release of assets due to the closing of the fiduciary account in Luxembourg following settlement of the 1988 New Financing Agreement in June.

            2/ Foreign exchange reserves include currency, deposits abroad and foreign securities. Balances on fiduciary accounts are included in other foreign assets.

            3/ Valued according to national practice.

Sources: Bank of Slovenia; IMF International Financial Statistics.

Table 3.10. International Investment Position, 1994–97

	1994	1995	1996	1997
	(In millions of dollars)			
Net	141	-238	-1,029	-272
Assets	5,450	6,324	6,856	7,734
Direct investment abroad	281	404	366	352
Portfolio investment	63	108	102	106
Other investment	3,607	3,992	4,092	3,961
Reserve Assets	1,499	1,821	2,297	3,315
Liabilities	5,310	6,562	7,885	8,006
Direct investment in reporting econo	1,331	1,745	1,934	2,120
Portfolio investment	86	112	1,121	1,321
Other investment	3,893	4,705	4,830	4,566
	(In percent of GDP)			
Net	1.0	-1.3	-5.5	-1.5
Assets	37.9	33.7	36.4	42.4
Direct investment abroad	2.0	2.2	1.9	1.9
Portfolio investment	0.4	0.6	0.5	0.6
Other investment	25.1	21.3	21.7	21.7
Reserve Assets	10.4	9.7	12.2	18.2
Liabilities	36.9	35.0	41.8	43.9
Direct investment in reporting econo	9.3	9.3	10.3	11.6
Portfolio investment	0.6	0.6	5.9	7.2
Other investment	27.1	25.1	25.6	25.0

Source: Bank of Slovenia.

Table 4.1. External Debt, 1993–98

	1993	1994	1995	1996	1997	1998 Aug.
	(In millions of U.S. dollars)					
Debt Outstanding and Disbursed	1,873	2,258	2,970	4,010	4,176	4,488
Total Medium- and Long-Term [1]	1,744	2,172	2,916	3,960	4,041	4,378
Public and publicly guaranteed	1,206	1,331	1,437	2,025	2,067	2,212
Official creditors	723	749	702	770	711	730
Multilateral [2]	442	472	482	541	569	557
IBRD	129	143	165	153	151	141
EBRD	1	55	127	158	151	151
EIB	196	213	235	279	313	358
IFC	80	49	33	14	1	...
EUROFIMA	36	39	22	15	9	8
Bilateral	281	277	220	229	142	173
Paris Club rescheduled debt	234	218	171	181	101	129
Austria	23	21	18	13	8	7
Belgium	3	3	3	3	0	0
France	33	31	28	22	3	1
Germany	34	32	27	82	56	51
Italy	2	8	6	4	2	1
Netherlands	18	16	14	11	8	8
Sweden	5	5	6	6	0	0
Switzerland	12	10	9	6	2	0
USA	104	92	60	34	5	5
Paris Club non-rescheduled debt	28	28	0	0		
Private creditors	483	582	735	1,255	1,356	1,482
Bonds	0	0	0	974	1,116	1,215
Commercial Banks	470	569	725	275	238	266
Others	13	13	10	6	2	1
Private non-guaranteed	538	841	1,479	1,935	1,974	2,166
Commercial banks	357	586	1,044	1,432	1,447	1,618
Others	181	255	435	503	527	548
Short-term	117	79	50	49	135	110
	(In percent of GDP)					
Memorandum items:						
Total external debt	14.8	15.7	15.8	21.3	23	...
Medium- and long-term debt	13.8	15.1	15.6	21.0	22	...

Notes: 1/ Excludes non-allocated debt of the former SFRY and the IMF through 1995; 1996 excludes
non-allocated SFRY debt not yet formally assumed by Slovenia.
2/ Excludes IFC credits from 1995, which are included in private non-guaranteed debt.
Source: Bank of Slovenia.

Table 4.2. Debt Service, 1993-97

	1993	1994	1995	1996	1997
Principal Repayments	249	315	542	735	691
Public and publicly guaranteed	96	128	184	384	232
Official creditors	95	105	139	167	117
Multilateral	60	70	51	42	50
Of which:					
IBRD	16	24	21	20	19
Bilateral	35	35	88	125	67
Of which:					
Concessional	0	0	1	51	13
Private creditors	1	23	45	217	115
Commercial banks	0	20	41	52	52
Other private	1	3	4	165	63
Private non-guaranteed	153	187	358	351	459
Commercial banks	140	179	201	240	356
Other private	13	8	157	111	103
Interest Payments	125	111	159	193	224
Public and publicly guaranteed	79	62	74	92	124
Official creditors	59	54	60	48	45
Multilateral	44	42	40	40	37
Of which:					
IBRD	11	13	13	13	10
Bilateral	15	12	20	8	8
Of which:					
Concessional	0	0	1	2	1
Private creditors	20	8	14	44	79
Commercial banks	20	7	13	19	16
Other private	0	1	1	25	63
Private non-guaranteed	46	49	85	101	100
Commercial banks	41	40	58	75	76
Other private	5	9	27	26	24
Memo Items:					
Total Debt Service Ratio[1]	5.0	4.9	6.8	8.9	8.7

Note:　1/ In percent of exports of goods and non-factor services.
Source: Bank of Slovenia.

Table 5.1. Consolidated General Government Operations, 1993-98

	1993 Actual	1994 Actual	1995 Actual	1996 Actual	1997 Actual	1998 Budget	1998 Outturn Jan.-Oct.
	(In billions of tolars)						
Total revenue [1]	674.8	849.8	1,015.5	1,153.8	1,295.9	1,479.0	1,182.5
Central government	319.9	421.1	529.2	624.2	721.9	841.2	656.0
Tax revenue	273.8	389.9	481.1	570.0	659.3	766.5	584.8
Contributions	21.1	11.0	9.1	4.9	4.8	5.4	4.3
Non-tax revenue	25.0	20.2	30.5	38.9	42.0	61.3	53.3
Extrabudgetary funds [1]	293.0	348.2	404.9	426.3	457.3	509.2	418.7
Pension Fund [1]	185.6	225.5	265.3	255.8	267.7	300.8	247.0
Health Fund [1]	105.3	120.6	139.6	170.5	189.6	208.4	171.7
Solidarity Fund	2.1	2.1	...	...	...	...	...
Local governments	62.0	80.5	81.2	103.3	116.7	128.7	107.8
Revenue from privatization	0.0	0.0	8.6	10.4	15.8	8.0	13.5
Total expenditure [1]	670.2	853.7	1,020.8	1,147.1	1,328.4	1,511.5	1,191.9
Central government [1]	300.7	373.7	457.8	508.0	603.5	701.5	531.3
Current expenditure	256.7	309.1	383.0	431.0	517.8	594.8	461.7
Capital expenditure	42.3	64.2	74.5	76.0	85.3	103.2	65.8
Reserves	1.8	0.4	0.4	1.0	0.4	3.5	3.9
Extrabudgetary funds [1]	295.4	382.0	455.8	515.2	585.0	654.1	538.2
Pension Fund [1]	186.1	248.0	302.5	341.6	387.5	435.0	360.7
Health Fund [1]	107.3	131.9	153.2	173.6	197.5	219.1	177.6
Solidarity Fund	2.1	2.1	0.0	0.0	0.0	0.0	0.0
Local government [1]	74.1	98.0	102.4	123.9	139.9	155.9	122.3
Expenditure from privatization	0.0	0.0	4.9	11.0	6.4		
Overall balance	4.7	-4.2	0.7	6.7	-32.6	-32.5	-9.4
Financing (net)	-4.7	-4.2	0.7	-6.7	32.6	32.5	9.4
Foreign	8.5	5.7	6.3	23.1	20.1	15.7	17.1
Borrowing	13.0	14.1	18.8	44.2	39.2	50.0	40.7
Amortization	-4.5	-8.4	-12.6	-21.1	-19.1	-34.3	-23.6
Domestic	-13.1	-1.5	-5.6	-29.8	12.5	16.8	-7.7
Borrowing	-6.4	7.5	6.9	-16.5	24.6	68.6	58.0
Amortization	-6.7	-9.0	-12.5	-13.3	-12.1	-51.8	-65.7
	(In percent of GDP)						
Total revenue [1]	47.0	45.9	45.7	45.9	44.6	45.1	...
Total expenditure [1]	46.7	46.1	45.7	45.7	45.7	46.1	...
Central government [1]	21.0	20.2	20.6	20.2	20.8	21.4	...
Pension Fund [1]	13.0	13.4	13.6	13.6	13.3	13.3	...
Health Fund [1]	7.5	7.1	6.9	6.9	6.8	6.7	...
Local governments [1]	5.2	5.3	4.6	4.9	4.8	4.8	...
Overall balance	0.3	-0.2	0.0	0.3	-1.1	-1.0	...
Foreign financing, net	0.6	0.3	0.3	0.9	0.7	0.5	...
Domestic financing, net	-0.9	-0.1	-0.3	-1.2	0.4	0.5	...
Memorandum item:							
GDP (in billions of tolars)	1,435.1	1,853.0	2,221.5	2,512.0	2,906.7	3,279.9	...

Note: 1/ Transfers between the different levels of government and the funds are netted out (consolidated).
Source: Ministry of Finance.

Table 5.2. General Government Revenue, 1993–98

(In billions of tolars)

	1993 Actual	1994 Actual	1995 Actual	1996 Actual	1997 Actual	1998 Budget	1998 Outturn Jan.-Oct.
Total revenue (consolidated)	674.8	849.8	1,015.4	1,153.8	1,295.9	1,479.0	1,182.5
Central government	319.9	421.1	529.2	624.2	721.9	841.2	656.0
Tax revenue	273.8	389.9	481.1	570.0	659.3	766.5	584.8
Corporate income tax	6.7	15.0	12.9	22.3	33.6	39.9	33.1
Payroll tax	0.0	5.9	3.8	18.3	37.5	41.4	37.1
Personal income tax	57.4	75.8	101.0	119.3	135.8	153.0	121.4
Sales taxes	158.2	228.9	285.1	333.7	394.0	472.1	351.2
General	103.9	144.9	185.6	215.2	256.5	297.0	226.8
Petroleum	41.7	56.6	67.0	84.5	93.5	122.2	82.9
Tobacco and alcohol	11.2	25.9	32.5	34.0	35.9	39.7	27.6
Other taxes	1.5	1.5	0.0	0.0	8.1	13.2	13.8
Tax on bank assets	0.0	0.0	0.0	0.0	0.0	7.2	2.7
Customs duties	51.5	64.3	78.2	76.6	58.5	53.0	39.4
Contributions	21.1	11.0	9.1	4.9	4.8	5.4	4.3
Unemployment	21.1	9.9	7.3	2.8	2.4	2.7	2.2
Health	0.0	0.0	0.0	0.0	0.0	0.0	0.0
Maternity leave	0.0	1.1	1.8	2.1	2.4	2.7	2.2
Non-tax revenue	25.0	20.2	30.5	38.9	42.0	61.3	53.3
Registration, road charges	7.4	5.8	6.4	7.2	8.0	12.4	10.6
Fees and charges	5.0	6.9	13.5	14.8	14.8	18.3	14.5
Bank of Slovenia profit transfers	3.6	1.0	0.0	0.0	0.0	0.0	0.0
Interest income	1.5	3.2	1.9	1.7	1.4	1.6	2.4
Other	4.4	3.4	8.8	15.2	17.8	25.5	25.1
Capital revenue	3.1	0.0	0.0	0.0	0.0	3.5	0.7
Extrabudgetary funds	303.5	368.7	430.9	500.5	576.6	646.3	547.0
Pension Fund revenue	207.0	260.9	308.4	352.3	410.2	462.3	396.5
Of which:							
Pension Fund contributions	192.4	238.5	283.7	280.2	291.6	327.5	268.5
Health Fund revenue	109.4	125.0	145.7	176.4	198.0	219.1	179.7
Of which:							
Health Fund contributions	87.6	98.3	116.1	139.9	157.1	174.6	143.5
Solidarity Fund contributions	2.1	2.1	0.0	0.0	0.0	0.0	0.0
Local governments	75.6	100.7	108.9	131.0	149.1	163.3	136.9
Of which:							
Income taxes	40.6	52.4	46.6	55.4	58.2	64.6	52.0
Revenue from privatization	0.0	0.0	8.6	10.4	15.8	8.0	13.5

Source: Ministry of Finance.

Table 5.3. General Government Expenditure, 1993–98
(In billions of tolars)

	1993 Actual	1994 Actual	1995 Actual	1996 Actual	1997 [1] Actual	1998 Budget	1998 Outturn Jan.-Oct.
Total expenditure (consolidated)	670.2	854.0	1,016.0	1,147.1	1,328.4	1,511.5	1,191.9
Central government	323.5	413.1	507.1	608.5	754.1	870.5	686.5
Current expenditures	278.8	345.6	427.3	524.2	662.7	761.9	615.8
Wages	81.5	89.5	142.9	171.6	205.7	232.6	187.5
Other goods and services	17.2	24.7	36.9	42.5	48.8	58.7	42.7
Transfers to individuals	59.3	73.9	76.5	88.5	115.0	130.2	107.4
Transfers to nonprofit organizations	29.1	36.4	31.5	36.4	47.0	52.5	39.1
Transfers to Pension Fund	6.4	16.1	19.9	67.1	111.7	126.3	120.3
Interest	18.7	28.0	24.9	30.4	33.9	43.4	37.9
Domestic	13.7	21.0	19.1	20.9	21.0	26.3	24.7
Foreign	4.9	7.0	5.8	9.6	12.9	17.1	13.2
Payments of guarantees	4.1	3.7	0.9	2.2	1.4	2.8	2.2
Transfers to enterprises	31.5	30.1	36.4	29.8	36.7	46.0	28.4
Transfers to local communities	13.4	19.0	24.7	23.0	28.0	31.6	26.2
Refugees	2.1	2.4	2.2	1.9			
Other	17.5	24.3	32.9	33.7	34.0	37.8	24.2
Capital expenditures	43.0	67.1	79.4	82.3	91.5	105.2	66.8
Budget reserves	1.8	0.4	0.4	1.0	0.4	3.5	3.9
Extrabudgetary funds	295.8	381.9	455.6	515.2	585.0	654.1	538.2
Pension Fund	201.6	267.3	325.8	369.7	419.1	470.1	389.9
Health Insurance Fund	107.3	131.9	153.2	173.6	197.5	219.1	177.6
Solidarity Fund	2.1	2.1	0.0	0.0	0.0	0.0	0.0
Local budgets	75.1	99.2	103.8	125.6	141.9	158.2	124.3
Expenditure of revenues from privatization	0.0	0.0	4.9	11.0			
Memorandum item: Consolidation items	24.2	40.2	50.5	102.2	152.6	171.3	157.2

Note: 1/ The 1997 estimates of the central government accounts are identical to the accepted budget.
Source: Ministry of Finance.

Table 5.4. Central Government Expenditure on Restructuring Programs, 1993-97

	1993	1994	1995	1996	1997
	(In billions of tolars)				
Total	60.5	70.6	73.9	88.3	93.9
Banks	9.7	15.5	14.6	18.5	14.1
Enterprises	11.7	11.6	11.5	14.9	15.9
Social safety net [1]	35.3	37.4	34.5	34.6	41.4
Active programs	15.4	12.9	12.2	8.4	9.0
Passive programs	19.9	24.6	22.3	26.2	32.4
Amortization of debt [1]	3.7	6.1	13.2	20.3	22.5
	(In percent of GDP)				
Total	4.2	3.8	3.4	3.6	3.3
Banks	0.7	0.8	0.7	0.9	0.5
Enterprises	0.8	0.6	0.5	0.6	0.6
Social safety net [1]	2.5	2.0	1.6	1.4	1.5
Active programs	1.1	0.7	0.6	0.4	0.3
Passive programs	1.4	1.3	1.0	1.0	1.1
Amortization of debt [1]	0.3	0.3	0.6	0.8	0.8
	(In percent of total expenditure) [2]				
Total	9.0	8.3	7.3	7.5	7.1
Banks	1.5	1.8	1.4	1.4	1.1
Enterprises	1.7	1.4	1.1	1.3	1.2
Social safety net [1]	5.3	4.4	3.4	3.0	3.1
Active programs	2.3	1.5	1.2	0.8	0.7
Passive programs	3.0	2.9	2.2	2.2	2.4
Amortization of debt	0.5	0.7	1.3	1.8	1.7

Note: 1/ Related to restructuring programs only.
Source: Ministry of Finance.

Table 5.5. Social Security Contribution Rates, 1992-98
(In percent of gross wage)

	1992	1993	1994	1995	1996	1997	1998
Pension and disability insurance	28.8	30.8	31.0	31.0	24.4	24.4	24.4
Employees	14.4	15.4	15.5	15.5	15.5	15.5	15.5
Employers	14.4	15.4	15.5	15.5	8.9	8.9	8.9
Obligatory health insurance	18.2	13.8	12.8	12.7	13.3	13.3	13.3
Employees	8.7	6.6	6.1	6.1	6.4	6.4	6.4
Employers	9.5	7.2	6.6	6.6	6.9	6.9	6.9
Unemployment insurance	3.4	3.4	1.3	0.8	0.2	0.2	0.2
Employees	1.7	1.7	0.6	0.4	0.1	0.1	0.1
Employers	1.7	1.7	0.6	0.4	0.1	0.1	0.1
Maternity leave	0.0	0.0	0.2	0.2	0.2	0.2	0.2
Employees	0.0	0.0	0.1	0.1	0.1	0.1	0.1
Employers	0.0	0.0	0.1	0.1	0.1	0.1	0.1
Total	50.4	48.0	45.2	44.7	38.0	38.0	38.0
Employees	24.8	23.7	22.4	22.1	22.1	22.1	22.1
Employers	25.6	24.3	22.9	22.6	15.9	15.9	15.9

Source: Ministry of Finance.

Table 6.1. Monetary Survey, 1993-98

	1993	1994	1995	1996	1997	1998 Sept.
	(In billions of tolars, end-of-period)					
Net foreign assets	99.0	269.3	335.2	457.3	636.9	679.9
Net foreign assets of BOS	102.5	189.1	250.3	329.6	559.2	601.5
Net foreign assets of DMBs (net)	-3.4	80.2	84.8	127.7	77.7	78.4
Net domestic assets	333.9	357.4	478.0	545.6	600.0	717.8
Domestic assets	534.1	643.3	841.5	948.8	1,071.9	1,248.3
Claims on government (net)	162.9	158.9	188.8	172.1	197.1	225.4
Claims on NBY	52.6	51.7	30.1	31.1	32.3	32.3
Claims on NFMIs	2.0	5.5	12.7	9.4	12.4	13.7
Claims on enterprises	260.7	335.0	448.3	527.3	586.5	684.8
Claims on private sector	55.8	92.2	161.5	208.9	243.7	292.2
Less: Bonds	69.4	120.5	171.7	215.5	417.4	444.6
Restricted deposits	9.9	12.1	12.9	17.9	19.9	24.4
Other items (net)	120.9	153.3	178.8	169.8	34.6	61.4
M1	98.0	132.5	165.4	195.9	231.6	264.5
Currency in circulation	32.7	47.3	60.0	66.8	78.1	89.2
Demand deposits	64.4	84.2	104.1	127.4	151.4	171.1
Other	0.9	1.1	1.4	1.6	2.1	4.2
M2 (= M1 + tolar deposits)	235.9	389.9	496.6	633.6	847.4	1,002.1
Of which: Tolar Deposits	138.0	257.3	331.1	437.7	615.8	737.6
M3 (= M2 + foreign currency deposits)	432.9	626.7	813.2	1,002.9	1,236.9	1,397.7
Of which: Foreign currency deposits	197.0	236.8	316.6	369.3	389.5	395.6
	(Annual growth, in percent)					
M1 growth	40.9	35.3	24.8	18.4	18.3	24.0
M2 growth	58.8	65.2	27.4	27.6	33.7	31.6
M3 growth	62.0	44.7	29.8	23.3	23.3	22.6
Contributions to M3 growth (in %)						
NFA	22.1	39.3	10.5	15.0	17.9	6.2
NDA	39.9	5.4	19.3	8.3	5.4	16.4
Contributions to M3 growth (in % points)						
NFA	35.6	87.9	35.3	64.4	76.8	27.3
NDA	64.4	12.1	64.7	35.6	23.2	72.7

Source: IMF.

Table 6.2. Balance Sheet of the Bank of Slovenia, 1993-98

	1993	1994	1995	1996	1997	1998 Sept.
	\multicolumn{6}{c}{(In billions of tolars)}					
Assets	138.8	235.6	309.2	361.0	593.0	630.1
Foreign Assets	104.0	190.1	250.9	329.8	559.3	601.6
Of which:						
Convertible foreign exchange	101.5	174.8	227.2	322.6	549.7	588.1
Investment in foreign treasury bills	6.7	11.6	26.3	54.7	187.1	259.6
Claims on central government	18.8	15.6	15.3	15.5	15.7	15.5
Claims on deposit money banks	16	29.9	43.1	15.7	18.1	13.0
Of which: Lombard	0.4	0.0	0.1	0.2	0.0	0.0
Liquidity loans	13.6	13.8	7.7	1.3	0.0	0.5
Repurchase agreements	1.5	12.6	16.8	13.6	13.7	12.0
Liabilities	138.8	235.6	309.2	361.0	593.0	630.1
Reserve money	51.3	80.5	100.8	116.5	143.4	162.3
Of which: Currency outside banks	32.7	47.3	60.0	66.8	78.1	89.2
Deposit money banks' cash	2.1	3.6	4.3	5.0	8.0	9.9
Deposit money banks' deposits	15.6	28.5	35.2	43.1	55.1	59.0
Bonds	50.4	99.8	126.7	178.4	365.0	390.2
Import and restricted deposits	0.4	1.8	1.9	0.9	2.3	2.7
Foreign liabilities	1.5	0.9	0.5	0.2	0.1	0.1
Central government deposits	6	27.4	47.5	22.3	23.1	24.9
Capital accounts	29.3	27.2	31.8	43.3	58.6	49.6
Of which: SDR allocation	4.6	4.7	4.8	5.2	5.8	5.5
Other items (net)	-0.1	-2.0	0.0	-0.7	0.6	0.2
Memorandum items:						
Reserve money	51.3	80.49339	100.8	116.5	143.4	162.3
NFA	102.5	189.1	250.3	329.6	559.2	601.5
NDA	-51.2	-108.6	-149.5	-213.0	-415.9	-439.2
	\multicolumn{6}{c}{(Annual percentage change)}					
Reserve money growth	38.3	43.1	10.3	14.3	11.6	5.4
Contributions to growth:						
NFA	85.4	60.9	31.4	14.7	10.3	-14.9
NDA	-47.2	-17.8	-21.1	-0.4	1.2	20.3

Source: Data provided by the Bank of Slovenia.

Table 6.3. Balance Sheet of Deposit Money Banks, 1993-98
(In billions of tolars, end of period)

	1993	1994	1995	1996	1997	1998 Sept.
Reserves	55.4	31.1	38.1	48.1	63.1	68.9
Currency	2.1	3.6	4.3	5.0	8.0	9.9
Deposits with central bank	53.3	27.5	33.8	43.1	55.1	59.0
Foreign assets	136.2	239.3	271.7	334.1	284.0	274.7
Claims on nonresident banks	130.4	202.7	226.5	289.6	243.2	236.3
Claims on nonresident nonbanks	5.7	36.6	45.2	44.5	40.8	38.5
Claims on central government	208.1	257.8	315.9	319.6	372.5	408.4
Government securities	188.7	224.9	264.6	278.7	302.4	320.1
Loans and advances	19.4	32.9	51.3	40.9	70.1	88.4
Claims on National Bank of Yugoslavia	52.6	51.7	30.1	31.1	32.3	32.3
Claims on private sector	316.5	427.0	609.7	736.0	830.0	976.7
Businesses (corporate)	261.2	334.9	448.2	527.2	586.3	684.6
Private households	55.2	92.2	161.5	208.9	243.7	292.2
Claims on nonmonetary financial institutions	2.0	5.5	12.7	9.4	12.4	13.7
Assets = Liabilities	770.7	1012.5	1278.3	1478.3	1594.2	1774.8
Deposit liabilities	399.3	578.3	751.9	934.5	1156.6	1304.4
Demand deposits	64.4	84.2	104.1	127.4	151.4	171.1
Foreign currency deposits	197.0	236.8	316.6	369.3	389.5	395.6
Time deposits	103.7	210.1	270.2	366.4	530.9	631.0
Savings deposits	29.9	41.9	54.7	65.2	79.1	100.7
Margin deposits	4.3	5.4	6.3	6.2	5.9	6.0
Money market instruments	16.4	12.5	27.0	13.2	18.5	19.0
Bonds	2.6	8.3	18.1	23.8	34.0	35.4
Import and restricted deposits	9.5	10.3	11.0	17.0	17.6	21.7
Foreign liabilities	139.6	159.2	186.9	206.4	206.3	196.3
Nonresident banks	114.7	128.6	146.9	156.2	150.1	142.6
Nonresident nonbanks	24.9	30.5	40.0	50.1	56.2	53.8
Central government deposits	57.9	87.2	94.9	140.7	168.0	173.7
Government lending funds	2.4	4.9	8.3	12.3	14.0	21.6
Credit from the central bank	15.5	29.6	41.7	15.3	17.8	12.7
Liabilities to nonmonetary financial institutions	9.9	5.5	10.4	15.4	23.3	32.1
Capital accounts	151.1	209.5	248.3	273.2	303.7	325.7
Other items (net)	-33.5	-92.7	-120.0	-173.6	-365.7	-367.8

Source: Data provided by the Bank of Slovenia according to IFS classification.

Table 7.1. Price Developments, 1993-97 (Page 1 of 2)

(Percentage change)

		Retail prices			Industrial Producer Prices		Agricultural Producer Prices		Cost of Living	
		Annual Growth	Monthly Growth	Controlled Sectors	Uncontrolled Sectors	Annual Growth	Monthly Growth	Annual Growth	Monthly Growth	Annual Growth	Monthly Growth
1991		117.7	10.9	...	...	124.1	12.5	108.2	11.4	114.8	10.8
1992		201.3	5.6	1.2	4.4	215.7	4.8	213.6	4.7	207.3	5.6
1993		32.3	1.7	0.7	1.0	21.6	1.4	18.7	1.4	32.9	1.7
1994		19.8	1.4	0.4	1.0	17.7	1.4	24.7	1.5	21.0	1.5
1995		12.6	0.7	...	...	12.8	0.6	13.3	0.6	13.5	0.7
1996		9.7	0.7			6.8	0.5	10.8	1.0	9.9	0.7
1997		9.1	0.7			6.1	0.6	6.7	0.5	8.4	0.7
	Jan.	269.1	15.2	6.1	9.1	314.3	10.8	306.3	15.5	269.2	14.6
	Feb.	276.8	11.0	2.7	8.3	348.8	17.5	342.6	16.0	278.2	12.6
1992	March	303.5	11.5	3.2	8.3	375.5	12.4	358.5	10.2	303.0	10.7
	April	301.7	5.1	0.2	5.0	386.4	4.3	365.5	6.7	309.4	6.4
	May	287.9	6.5	1.0	5.6	331.6	5.9	319.8	5.3	292.3	7.1
	June	261.7	5.9	1.0	4.9	299.9	2.5	292.0	2.3	267.4	4.4
	July	249.7	2.0	0.3	1.7	274.9	1.2	236.6	-4.4	250.5	0.7
	Aug.	229.2	1.4	0.2	1.2	252.8	1.4	232.1	0.1	233.9	0.2
	Sept.	191.5	2.7	0.2	2.6	203.5	1.1	218.0	2.7	202.5	3.5
	Oct.	150.0	3.4	0.4	3.0	144.2	1.1	159.5	4.2	157.8	3.9
	Nov.	116.0	2.8	0.2	2.6	106.2	1.2	102.9	-1.0	121.9	3.5
	Dec.	92.9	1.1	-0.2	1.3	76.2	0.4	74.1	-0.2	92.0	0.7
	Jan.	71.7	3.7	2.5	1.3	66.1	4.6	49.3	0.8	73.2	3.8
	Feb.	57.2	1.6	0.3	1.3	43.7	1.5	30.6	0.6	56.6	1.8
1993	March	42.5	1.4	0.1	1.3	27.7	-0.2	18.6	-0.1	43.3	1.6
	April	36.6	1.0	0.5	0.5	21.7	-0.6	9.6	-0.4	35.4	0.8
	May	30.2	1.4	0.3	1.1	15.0	0.1	1.5	0.0	28.9	2.0
	June	26.2	1.5	0.6	0.9	14.4	1.9	4.4	3.5	25.1	0.6
	July	24.6	0.8	0.3	0.5	14.0	0.8	13.8	4.5	25.1	0.8
	Aug.	25.2	1.7	1.7	0.0	13.3	0.8	19.0	4.7	25.6	0.7
	September	24.0	1.7	0.4	1.4	13.6	1.2	16.5	-0.2	24.0	2.1
	Oct.	24.2	2.9	1.4	1.5	16.0	3.3	17.3	2.6	23.0	2.6
	Nov.	22.4	1.6	0.4	1.2	16.2	1.4	20.0	1.6	21.6	2.3
	December	22.9	1.5	0.5	1.0	18.6	2.4	18.8	-0.1	22.8	1.8
	Jan.	20.3	1.5	0.1	1.4	14.5	1.1	24.2	2.2	20.7	1.9
	Feb.	19.9	1.3	0.1	1.2	15.3	2.2	23.9	0.4	20.1	1.3
1994	March	19.5	1.1	0.1	1.0	19.9	0.5	26.0	1.0	19.9	1.5
	April	20.8	2.1	0.3	1.8	21.5	0.7	29.2	2.6	21.8	2.4
	May	20.4	1.0	0.1	0.9	22.2	0.7	32.9	0.9	20.8	1.1
	June	20.5	1.6	0.5	1.1	23.8	1.3	36.7	3.5	21.8	1.5
	July	20.8	1.1	0.5	0.6	18.2	1.3	29.3	1.2	22.5	1.4
	Aug.	20.1	1.1	0.5	0.6	18.5	1.1	22.6	0.2	22.6	0.8
	September	19.9	1.5	0.6	0.9	19.1	1.6	18.9	-0.5	22.1	1.7
	Oct.	18.9	2.0	1.4	0.6	19.1	3.3	18.4	2.9	21.0	1.7
	Nov.	18.9	1.5	0.1	1.4	19.3	1.6	18.9	3.2	20.5	1.9
	December	18.3	1.1	0.5	0.6	18.2	1.5	20.0	1.0	19.5	0.9
	Jan.	17.8	1.1	0.0	1.1	18.2	1.1	24.1	4.8	19.8	2.0
	Feb.	17.5	0.9	0.1	0.8	16.4	0.6	22.8	-0.7	19.6	1.2
1995	March	16.6	0.5	0.0	0.6	16.6	0.7	20.8	-0.3	18.3	0.4
	April	14.2	-0.1	-0.5	0.5	15.9	0.1	18.8	1.0	15.3	-0.2
	May	13.6	0.5	0.0	0.5	15.0	-0.1	19.3	1.0	15.2	1.1
	June	12.6	0.8	0.5	0.3	13.7	0.2	10.7	-2.3	14.1	0.5
	July	11.7	0.3	0.0	0.3	12.3	0.0	8.7	-4.2	12.7	0.1
	Aug.	11.1	0.5	0.1	0.4	11.5	0.4	7.7	-0.2	11.4	-0.3
	September	10.8	1.3	0.9	0.5	10.9	1.1	6.2	0.2	10.7	1.0
	Oct.	9.3	0.6	0.3	0.3	8.6	1.2	6.0	2.1	9.4	0.5
	Nov.	9.1	1.3	0.8	0.5	8.2	1.2	8.4	3.0	8.9	1.4
	December	8.6	0.6	0.1	0.5	7.9	1.2	7.8	3.1	9.0	1.0

Table 7.1. Price Developments, 1993-97 (Page 2 of 2)
(Percentage change)

		Retail prices			Industrial Producer Prices		Agricultural Producer Prices		Cost of Living	
		Annual Growth	Monthly Growth	Controlled Sectors	Uncontrolled Sectors	Annual Growth	Monthly Growth	Annual Growth	Monthly Growth	Annual Growth	Monthly Growth
1996	January	8.5	1.0	0.1	0.9	7.1	0.3	2.9	-0.3	8.4	1.4
	February	8.5	0.9	0.6	0.9	7.6	1.1	5.9	2.1	8.4	1.2
	March	9.3	1.3	0.6	1.2	6.8	-0.1	8.4	2.1	9.6	1.6
	April	10.7	1.2	0.1	0.6	7.1	0.4	10.4	2.2	11.4	1.4
	May	10.9	0.7	0.0	0.3	6.5	-0.7	11.0	0.5	10.8	0.6
	June	10.5	0.5	0.1	0.3	7.0	0.7	12.8	2.4	10.5	0.2
	July	10.7	0.5	0.1	0.4	7.4	0.4	10.5	-4.1	10.7	0.3
	August	10.3	0.1	0.2	-0.2	7.3	0.3	10.9	0.0	10.4	-0.6
	September	9.4	0.5	0.1	0.4	6.8	0.6	15.2	3.7	9.7	0.4
	October	9.7	0.8	0.2	0.6	6.7	1.2	15.1	1.3	10.2	0.9
	November	8.6	0.4	0.1	0.3	5.9	0.4	11.8	0.4	9.2	0.5
	December	8.8	0.7	0.3	0.4	5.8	1.1	12.9	3.2	9.0	0.8
1997	January	9.0	1.1	0.4	0.7	5.8	0.3	11.1	-0.8	8.9	1.3
	February	8.5	0.4	0.4	0.1	5.4	0.7	7.6	-1.4	8.4	0.7
	March	7.4	0.3	0.0	0.3	5.0	-0.5	5.0	-0.1	7.2	0.5
	April	8.2	2.0	1.2	0.8	5.0	0.4	2.0	-0.7	7.0	1.2
	May	8.9	1.3	0.9	0.4	6.2	0.4	2.4	1.0	8.1	1.6
	June	8.8	0.4	0.2	0.2	6.2	0.8	1.7	2.1	7.8	0.0
	July	9.4	1.0	0.8	0.3	5.9	0.1	10.9	3.1	8.1	0.6
	August	9.6	0.3	0.1	0.2	5.8	0.2	11.7	0.7	9.0	0.2
	September	10.1	0.9	0.3	0.6	6.6	1.4	7.6	-1.0	9.2	0.6
	October	9.7	0.5	0.1	0.4	7.3	1.8	7.8	0.9	8.7	0.5
	November	9.9	0.6	0.0	0.6	7.1	0.2	8.3	0.9	9.1	0.8
	December	9.4	0.3	0.0	0.3	6.8	0.8	5.5	1.1	8.8	0.6

Source: Statistical Office of the Republic of Slovenia, Institute of Macroeconomic Analysis and Development and Bank of Slovenia.

Table 7.2. Average Monthly Net Wages
Per Worker in the Enterprise and Public Sectors, 1993–98

| | Nominal | | Real [1] | |
	Tolars month	Percent change [2]	Index 1992=100	Percent change [2]
1992	30,813	198.7	100.0	..
1993	46,826	52.0	114.3	14.3
1994	60,089	28.3	121.3	6.1
1995	71,279	18.6	126.8	4.6
1996	81,830	14.8	132.5	4.5
1997	91,199	11.4	136.3	2.9
1998 January	96,770	10.2	138.1	1.2
February	97,188	11.6	137.4	2.3
March	97,375	10.6	136.6	1.1
April	97,993	9.8	136.3	0.6
May	98,336	8.9	135.6	0.6
June	99,811	9.9	137.7	1.5
July	100,178	9.3	138.2	1.5
August	99,488	9.3	137.1	1.6
September	100,000	8.4	137.7	1.5
October	100,365	7.4	137.8	0.5
November	103,373	10.1	141.4	3.5

Notes: 1/ Average net personal income deflated by the consumer price index.
2/ Change from corresponding period of preceding year.
Source: Statistical Office of the Republic of Slovenia.

Table 7.3. Selected Interest Rates, 1993–98 [1]

(Annualized, in percent)

	1993	1994	1995	1996	1997	1998 Sept.
Interbank market rate						
Real [2]	12.8	8.3	...	...		
Nominal	39.1	29.0	15.9	10.2	9.8	6.4
Deposit rates						
Demand deposits	9.4	8.3	5.3	1.4	1.0	1.0
Time deposits (31-90 days)						
Real	7.9	7.8	6.2	4.9	3.7	0.9
Nominal	33.0	28.1	20.8	11.2	13.9	8.5
Time deposits (over 1 year)						
Real	11.2	11.0	9.4	7.1	6.2	4.2
Nominal	37.1	31.9	24.4	13.6	16.6	12.1
Foreign exchange deposits	6.5	5.2	4.2	3.0	3.6	3.1
Lending rates						
Short term						
Real	20.4	16.9	12.5	11.5	9.6	5.9
Nominal	48.6	38.9	28.0	18.3	20.3	13.9
Long term						
Real	21.2	17.3	13.6	12.5	10.7	7.3
Nominal	49.6	39.4	29.2	19.3	21.6	15.4
Consumer credits						
Real	19.3	16.3	11.7	10.3	8.0	4.3
Nominal	47.2	38.2	27.1	17.0	18.7	12.2
Bank of Slovenia interest rates						
Lombard rate	21.3	17.2	11.0	11.0	11.0	11.0
Penalty rate						
Real [2]	25.8	25.0	...	...		
Nominal	55.3	48.5	31.8	24.1	27.8	25.6
Liquidity loans (overnight)						
Real [2]	9.0	5.8	...	...		
Nominal	34.4	25.7	10.5	10.5	10.5	10.5
Tolar bills (14 days)						
Real [2]	8.8	8.0	...	...		
Nominal	34.2	28.3	5.5	5.0	5.0	4.7
Foreign exchange bills (60 days)	6.7	5.2	3.8	3.1	3.6	3.3

Notes: 1/ Nominal rates are calculated by adding a "revaluation clause" to the real component. The revaluation clause is calculated on the basis of past inflation (one-month through May 1995, average of 3 months through January 1996, average of 4 months through November 1996, average of 6 months through April 1997, and average of 12 months thereafter).

2/ Interest rates on financial assets with less than one-month maturity began to be determined in nominal terms in May 1995.

Source: Bank of Slovenia.

Table 7.4. Average Monthly Net Wage By Sector of Activities, 1992-97 [1]

Standard Classification of Activities [2]	1992	1993	1994	1995	1996	1997
Total	30,813	46,826	60,089	71,279	81,830	91,199
A. Agriculture, hunting, and forestry	33,165	49,347	60,731	69,709	79,847	87,650
B. Fishing	33,437	48,952	61,812	69,499	78,223	86,937
C. Mining and quarrying	36,972	57,184	73,314	86,006	95,330	106,359
D. Manufacturing	26,575	39,489	51,624	60,658	69,247	77,325
E. Electricity, gas, and water supply	35,343	54,208	71,736	84,198	93,582	102,600
F. Construction	25,768	39,677	52,405	61,863	71,601	78,880
G. Wholesale, retail; certain repair	31,857	48,702	61,758	71,282	80,821	87,594
H. Hotels and restaurants	27,666	42,692	57,829	68,597	76,650	80,315
I. Transport, storage, and communications	36,915	53,470	69,135	79,639	90,369	99,387
J. Financial intermediation	43,670	64,880	83,342	100,735	115,844	126,973
K. Real estate, renting, and business activities	33,743	51,920	69,959	78,728	86,670	95,029
L. Public administration and defense; comp. social security	41,352	64,389	76,583	90,369	104,743	116,070
M. Education	35,779	53,433	65,233	75,713	87,810	102,446
N. Health and social work	33,817	51,143	63,372	80,845	94,544	105,023
O. Other social and personal services	36,088	54,831	67,469	88,644	102,110	114,213

(Percentage changes)

	1992	1993	1994	1995	1996	1997
Total	-	52.0	28.3	18.6	14.8	11.4
A. Agriculture, hunting, and forestry	-	48.8	23.1	14.8	14.5	9.8
B. Fishing	-	46.4	26.3	12.4	12.6	11.1
C. Mining and quarrying	-	54.7	28.2	17.3	10.8	11.6
D. Manufacturing	-	48.6	30.7	17.5	14.2	11.7
E. Electricity, gas, and water supply	-	53.4	32.3	17.4	11.1	9.6
F. Construction	-	54.0	32.1	18.0	15.7	10.2
G. Wholesale, retail; certain repair	-	52.9	26.8	15.4	13.4	8.4
H. Hotels and restaurants	-	54.3	35.5	18.6	11.7	4.8
I. Transport, storage, and communications	-	44.8	29.3	15.2	13.5	10.0
J. Financial intermediation	-	48.6	28.5	20.9	15.0	9.6
K. Real estate, renting, and business activities	-	53.9	34.7	12.5	10.1	9.6
L. Public administration and defense; comp. social security	-	55.7	18.9	18.0	15.9	10.8
M. Education	-	49.3	22.1	16.1	16.0	16.7
N. Health and social work	-	51.2	23.9	27.6	16.9	11.1
O. Other social and personal services	-	51.9	23.0	31.4	15.2	11.9
Memorandum items:						
Retail price index	201.3	32.2	19.8	12.6	9.8	9.1
Consumer price index	207.3	32.9	21.0	13.5	9.9	8.4

Notes: 1/ Includes socially-owned, state-owned and private enterprises with more than 2 employees.
2/ From January 1, 1997 the Standard Classification of Activities is used for statistical and analytical purposes. In order to assure comparison of data which correspond in view of time, we have classified the data on average net wages of persons in paid employment in enterprises, companies, and organizations in the period from 1992 to 1996 into sections of activities of the SCA with crosstables.

Source: Statistical Office of the Republic of Slovenia.

Table 8.1. Number of Enterprises by Ownership and Activity, 1995–97

Activities	Total 1/			Social			Private			Cooperative		
	1995	1996	1997	1995	1996	1997	1995	1996	1997	1995	1996	1997
Total	33,609	35,786	36,717	2,317	1,916	1,399	29,978	32,243	33,256	36	35	38
Agriculture, hunting, and forestry	364	382	401	53	42	24	297	320	331	5	6	9
Fishing	18	18	19	6	4	4	12	12	12	-	-	1
Mining and quarrying	38	42	42	18	19	15	16	19	18	-	-	-
Manufacturing	5,594	5,876	6,121	843	673	456	4,456	4,792	5,061	4	4	3
Electricity, gas, and water supply	110	117	120	76	72	66	23	29	31	1	1	1
Construction	1,855	2,013	2,180	166	138	88	1,632	1,793	1,968	4	4	3
Wholesale, retail, certain repair	14,113	14,821	14,904	370	278	192	13,411	14,151	14,292	6	7	8
Hotels and restaurants	928	1,045	1,108	108	99	76	785	902	965	1	1	1
Transport, storage, and communication	1,722	1,915	1,866	89	72	49	1,539	1,733	1,702	5	4	4
Financial intermediation	237	280	315	11	9	9	185	217	247	-	-	-
Real estate, renting, and business services	7,340	7,812	8,031	431	374	291	6,535	7,030	7,276	10	8	8
Public administration and defense; compulsory social security	4	5	4	2	2	1	1	2	1	-	-	-
Education	432	449	460	12	10	10	411	429	444	-	-	-
Health and social work	194	256	319	55	55	51	128	182	227	-	-	-
Other social and personal services	660	755	827	77	69	67	547	632	681	-	-	-

Note: 1/ Includes the number of companies of mixed ownership and from 1997 also state-owned companies.
Source: Agency for Payments, Supervision, and Information.

Table 8.2. Distribution of Enterprises by Size in 1997

		Number of employees per Enterprise	Revenue per employee (In thousands of tolars)	Wages per employee (In thousands of tolars)	Net Profits (In millions of tolars)	Number of enterprises	Revenues (In percent)	Exports/ revenues (In percent)	Capital/ capital and liabilities (In percent)
Total	Total	13	14,153	1,547	177,258	36,717	100.0	23.8	51.6
	Large	311	14,863	1,681	108,433	869	61.6	29.3	56.8
	Medium	56	12,138	1,543	27,018	1,478	15.6	19.0	51.5
	Small	3	13,930	1,211	41,807	34,370	22.8	12.1	29.0
Agriculture	Total	23	10,043	1,543	2,383	432	100.0	9.3	65.8
	Large	264	10,445	1,586	1,593	25	67.5	12.1	68.1
	Medium	78	7,737	1,608	520	32	19.0	3.0	68.7
	Small	3	12,973	1,130	270	375	13.5	4.4	43.4
Industry	Total	35	11,618	1,488	68,958	6,792	100.0	38.5	59.3
	Large	383	12,579	1,566	50,838	446	76.9	42.9	63.5
	Medium	75	8,685	1,388	9,087	552	12.8	30.8	44.3
	Small	5	10,112	1,169	9,033	5,794	10.3	15.7	29.4
Services	Total	7	17,263	1,615	105,917	29,493	100.0	12.8	45.0
	Large	233	19,392	1,902	56,002	398	49.7	13.8	48.6
	Medium	44	16,027	1,701	17,411	894	17.5	12.8	53.8
	Small	3	15,346	1,228	32,504	28,201	32.8	11.4	28.7

Source: Agency of the Republic of Slovenia for Payments: Statistical data from balance sheets and loss accounts of commercial companies.

Table 8.3. Distribution of Enterprises by Ownership in 1997

Activities		Number of employees per enterprise	Revenue per employee (In thousands of tolars)	Net profits (In millions of tolars)	Number of enterprises	Revenues (In percent)	Exports/ Revenues (In percent)
Total	Total	13	14,153	177,258	36,717	100.0	23.8
	Social	104	11,508	39,777	1,399	25.8	20.8
	Private	4	18,131	60,629	33,256	32.5	15.6
	Cooperative	6	13,061	25	38	0.0	3.5
	Mixed	97	13,721	75,573	1,972	40.1	32.6
	Public	134	14,567	1254	52	1.6	17.5
Agriculture	Total	24	10,044	2,383	432	100.0	9.3
	Social	124	8,868	288	31	33.3	4.9
	Private	3	14,019	401	349	14.2	3.8
	Cooperative	1	55,241	2	8	0.2	4.5
	Mixed	122	10,112	1687	43	52.0	13.8
	Public	44	7,881	5	1	0.3	0.0
Industry	Total	35	11,618	68,958	6,792	100.0	38.5
	Social	161	11,567	16,597	516	34.4	27.8
	Private	7	12,625	15,246	5,662	17.3	27.5
	Cooperative	15	21,297	19	6	0.1	0.6
	Mixed	194	11,163	36,231	588	45.4	52.3
	Public	266	14,714	865	20	2.8	16.5
Services	Total	7	17,264	105,917	29,493	100.0	12.8
	Social	69	11,597	22,892	852	18.9	11.7
	Private	3	20,911	44,982	27,245	44.8	12.2
	Cooperative	6	6,654	4	24	0.0	9.4
	Mixed	53	18,067	37,655	1,341	35.6	14.0
	Public	52	14266	384	31	0.7	21.1

Source: Agency of the Republic of Slovenia for Payments: Statistical data from balance sheets and loss accounts of commercial companies.

Table 8.4. Ownership Structure, 1992-97

	1992	1993	1994	1995	1996	1997
	(Number of enterprises)					
Socially owned	2,635	2,524	2,479	2,317	1,916	1,399
Privately owned	16,404	23,907	27,179	29,978	32,243	33,256
Cooperatives	169	257	41	36	35	38
Mixed	1,094	1,214	1,242	1,278	1,592	1,972
Total	20,302	27,902	30,941	33,609	35,786	36,717
	(In percent)					
Socially owned	13.0	9.0	8.0	6.9	5.4	3.8
Privately owned	80.8	85.7	87.8	89.2	90.1	90.6
Cooperatives	0.8	0.9	0.2	0.1	0.1	0.1
Mixed	5.4	4.4	4.0	3.8	4.4	5.4
Total	100.0	100.0	100.0	100.0	100.0	100

Source: Agency of the Republic Slovenia for Payments: Statistical data from balance sheets and loss accounts of commercial companies.

Table 9.1. GDP Growth in Central Europe and Asia

(in percent change)

	1990	1991	1992	1993	1994	1995	1996	1997	1998^p
Central Europe and Baltic States */	*-7.4*	*-10.9*	*-5.3*	*0.3*	*4.0*	*5.5*	*3.5*	*1.8*	*3.1*
Albania	-10.0	-27.7	-7.2	9.6	9.4	8.9	8.2	-7.0	10.0
Bosnia	--	--	--	--	--	33.0	50.0	30.0	--
Bulgaria	-9.1	-8.4	-7.3	-1.5	1.8	2.9	-10.1	-6.9	5.0
Croatia	--	--	-2.1	-2.5	6.0	2.6	4.3	6.3	4.0
Czech Republic	-1.2	-14.2	-6.4	0.6	2.7	6.4	3.9	1.0	-2.0
Estonia	-8.1	-11.0	-25.8	-8.5	-1.8	4.3	4.0	11.4	8.0
Hungary	-3.5	-11.9	-3.1	-0.6	2.9	1.5	1.3	4.4	5.2
Latvia	-3.5	-8.0	-35.0	-16.0	2.0	-0.8	2.8	6.2	6.0
Lithuania	-6.9	-15.0	-39.0	-16.2	1.0	3.0	3.6	4.7	4.7
FYR Macedonia	--	--	--	-9.4	-1.7	-1.2	0.8	1.5	3.5
Poland	-11.6	-7.0	2.6	3.8	5.2	7.0	6.1	6.9	6.2
Romania	-5.6	-12.9	-8.8	1.5	3.9	7.1	3.9	-6.6	-4.0
Slovak Republic	-2.5	-14.6	-6.5	-3.7	4.9	6.8	6.6	6.5	4.0
Slovenia	-4.7	-8.1	-5.5	2.8	5.3	4.1	3.3	3.8	4.0
Community of Independent States */	*-3.2*	*-6.3*	*-15.2*	*-10.5*	*-14.7*	*-6.0*	*-3.2*	*0.7*	*-1.6*
Armenia	-8.5	-8.8	-52.3	-15.0	5.4	6.9	5.8	3.1	5.5
Azerbaijan	-11.7	-0.7	-35.2	-23.1	-19.7	-13.3	1.2	5.8	7.0
Belarus	-3.0	-3.0	-9.6	-7.6	-12.6	-10.4	2.8	10.4	5.0
Georgia	-11.1	-28.1	-43.4	-39.4	-11.4	2.4	10.5	11.0	10.0
Kazakhstan	-1.1	-11.8	-13.0	-12.9	-18.0	-8.2	0.5	2.1	1.6
Kyrgyz Republic	3.2	-5.0	-19.0	-15.5	-20.1	-5.4	7.1	6.5	6.0
Moldova	-1.5	-18.7	-29.1	-1.2	-31.2	-3.0	-10.0	1.3	-1.0
Russia	-3.6	-5.0	-14.5	-8.7	-12.6	-4.1	-3.5	0.8	-6.0
Tajikistan	-0.6	-7.0	-29.0	-11.0	-18.9	-12.5	-4.4	1.7	3.4
Turkmenistan	1.5	-5.0	-5.0	-10.0	-19.0	-8.2	-3.0	-25.9	20.0
Ukraine	-4.0	-8.7	-9.9	-14.2	-22.9	-12.2	-10.0	-3.2	1.0
Uzbekistan	1.6	-0.5	-11.1	-2.3	-4.2	-0.9	1.6	2.4	2.0

Notes: */ Population-weighted averages.
        p/ projection.
Source: The World Bank.

Table 9.2. Annual Inflation in Central Europe and Asia
(Percentage change in period-average Consumer Price Index)

	1990	1991	1992	1993	1994	1995	1996	1997	1998 [p]
Central Europe and Baltic States */	*16.1*	*120.2*	*226.0*	*85.0*	*35.9*	*25.0*	*17.6*	*9.1*	*11.0*
Albania	0.0	35.5	226.0	85.0	22.5	7.8	12.7	33.2	21.9
Bosnia	--	--	--	--	--	--	--	--	--
Bulgaria	64.0	338.5	79.4	56.1	87.1	62.1	123.0	1,082.3	23.0
Croatia	--	122.6	663.6	1,517.1	97.0	2.0	3.4	3.7	5.0
Czech Republic	9.6	56.6	11.1	20.8	10.0	9.1	8.8	8.5	11.3
Estonia	23.1	210.6	1,069.0	89.0	47.7	28.9	23.1	11.2	11.0
Hungary	28.9	35.0	23.0	22.5	18.8	28.2	23.6	18.3	13.0
Latvia	10.5	172.2	958.7	109.2	35.9	25.0	17.6	8.0	6.5
Lithuania	16.1	224.0	1,162.7	291.4	72.2	40.0	25.0	9.0	7.0
FYR Macedonia	--	--	1,975.0	355.0	121.9	16.0	3.1	4.0	3.0
Poland	585.8	70.3	43.0	35.3	32.2	27.8	19.9	14.8	12.7
Romania	4.7	270.1	310.4	356.1	236.8	132.3	138.8	254.8	160.0
Slovak Republic	10.4	61.2	10.0	23.2	13.4	9.9	5.8	6.2	7.1
Slovenia	549.7	117.7	201.3	32.9	19.8	12.6	9.7	9.1	8.0
Community of Independent States */	*5.2*	*91.2*	*1,156.7*	*1,190.0*	*1,497.9*	*246.9*	*49.2*	*16.5*	*14.8*
Armenia	10.1	80.1	677.9	3,731.9	5,273.4	176.7	19.0	14.0	15.6
Azerbaijan	7.5	82.8	1,350.9	980.9	1,427.7	411.7	24.6	4.0	5.0
Belarus	4.5	94.1	971.0	1,190.0	2,221.0	709.0	52.7	64.0	70.0
Georgia	3.3	78.7	637.3	3,125.0	15,606.5	162.7	39.3	6.9	6.5
Kazakhstan	18.9	87.4	1,622.6	1,255.5	1,880.0	176.0	51.0	17.0	11.0
Kyrgyz Republic[a]	4.8	113.7	1,007.0	782.1	95.7	31.9	30.0	26.0	14.0
Moldova	14.8	136.1	1,276.0	788.5	330.0	30.6	23.5	12.0	7.0
Russia	5.6	92.6	1,354.0	895.3	303.2	188.7	47.4	15.1	48.0
Tajikistan	--	111.1	1,156.7	2,194.8	350.4	609.3	418.3	88.0	58.3
Turkmenistan	--	--	--	--	1,748.0	1,005.0	992.0	84.0	21.0
Ukraine	4.2	91.2	1,627.0	4,834.9	991.2	476.7	180.2	16.0	13.0
Uzbekistan	3.1	82.2	645.0	534.0	1,568.0	305.0	54.0	72.0	37.0

Notes: */ Median of countries included.
  p/ projection.
  a/ Retail price inflation.
Source: The World Bank.

Table 9.3. Fiscal Balances in Central Europe and Asia

(In percent of GDP)

	1990	1991	1992	1993	1994	1995	1996	1997
Central Europe and Baltic States */	*0.5*	*-4.5*	*-4.9*	*-2.3*	*-1.9*	*-1.8*	*-1.4*	*-1.2*
Albania	-3.7	-43.7	-20.4	-14.6	-11.8	-10.3	-11.9	-13.6
Bulgaria	-9.1	-4.5	-4.9	-12.1	-4.6	-5.2	-15.4	2.1
Croatia	--	-4.6	-3.4	-1.5	1.7	-0.8	-0.5	-1.3
Czech Republic	--	--	-1.0	2.6	0.8	0.4	-0.4	-1.2
Estonia	--	--	--	-0.7	1.3	-1.2	-1.5	2.0
Hungary	0.5	-2.1	-5.4	-6.6	-7.5	-3.5	0.8	-4.7
Latvia	--	--	--	0.6	-4.0	-3.3	-1.3	1.3
Lithuania	--	--	--	-2.4	-1.5	-1.8	-2.0	-1.0
FYR Macedonia	--	--	--	-13.8	-2.9	-1.2	-0.4	-0.4
Poland	3.7	-6.7	-4.9	-2.3	-2.2	-1.8	-2.3	-2.9
Romania	1.0	3.2	-4.6	-0.4	-1.9	-2.6	-3.9	-3.6
Slovak Republic	--	--	-11.9	-7.0	-1.3	0.2	-1.4	-4.5
Slovenia	--	2.6	0.2	0.1	-0.3	-0.5	-0.2	-1.1
Community of Independent States */	*0.4*	*-3.6*	*-17.4*	*-9.5*	*-10.0*	*-5.5*	*-6.6*	*-4.0*
Armenia (excl. grants)	--	-1.8	-8.1	-56.1	-16.4	-12.0	-9.3	-6.5
Azerbaijan	-5.5	-5.0	-4.1	-14.0	-16.4	-4.1	-4.3	-1.5
Belarus	--	--	--	-1.9	-2.5	-1.9	-1.6	-0.7
Georgia (incl. grants)	--	--	--	-26.2	-16.5	-5.3	-4.5	-4.2
Kazakhstan	--	-9.0	-6.9	-0.7	-6.5	-2.5	-11.9	-3.8
Kyrgyz Republic[1]	--	5.0	-17.4	-14.4	-11.6	-17.3	-9.5	-9.4
Moldova	2.8	0.0	-27.3	-8.4	-9.7	-5.7	-7.6	-8.0
Russia	--	--	-21.8	-8.7	-11.3	-5.6	-8.7	-7.6
Tajikistan	--	-16.4	-31.2	-24.8	-10.2	-11.2	-5.8	-3.3
Turkmenistan	1.8	2.5	--	-0.4	-2.0	-3.0	-1.0	-1.0
Ukraine	--	-13.8	-13.8	-5.1	-8.9	-6.6	-4.9	-6.7
Uzbekistan	-1.1	-3.6	-18.4	-10.4	-6.1	-4.1	-7.3	-2.3
Turkey	--	--	-10.7	-12.4	-7.7	-4.8	-8.3	-7.5

Note: */ Median of countries included.

1/ Includes foreign financial public investment program and the net deficit of the social fund.

Source: The World Bank.

Table 9.4. Current Account Balances in Central Europe and Asia
(In percent of GDP)

	1990	1991	1992	1993	1994	1995	1996	1997
Central Europe and Baltic States */	*-2.4*	*-3.2*	*0.0*	*-2.9*	*-2.2*	*-5.0*	*-7.3*	*-6.9*
Albania	-5.8	-25.7	-55.7	-26.2	-11.8	-6.1	-9.0	-12.0
Bulgaria	-5.9	-4.5	-4.9	-12.1	-4.6	-5.2	-15.4	2.1
Croatia	--	-3.2	8.1	5.5	5.4	-6.8	-4.5	-12.6
Czech Republic	--	--	-1.7	1.3	-2.0	-2.7	-7.6	-6.1
Estonia	--	--	-1.0	1.3	-7.1	-4.7	-9.1	-12.0
Hungary	1.0	0.8	0.9	-9.0	-9.5	-5.6	-3.7	-2.2
Latvia	--	--	15.2	6.9	-2.4	-3.7	-4.4	-6.9
Lithuania	--	--	5.4	-3.2	-2.2	-10.3	-9.3	-10.3
FYR Macedonia	--	--	--	--	-5.7	-5.7	-7.3	-8.2
Poland ªª/	1.1	-1.0	-0.3	-2.7	-1.0	4.6	-1.0	-3.5
Romania	-8.7	-3.5	-8.0	-4.5	-1.4	-5.0	-7.3	-6.7
Slovak Republic	--	--	0.4	-5.0	4.8	2.3	-11.1	-6.9
Slovenia	3.0	1.5	7.4	1.5	4.2	-0.1	0.2	0.2
Community of Independent States */	*-2.2*	*1.6*	*-10.4*	*-7.4*	*-9.7*	*-6.3*	*-7.3*	*-7.1*
Armenia (excluding grants)	--	--	-84.1	-54.6	-35.5	-37.5	-26.9	-29.0
Azerbaijan	--	9.8	--	-2.8	-15.8	-10.1	-18.2	-18.9
Belarus	--	--	4.0	-30.4	-13.2	-2.4	-3.6	-6.0
Georgia (excluding grants)	--	--	-21.0	-11.0	-34.1	-14.1	-9.1	-10.2
Kazakhstan	--	-25.3	2.9	-4.3	-8.0	-4.0	-3.6	-4.7
Kyrgyz Republic	-19.5	0.5	-9.1	-6.9	-11.3	-16.2	-23.2	-8.1
Moldova	-2.2	21.4	-13.7	-12.2	-5.7	-8.6	-9.1	-14.9
Russia	0.4	2.8	0.5	1.5	3.2	1.8	2.1	0.6
Tajikistan	--	--	-18.0	-31.0	-21.0	-9.0	-7.4	-5.5
Turkmenistan	--	--	--	18.5	8.0	1.3	1.1	-21.3
Ukraine	--	-2.2	-0.3	-0.8	-3.1	-3.1	-2.7	-2.7
Uzbekistan ᵇ/	--	--	-11.8	-7.8	2.1	-0.2	-7.2	-4.1
Turkey	--	--	-0.6	-3.5	-2.0	-1.4	-3.0	-2.5

Note: */ Median of countries included.
        a/ Figures for 1995-96 includes estimate of non-registered trade surplus.
        b/ 1991 figure represents resource balance as % GDP.
Source: The World Bank.

Table 9.5. Tax Rates in Selected Countries

	PIT	CIT	VAT	Total pension to to total labor cost [1]	Total payroll tax for SS to total labor cost [1]
Czech Republic	40.0	39.0	22.0	20.1	35.9
Hungary	48.0	20.5	25.0	20.5	40.6
Poland	45.0	40.0	22.0	30.4	32.4
Slovakia	42.0	40.0	23.0	19.6	34.1
Slovenia	50.0	25.0	N/A.	25.2	37.2
OECD average	43.9	40.6	8.2	12.9	24.9
EU 15 average	43.9	39.5	18.1	15.3	32.5

Note: 1/ OECD and EU averages do not include Denmark.

Sources: Individual taxes-A Worldwode Summary. Price Waterhouse, 1996;
Corporate Taxes-A Worldwide Summary. Price Waterhouse, 1996; IMF.

MAP SECTION

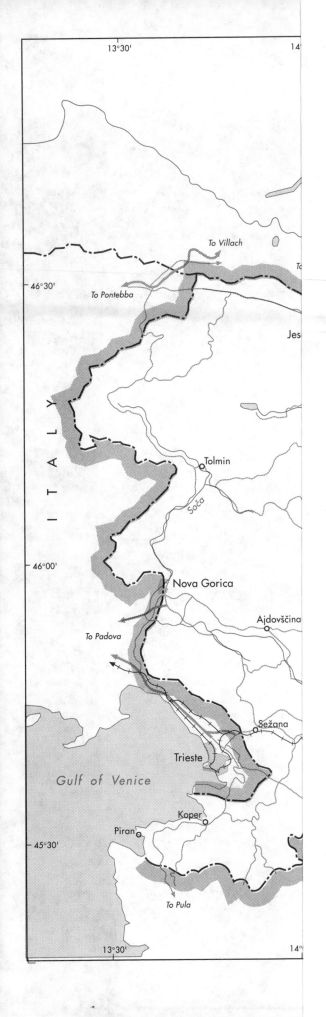